DANCING

with FIRE

DANCING with FIRE

A Mindful Way to Loving Relationships

JOHN AMODEO, PhD

QUEST

BOOKS

Theosophical Publishing House
Wheaton, Illinois * Chennai, India

Quest Books
Theosophical Publishing House
PO Box 270
Wheaton, IL 60187-0270

www.questbooks.net

Cover design by Mary Ann Smith
Typesetting by Datapage, Inc.

Library of Congress Cataloging-in-Publication Data

Amodeo, John.
    Dancing with fire: a mindful way to loving relationships / John Amodeo.—1st Quest ed.
        p. cm.
    Includes index.
        ISBN 978-0-8356-0914-2
    1. Interpersonal relations.   2. Intimacy (Psychology)   3. Spirituality.   I. Title.
    HM1106.A54 2013
    302—dc23   2012043550

5   4   3   2   1   *   13   14   15   16   17   18

Printed in the United States of America

Table of Contents

Dedication

This book is dedicated to all those who feel deeply the anguish in today's world and who feel moved to make some small contribution to improving the quality of life for all and protecting our precious planet.

I also dedicate this book to my clients, who have allowed me to accompany them on their sacred journeys toward themselves, toward others, and toward life itself. I'm deeply grateful for the trust they have placed in me.

Acknowledgments

I want to express my deep appreciation to the following people, who generously spent time poring over the manuscript to offer helpful feedback and suggestions: Leona Dawson, Joya D'Cruz, Bruce Gibbs, and Jean Holroyd.

I also want to thank those who offered invaluable input and important help with various parts of the manuscript: Pamela Meigs, Kye Nelson, Laury Rappaport, Steven Ruddell, and Jim Wilson.

Special thanks to Madelaine Fahrenwald for her astute refinements and brilliant editing of the manuscript.

Profuse thanks to my devoted literary agent, John White, for his longtime support of me and my work.

I also feel great appreciation for the magnificent staff at Quest Books, especially Sharron Dorr, publishing manager; Jessica Salasek, publicist; and Joanne Asala, editor. Their enthusiastic support of the book was most heartening.

Someday, after mastering the winds, the waves, the tides and gravity, we shall harness for God the energies of love, and then, for a second time in the history of the world, man will have discovered fire.

—Pierre Teilhard de Chardin

Introduction

For many years, I awkwardly straddled two worlds without being fully comfortable in either one. My spiritual buddies made a convincing case: the key to life is finding inner peace and liberation through meditation and spiritual practice. My psychologically minded friends made an equally compelling argument: to love and be loved is what life is all about; contacting and expressing our human feelings and needs bring the love, joy, and juiciness that our heart longs for.

My spiritual friends echoed teachers who dismissed the value of personal growth. People who pursued interpersonal fulfillment were affectionately known as "relationship junkies." This path was viewed as feeding the ego and strengthening the personality—a seductive distraction from the awakening offered by meditation and spiritual work. Scowling from the other camp were the psychologically minded who viewed spirituality as an avoidance of feelings and a denial of basic needs for love and intimacy. They dismissed meditation as self-centered navel-gazing—a narcissistic path of self-absorption.

For many years, I wondered if we are working at cross-purposes if we pursue a spiritual practice *and* loving relationships. Over the course of many decades, what I once viewed as an unbridgeable gap I now see as converging paths. Suggesting that we must choose between interpersonal fulfillment and spiritual development is to overlook how these are two sides of the same coin of awakening. This book explores how the path of liberation—a vibrant and intimate connection with life—is synonymous with satisfying love relationships.

A Love Affair with Life

During shining moments, when our defenses melt and our heart opens wide, we may make a startling discovery: the path toward love and intimacy leads naturally toward a spiritual life. Conversely, the path of spirituality leads naturally toward deeper love and intimacy—*if* we learn to attend to our experience in a certain mindful way.

"Spirituality" is a term used so casually that we are in danger of losing its sacred meaning. Unlike "religion," which binds us to a creed of beliefs that often divide us, spirituality points to a deeply felt experience that connects us. Living with spiritual sensitivity means having a love affair with life. It is the juiciness of being alive—a vibrant intimacy with ourselves, others, and life itself.

Attuning to life with exquisite sensitivity and a loving openness is the essence of spirituality. We awaken to the poignancy of each sacred moment. We are available to touch and be touched by life and love. Living and breathing in harmony with existence itself, we recognize that our lives are interconnected with the life that thrives around us.

Honoring Desire

A Chinese Zen story portrays a common pitfall of the spiritual path. A devoted old woman supported a monk for twenty years. She built a hut for him and brought him food every day. Wondering what progress he had made, she sent a beautiful young girl "rich in desire" to visit him and instructed her to embrace him and report his response.

The young seductress visited the monk and, without hesitation, caressed him and asked how he felt. Standing utterly stiff and lifeless, he replied poetically that he felt "like a withering tree on a rock in winter, totally without warmth." Hearing of the monk's heartless response, the old woman was quite displeased. "To think I fed that fellow for twenty years!" Concluding that he was a fraud, she straightaway evicted him and burned down his hut.[1]

The monk's chilly response seemed to convey that he had transcended desire, but the old woman recognized that he had merely replaced one desire with another. He was now clinging so tightly to meditative absorption that he was dissociated from his human longings and feelings. Here we see the common hazard of denying our fiery desires rather than finding peace with them.

Life is a dance with fire. Trying to extinguish human passions rather than dancing with them propelled them underground, where they soon returned with greater ferocity in the form of a firestorm that destroyed the monk's home. We can also imagine that if he had surrendered to the young woman's seduction, he might have faced a different peril—becoming attached to an unaccustomed pleasure or allowing himself to fall in love and then facing love's potential loss. There is no escaping life and the longings that are hinged to it. Life invites us to give desire its proper due and engage with it in ways that nourish us rather than sabotage us.

Rather than becoming monks, most people are drawn to a spiritual life that includes emotional and sexual intimacy. However, our longing for loving connections may bump up against painful memories of lost love, frustrated desire, and unrequited passion. Much confusion reigns about how to reconcile our irrepressible yearning for love and intimacy with a path toward liberation. This book attempts to bridge this divide.

Spiritual awakening is not synonymous with the cessation of desire, emotional shutdown, or icy withdrawal. Modern neuroscience has made a compelling discovery, though not a surprising one: we are hard-wired for connection. We deny our need for bonded relationships at our own peril.

I believe that the major challenge faced by spiritually oriented people—and all of us—today is twofold:

- To be mindful of our longings and feelings and how they operate in us
- To engage with them in a way that furthers spiritual growth

By honoring our neurological wiring and what delights our heart, can we welcome our yearning for love and connection and dance with it in ways that move us toward each other and support awakening?

Integrating Spirituality with Intimacy

Working as a psychotherapist for over thirty years, as well as observing myself and my friends, I have often noticed a gap between our spiritual paths and how we live our lives. For example, a client commented that the residents he met in a spiritual community seemed emotionally unbalanced and immature. A friend reported that her husband seemed distant after meditation retreats. Whenever she wanted to discuss their relationship, he would flee to his other lover: the meditation cushion. Clueless about the depth of her dissatisfaction, he was stunned when she filed for divorce.

Echoing many people's experiences, meditation teacher Gregory Kramer describes the rift he experienced between meditation retreats and his own life: "Long retreats were notorious for heightening the contrast between meditation and the rest of my life. . . . My wife commented that I seemed unhappier after retreats and wondered why I was doing this to myself."[2]

In the arena of human relating, the spiritually inclined appear to suffer as much as everyone else. I have come to wonder whether there is something in traditional Eastern teachings about attachment and desire—or more likely, in how they've been interpreted—that inhibits our movement toward each other. I have come to realize that traditional meditation and spiritual practices are not enough if we want deeply loving relationships. What would it look like to expand our spiritual practice to include our life of feelings and longings so that our humanity becomes an integral part of our spirituality? Throughout the book, I will reference clients, friends, and even myself through composite examples culled over many years.

Intimacy with Life

A healthy spirituality includes accommodating our yearnings and emotions rather than pushing them away. By connecting intimately with what lives within ourselves, we begin to experience life's bounty around us.

We savor a deeper connection with our fellow humans, the myriad creatures with whom we share this planet, and our precious environment.

As our heart embraces living, we are touched by the quiet thrill of a spontaneously arising intimacy with life. As our familiar separateness dissolves, we register and receive others' humanity. We relish moments of connection without eradicating differences and diversity, which adds richness to our lives. We embrace the dance of union and otherness—autonomy and intimacy—without getting lost in either.

Living with spiritual depth invites us to be mindful of our feelings, dance with them skillfully, and share the rich texture of our felt experience with others. The gift of being human endows us with the creative capacity to convey the glistening nuances of our felt experience—perhaps through an expressive glance, a radiant smile, a gentle touch, our tone of voice, or resonant words. If our communication is graciously received, we may glow in a shining moment of loving connection.

Embracing the Personal Within

Religious and spiritual perspectives can move us toward healing and transformation. But herein lies the rub: if our motivation is to find security or be special, we may latch onto beliefs and practices that supplant our *felt experience* of life with petrified ideas *about* it. We might ignore a sacred intelligence that continually tries to break through in the form of fertile feelings and longings. The spiritual path involves embracing the insecurity, anxiety, and uncertainty that accompanies being alive.

Cross-pollinating spiritual teachings with sound psychology can enrich our personal lives and interpersonal connections. I've become heartened to see that spiritual teachers have become increasingly interested in helping people integrate their spiritual practice with loving relationships and the feelings they evoke.

Bringing personal relationships into spiritual life is notable among Western teachers who have immersed themselves in Eastern practices.

For example, a student of the American Zen teacher Charlotte Joko Beck approached her during a retreat. As this student excitedly shared a profound experience she had while meditating, Joko responded rather tepidly: "Oh, that's very nice." Pausing a moment, Joko inquired with keener interest, "How is your relationship with your mother going?" This student came to appreciate how she was prone to get so attached to her spiritual experiences that she overlooked what was happening in her life.

Finding inner freedom means integrating the personal with the spiritual in a way where the boundary between them gradually fades. A foundation for intimacy is forged as we allow ourselves to *be* as we are and *be seen* as we are. Spiritual growth happens as we relinquish clinging to a fixed identity, freeing us to experience our inherent connection with ourselves, others, and life itself.

An Emotionally Engaged Spirituality

Finding skillful ways to bring the awareness gained through spiritual practice and self-inquiry into our relationships can heal the rifts that isolate us and divide the world. Questions to be explored include

- How can we develop an emotionally aware and interpersonally engaging spirituality?
- How can we integrate our spirituality with our daily life in the world?
- How do our relationships transform as we bring mindfulness into them?
- How can we engage with desire and longing in ways that deepen love, enhance intimacy, and foster liberation?

Attending to our interpersonal lives does not mean indulging in emotional drama or neglecting our need for solitude. It means pursuing a spirituality that includes emotional engagement, which requires experiencing and embracing our human feelings and longings just as they are. It means sharing our felt experience of life with selected people as a way to deepen connections and create a vibrant community.

Buddhism as a Path Toward Intimacy

More than most Buddhist teachers, Zen master Dōgen Zenji has portrayed Buddhism as a path of intimacy. By cultivating "soft-heartedness," we open ourselves to warm, fulfilling connections with people and nature. But "Buddhism" and "spirituality" are not usually spoken with the same breath that we utter the word "intimacy." Might a fresh perspective on Eastern notions about desire, attachment, and craving ease our way toward the ever-deepening intimacy that Dōgen encouraged?

Over the past few decades, Western psychology has made compelling discoveries about the importance of self-esteem, honoring our feelings, and communicating effectively. New light is also being shed on how shame, fear, and trauma undermine our capacity to love and be loved. Recent findings in neuroscience are offering compelling insights into the relationship between body, mind, and emotions, which prod us toward brain-friendly ways of understanding and pursuing spiritual practice.

A psychologically grounded spirituality can help us inquire into the seeming paradoxes that appear as we try to live a spiritual life while also desiring relationships that are emotionally and sexually satisfying. Some compelling questions arise:

- How can we reconcile our longing for emotional and sexual intimacy with spiritual warnings to beware of attachment and craving?
- Many spiritual teachings suggest that we are all "one" on a deeper, non-dual level. But how can we deal with differences and conflicts that generate heartache on the level of our personalities?
- Is the path toward liberation an ascetic one of abandoning desire or an alternately ecstatic and excruciating journey of becoming more fully human and embracing our experience with equanimity?

- How can we deal with passionate emotions in ways that deepen love and further spiritual development? Can we welcome life's challenge to mindfully dance with the fire of love rather than try to extinguish it or be burned by it?

A Spirituality for the West

Renowned psychiatrist Carl Jung has warned us about the wholesale adoption of Eastern paths. He has urged us to develop a yoga of the West—a spiritual path that resonates with our unique psyche and culture. Tibetan spiritual leader and Nobel Peace Prize recipient the Dalai Lama has also advised us to adapt Buddhism to our culture:

> It is very important to remember that you are a Westerner. Your social and cultural background and your environment are different from mine. . . . As you engage in spiritual practice (for example, Buddhism) over the course of time, you can gradually integrate it with your own culture and the values here, just as in the past occurred with Indian Buddhism, Tibetan Buddhism, and so on. There must gradually evolve a Western Buddhism or an American Buddhism.[3]

The pursuit of romantic love and rich friendships is deeply ingrained in our psyche. How might we understand and apply Eastern practices in ways that can help us become more awake in our relationships? How can relationships help us awaken?

Being raised Catholic, I grew up with an appreciation for the sacred. During college, I immersed myself in Christian, Hindu, Taoist, and especially Buddhist practices. Thus, while the bulk of my comments will apply to the Buddhist path, this book also speaks to spiritual paths influenced by Buddhism, including New Age spirituality and viewpoints popularized through books on spiritual love.

This work revisits Eastern perspectives in a way that guides us to connect not only with ourselves but also with our fellow humans. It borrows from the best of psychology, particularly a practice known as Focusing, to describe a path that can promote love and intimacy while helping our spiritual development. It invites us to look at the teachings of the Buddha with fresh eyes. Doing so, we might be surprised and delighted to discover that Buddhism is indeed a path toward intimacy. As we integrate Eastern wisdom into our Western psyche, we may take a path that feels more natural for us—one that leads toward liberation in a way that sustains and deepens loving connections.

These are exciting times. Scientific findings about what it means to be a healthy human being are mingling with Eastern views of what it means to be a spiritual being. The Dalai Lama has commented that if science makes discoveries that conflict with Buddhism, then Buddhism needs to change—not science. It appears that both Buddhism and Western views are transforming and enriching each other as they intermingle.

Part One

The Root of Suffering:
Disconnection and Isolation

What is to give light must first endure burning.

—Viktor Frankl

Every moment of our life is relationship.

—Charlotte Joko Beck

Chapter One

Off the Cushion and Into Life

I have never been a great meditator. A great meditator can sit for one hour in the morning and one hour in the evening—very still, back straight. A great meditator rises at dawn, bright-eyed and alert, eager to hit the cushion before a grueling day at the office. There is no grumbling when mornings are cold, traffic is bumper to bumper, and the hot coffee is not ready upon arrival. Everything is an opportunity for spiritual practice.

If you are a great meditator, then all day long you watch your thoughts, and you don't let them interfere with being here now. You never have judgments about other people, including your boss, who just promoted a younger, less-qualified employee to the position you wanted. Any disappointment is brief because you know that desire and ambition cause suffering. Besides, you are so compassionate that you're happy for him, as you figure that he needs the raise more than you do! Your life is blessedly serene—no worries that the polar ice caps are melting and that your elderly parents are running out of money and want to move in with you. After all, it's just the workings of karma—all part of the grand illusion.

Most notably, great meditators never slip out for pizza during a meditation retreat. Did I say pizza? Yes, I must humbly confess that I once committed that grievous breach of retreat protocol.

There we were, at a ten-day meditation course in the woods during a brutal New England winter. We arose before the birds and meditated well past their bedtime. All day long we watched our breath, which I discovered is much easier to do in the dead of winter because you can actually see it!

While attempting to observe the breath, we were instructed to notice any stray thoughts that were coming and going in our minds. One cold, lonely night, mine were straying toward pizza. I was having a thought that came but was reluctant to get going. I knew that I was a total meditation failure when not only did I *notice* this thought, I also felt compelled to act upon it!

Now, I must further confess that my desire wasn't limited to flaunting the rules and indulging in that pizza all by myself. I fully intended to corrupt an innocent retreatant, the friend I came with. Fortunately, I was saved from that perilous karma.

It just so happened that my friend and I were thinking of pizza at the same time. Endless hours of meditation must have connected our minds on some mysterious level. I'm not sure how the contact was made, but suddenly we found ourselves in his Volkswagen Bug headed for the local pizzeria. Was it a moment of shared illumination or a shared delusion that this expedition would somehow satisfy us? Whatever it was, that pizza sure hit the spot . . . and even more so, our conversation.

I don't remember exactly what we talked about, but the usual suspects would, of course, be women, our careers, and our complaints, including sitting and watching our breath for days on end in the middle of winter.

What a Little Pizza and Conversation Can Do

Fast-forward thirty-five years. How can I still maintain that slinking away for a late-night snack was an acceptable diversion amidst the serious undertaking of a meditation retreat? Well, maybe it wasn't. Maybe I was guilty of poor discipline, youthful rebellion, or unadorned self-indulgence. Perhaps I succumbed to the greed, aversion, and delusion that divert us from the spiritual path.

But another possibility is that there was something I needed that only comes through human contact. What lingers in my memory is not the quality of the pizza, although true to my heritage, I am fond of Italian food. More than the illicit food, it was something about the human connection that nurtured me. I felt less alone and less isolated. Something inside me was soothed.

But wait! The meditation practice is about sitting with the isolation, right? Just notice the aloneness, be mindful of it, maybe feel it a bit—and then let it go. We are not supposed to act upon anything but instead notice how experiences come and go without getting attached to any of them. Well, like I said, perhaps I'm a terrible meditator. Or maybe there is something to be said for not getting too attached to our familiar frame of reference or trying to fit ourselves neatly into some model of how we are supposed to be or what spiritual practice is supposed to look like. Maybe there's value in honoring *all* of our experience—and when it feels right, allowing ourselves to be moved by that experience into some mindful action. What would it be like if our life was our meditation?

When I returned to the retreat, something in me felt more settled. A certain longing for human contact was satisfied. I was glad that I listened to myself and honored the part of me that wanted to connect with another human being. But something else is profoundly true as well. The connection wouldn't have felt as rich if I had not been meditating. The stillness and presence cultivated by mindfulness practice allowed my friend and me to be more present and open with each other. Connecting more deeply with ourselves allowed a conversation that was slow-paced, poignant, and connecting.

I've been pleased to notice that since that time, many retreats now feature group interviews. One teacher even invited people to make eye contact during walking meditation. Meditation leaders, including Vietnamese meditation teacher Thich Nhat Hanh, have added periods of interpersonal sharing to their retreats. These teachers encourage mindfulness in daily living, rather than replicating the experience of monks.

On the Cushion, Off the Cushion

Having developed what philosopher Friedrich Schleiermacher calls a "sense and taste for the infinite," I was drawn to spiritual life. I recognized a longing to experience something more than my myopic, limited state of awareness. At the same time, I noticed another yearning not clearly addressed in spiritual communities: a longing to experience love, connection, and even ecstasy with another human being.

The spiritual path and intimate relating have often been viewed as incompatible—like mixing water and oil. Pursuing the sacred has often meant renouncing personal love and the seductive pleasures of the flesh. Yet what if the longings for spirituality and a loving, juicy intimacy turn out to be aspects of the same sacred longing, just pursued in different ways? It dawned on me that I don't have to choose between leading a spiritual life and enjoying intimacy—in fact, they complement and support each other. As it turns out, pursuing either one of these paths with open curiosity and a devotion to truth naturally intersects with the other path.

Spirituality: A Hazardous Word

I must confess that I hesitate to use the word "spiritual." It has been tossed around so carelessly that its meaning is often lost. Yet it is precisely because I feel so irked by its reckless use that I feel drawn to use the word to explore the deeper *felt sense* of spiritual life and to consider what it offers and what it requires from us. Rather than dispense with a word that has been used for millennia, I'd prefer to become sensitized to its routine abuse and to clarify its meaning.

It is always treacherous to define spirituality, for it points toward a domain of experience where words fail us. At the same time, if we relegate it to some otherworldly domain, we divorce ourselves from our human experience. While words can never quite capture it, they can perhaps point to it—as if with an awkwardly brandished elbow.

My use of the term "spirituality" refers not to any particular religious ideology but rather to something within us that feels irresistibly drawn toward having abundant love in our hearts and a luscious connection with life. As we come to realize that this burning inside is our innate yearning for awakening and happiness, we feel drawn to create conditions that support this sacred journey. We also come to realize what wise people throughout history have implored us to recognize: that this happiness, this awakening, is inextricably linked to loving others. As the Dalai Lama expresses it, "The purpose of life is to be happy . . . love and compassion bring us the greatest happiness . . . The need for love lies at the very foundation of our existence."[1] A path that leads us toward this resplendent love is an essential aspect of spirituality.

A spiritual life invites us to live according to values that encourage us to do our best to help people and the world we inhabit. But such values have little potency if they are limited to the confines of our heads; they become vibrantly alive only as they merge with our bodily, lived experience. A spiritual path means cultivating qualities that include compassion, joy, openness, and gratitude, which connect us deeply to people and the world. Happiness comes not by lunging toward fleeting pleasures but by coming to relish a growing gratitude for the gift of being alive.

Walking Our Talk

Pursuing a spiritual path has more to do with our walk than our talk. You may know people who are spiritually vibrant, but they are too self-effacing to identify themselves as such. They might cringe if you suggest that they are true embodiments of a spiritual life. Yet their expansive heart, humble speech, and responsiveness to others' feelings and needs may be more robust than those who preen themselves with the trappings of religiosity.

A spiritual sensitivity connects us with life in such a way that we are touched by the suffering in the world. We feel moved to respond in whatever ways we can, rather than holding the attitude that everyone is on their own and there is no human imperative to be engaged in helpful action. From this perspective, it saddens me to observe that even though we are a very religious nation, we're not a very spiritual one. As Mother Theresa has observed, "You in the West have the spiritually poorest of the poor. . . . I find it easy to give a plate of rice to a hungry person . . . but to console or to remove the bitterness, anger, and loneliness that comes from being spiritually deprived, that takes a long time."[2]

Most Americans would assert that they believe in spiritual values. But *embodying* such beliefs lags behind, which forestalls the momentum necessary for these beliefs to be translated into the larger realm of social policy.

A Spirituality that Embraces Intimacy

The time is ripe for us to pursue a spiritual life that is robustly, interpersonally engaging. Our spiritual quest receives its grounding through intimate connections, and at the same time, the fertile stream of spiritual practice nourishes our relationships. A spiritual path invites attention to our inner life in a way that inevitably connects us to what lives and breathes outside of ourselves.

Through a painful tragedy, the Jewish spiritual writer and teacher, Martin Buber, came to devote his life to being present and caring in his relationships. One day Buber was praying and meditating in his room when a student came to see him. Buber listened, but he was not there in spirit. Shortly thereafter, Buber was horrified to hear that the student had apparently committed suicide. Buber later learned that this young man had desperately sought to better understand his life.

The shocking realization that he had not been fully attentive and responsive to this man's suffering was a pivotal moment in shaping Buber's vision of bringing spirituality into relationships. The essence of faith, he realized, is not "the pursuit of ecstatic experiences but . . . a life of attentiveness to others, the life of 'I and thou' in encounter."[3] For Buber, being fully available and present to others, generously extending our loving attention and hearing another human being, is at the heart of living a spiritual life.

Vertical Spirituality

My initiation into the sacred was by way of teachings that might be called vertical spirituality. The emphasis was on mindfully following the breath into a deep state of stillness and equanimity. I found this to be invaluable. Never before had I experienced such deep states of peace, compassion, and even bliss.

Yet, during college, I was also involved in "sensitivity groups" that focused on feelings and relationships. I had deep openings and profound realizations about myself during these meetings. These experiences stirred up questions about how I might bring the mindfulness of meditation into my relationships as well as how to deal with my feelings on the spiritual path.

The response from the meditation teachers I consulted about these burning questions wasn't very satisfying. One teacher advised, "Just let the feelings go. See them as neutral objects and don't get attached to them." Others insisted that meditation and therapy are very different paths and lead to different results. These dismissive responses left me feeling not fully at home in the Buddhist world. But the dismissive views of spirituality offered by personal-growth leaders left me feeling even more confused and disheartened.

After much struggling, I realized that a whole and healthy spirituality is not just about taking the elevator to the heights of the penthouse and savoring the expansive view. It is also about taking it down to the basement and exploring the hidden nooks and crannies of our psyche. Liberation is about being drawn to the sunlight while also exploring the depths of the shadowlands.

Liberation From or To?

The invitation to pursue spiritual liberation implies that we are clear about what we're seeking. Much of the history of Western civilization, from the birth of democracy in Greece to the American Revolution to the storming of the Bastille, has been a quest for outer freedoms. The Hindu and Buddhist cultures have been more interested in inner freedom, liberation from the greed, hatred, and ignorance that bind us to the wheel of suffering. When we are pursuing either form of freedom, it becomes quite apparent that we cannot truly have one form of freedom without the other.

Oftentimes we see freedom as liberation *from* something, typically something unpleasant, rather than the freedom to move *toward* something that we see as positive. We want freedom from government control and oversight. Corporations and wealthy people clamor for deregulation and lower taxes. They want freedom from government restrictions so they do not have to consider how their actions or lifestyle disenfranchise others or affect the environment. They sometimes accomplish this by persuading the less privileged to believe that their own freedoms are at risk. A young view of freedom is that we are all on our own. In reality, our freedom and security are enhanced as we take care of each other.

An inevitable extension of this experiment in outer freedom is seeking total freedom from other people. We might think, "I want to be my own person and not be controlled by anyone." But what we may really be saying is, "I don't want to be affected by anyone. I don't want to be responsive to others' feelings or circumstances. I want rights without responsibilities." In this view of freedom, everyone is in it for themselves.

We confuse ourselves and others by broadcasting conflicting desires. We may claim that we want love and intimacy, but we don't want to be inconvenienced by having to consider others' needs and desires. Not surprisingly, we ultimately find that we can't have the love we want if we cling to personal desires without becoming sensitized to how we're affecting others and what they need to be happy.

What we often call freedom is being comfortably encapsulated within our own ego; we are desensitized to the life around us. A spiritual path runs the risk of reinforcing this narcissistic view of liberation if we end up trying to free ourselves from the desire for human connections in the mistaken belief that they will hold us back. The truth is that we need each other to awaken.

What needs to happen inside us and between us so that we are liberated from what constrains us from moving naturally toward deeper love and intimacy? What would our path look like if we realized that our quest for freedom is furthered as we help create conditions for others to be freer and happier?

Horizontal Spirituality

In contrast with a vertical spirituality of transcendence, which moves us away from people and the world, a horizontal spirituality is about being awake in our everyday lives and relationships. In the words of Harvard theologian Harvey Cox, it's about finding "the sacred in the imminent, the spiritual within the secular."[4] It is about attending to how we are relating to people and to our own lives. It is about being intimate with what lives outside ourselves and navigating through the joys and sorrows of our relationships with presence, awareness, and kindness.

In *A Path with Heart*, meditation teacher Jack Kornfield reveals his own personal dilemma:

> Meditation had helped me very little with my human relationships. . . . I could do loving-kindness meditation for a thousand beings elsewhere but had trouble relating intimately to one person here and now. I had used the strength of my mind in meditation to suppress painful feelings, and all too often, I didn't even recognize that I was angry, sad, grieving, or frustrated until a long time later. The roots of my unhappiness in relationships had not been examined. I had very few skills for dealing with my feelings or for engaging on an emotional level or for living wisely with my friends and loved ones.[5]

Kornfield's courageous disclosure reflects the experience of many people who have immersed themselves in Eastern teachings only to find that years of rigorous meditation practice did not do much for their emotional lives and intimate relationships.

In the same vein, meditation teacher Tara Brach reports that meditation was not enough to heal the emotional wounds of many of her students: "They assumed their feelings of inadequacy would be transcended through a dedicated practice of meditation. Yet even though meditation has helped them in important ways, they find that deep pockets of shame and insecurity have a stubborn way of persisting—sometimes despite decades of practice . . . perhaps they needed the additional support of psychotherapy to uncover and heal deep wounds."[6]

Kornfield paints a similar picture:

> Awareness doesn't translate automatically from one realm to another. You can be extremely conscious of your body and still be emotionally ignorant. You can have a great deal of emotional understanding and still be spiritually bereft. I've known dozens of meditators who can go completely empty in meditation, dissolve their bodies and mind into pure void and bliss—but then come back into the world and still act like emotional infants and sexual idiots in their relationships. In my view, they've done only half the dharma. There has to be a wedding of the personal and universal.[7]

Sadly, many people abandon their spiritual path when it doesn't deliver the anticipated rewards, but the fault may not lie in their chosen practice. No matter how hard they meditate, pray, repeat affirmations, or read sacred texts, the undertow of old traumas and emotional wounds may relentlessly undermine their spiritual intentions until they are finally addressed.

We Are Relational Creatures

To be human is to be relational. As we release what constrains us, our felt sense of relatedness becomes more than just a spiritual notion of oneness or a humanistic concept of interdependence. Sound spiritual practice moves us toward becoming richly connected, engaged, and empathic, which is the resounding opposite of detached and isolated.

Spirituality means relating to one another and ourselves with tender openness. In the Dalai Lama's oft-repeated words, "My religion is very simple. My religion is kindness." Kindness embodies a sacred intelligence. We inhabit our own heart in such a way that its loving warmth extends naturally toward others.

Our ultimate spiritual potential isn't to attain some extraordinary state of consciousness that is separate from our ordinary life in the world. Rather, it is to appreciate the precious gift of being alive in this very moment. It's to sense the wind on our face, smell the fragrant air on a summer's day, and delight in a chorus of birds calling the day to life. And as Buber discovered, spirituality is about receiving people with an available and undefended heart.

Moving toward liberation means being intimate with the life that flows within us and without us in its many colorful manifestations. It is being alive to our ever-changing felt experience as it unfolds from moment to moment. Being free means experiencing life with fewer encumbrances. Liberation is bringing the spirit of *vipassana*, a Pali word meaning "seeing things clearly," into our lives. As our life becomes our meditation, we live with an ever-greater clarity and lucidity. We are awakened by life and dance artfully with it.

Relating to Self, People, and Life

I find sitting meditation helpful, but the motive and method of my meditation have changed over the years. I am less driven to get somewhere. I include more awareness of my body and whatever feelings arise. Most importantly, I'm gradually closing the gap between sitting silently and living mindfully in the world. I do my best to maintain an availability to connect with others. Wonder-filled moments of poignant contact with people and life appear with greater regularity as I cultivate more intimacy with myself.

Connecting with ourselves is easier said than done. Many of us grew up in environments where criticism, abuse, or neglect overwhelmed our nervous system. Perhaps we were not supported in noticing and expressing our feelings and needs and we eventually gave up on being heard and seen. Due to a lack of positive mirroring from others, we may have difficulty valuing ourselves, knowing how we feel, and discerning what we really want. We may feel irritable or anxious without understanding the source of our feelings. We may carry a lingering loneliness, insecurity, or dullness that distracts us from being present and available for connection.

I have often seen clients desperately searching for some pivotal childhood experience that would explain why they feel so shut down or unhappy. Perhaps there were tangible forms of abuse that caused damage, but more commonly, there was ongoing emotional neglect or shaming that wore down the child's vibrancy. A sense of isolation became their background feeling, and it grew to be so familiar that it seemed normal.

Whether because of old trauma or developmental wounds, we may have dissociated from our bodies if it became too uncomfortable to experience the feelings that resided in it. An inner intelligence evoked a sentry within us, blessedly numbing us to unbearable emotions and shutting down longings that had little chance of being satisfied.

For some people, meditation and spiritual teachings provide a salve for their dissociation but do not necessarily heal it. Spiritual growth includes mending the splits within us, healing what was damaged, and reconnecting with what we've lost so that we might re-engage with the agony and ecstasy of loving and being loved. Spiritual practice helps us come alive.

Being Intimate with Our Experience

By disconnecting from our body and the feelings pulsating within it, we disengage from living. Spiritual teachings invite us to recognize that we are inextricably connected to others and life. The felt sense of this non-dual awareness is one of intimacy and engagement, the feeling of being alive and connected. By living more in our body and welcoming its vibrant (and sometimes uncomfortable) feelings, we become more present to ourselves and, therefore, to life.

The capacity to be intimate with our own felt experience provides the foundation for intimacy with life and others. As we walk down a tree-lined street with our mind still and heart open, we may feel delight as we notice the sunlight shimmering off the leaves as they wave in the wind. As our partner makes a critical comment, we may notice how her words create a feeling of tightness in our abdomen and a sense of hurt and distance. Waiting in line at the store, we may notice the difficult customer ahead of us and his negative effect on the clerk; feeling compassion, we may make a playful comment that tells the clerk that we noticed and cared: "Do you get many crabby customers like that?"

Spirituality is all about entering the rich depths of our inner world. But it is also about connecting more poignantly with what lies outside ourselves. Mindfulness practice helps us notice the curious things around us. As we awaken, we become aware of opportunities for ordinary intimacies that exist right in front of us, as well as deeper connections with people who touch us in special ways.

Finding Comfort in Human Connection

In a popular Buddhist story, a woman experiences grief over the death of her only son. She visits the Buddha, pleading for medicine to return him to life. The Buddha tells her that he can help if she brings him a handful of mustard seeds. But there's a small catch. It must come from a house where no one has suffered over a lost child, spouse, parent, or friend. She goes from house to house and finds people are eager to help, but then she asks, "Oh, by the way, has any family member died here?" One household after another tells their sad story. Realizing that there is no home where a loved one has not died, leaving people to grieve, she realizes that this is our common human fate.

The usual interpretation of this story is that life is impermanent and that there is a path that alleviates our suffering. But there is much more to it. The trickster Buddha invites this anguished woman into a relational inquiry that stirs her heart and leads to the comforting discovery that we're all in this together. He could have told her straight out that everything is impermanent and loss is unavoidable, but this *information* wouldn't have led to a *transformation* that can only come from the embodied experience of grieving. Hearing others' stories helps her realize deep in her bones that she is not alone in her grief. This liberates her from the suffering of isolation and moves her toward insight and connection.

A Path Toward Healing and Liberation

A simple way to avoid suffering in relationships is to avoid relating. But eventually our human longings will catch up with us. The need to interact with other living beings is cellular, genetically embedded through millions of years of evolution.

However lofty our spiritual aspirations might be, we are still mammals. Residing in these bodies, our lives go better with human contact. A flood of research on health and longevity has confirmed the obvious: our immune system beefs up through warm, human relations. According to several international studies, those experiencing isolation and loneliness had two to five times the risk of premature death compared to those who had a strong sense of connection and community.[8] People undergoing heart surgery who did not have regular group participation had a fourfold increased risk of dying six months after surgery. No wonder we long for intimacy; it heals our heart more than just metaphorically.

I have come to see relationships as the premier place for spiritual practice. The disruptions of trust and connection that visit every relationship reflect the ways we have learned to habitually distance ourselves from the vulnerable places within. The arena of relationships is where the fears, wounds, and resentments associated with our frustrated longings arise. Bringing loving-kindness to these shadowy places within the context of an intimate relationship and sound spiritual practice offers a rich opportunity to heal and grow. There is no better place to learn about ourselves and to untangle our inner knots, thereby easing our way toward the loving connections and liberation we long for.

Longing, fully felt, carries us to belonging. The more times we traverse this path—feeling the loneliness or craving, and inhabiting its immensity—the more the longing for love becomes a gateway into love itself.

—Tara Brach

The respectable view is that falling in love is full of delusion, projections, and misunderstandings. But if we reverse that idea, we can ask, how is love actually very much like enlightenment? . . . Love teaches you how to live down a level, to follow instructions that come from deep inside.

—John Tarrant Rōshi

Chapter Two

Sacred Longing: A Doorway to Connection

A new client enters my office and tells me something I have heard countless times: "Everyone I meet is happier than me. Their lives are working. They're in great relationships. Why can't I be like them?" Hearing these words, I wonder, "Whom is she talking about? I wish she could have been a fly on the wall during my previous session."

Like many couples I have seen, Ashley and Tony were loathe to reveal how difficult their relationship had become. As Ashley explained, "Everyone sees us as the perfect couple. But they have no clue how unhappy we are. Sure, things were great at first. But now there's all this distance. We put on a good show when we're out in public, but when we get home the wall goes back up. There's no intimacy."

People who appear unruffled are often adept at hiding things not only from others but also from themselves. Carrying with them a silent shame and a fear of being real, they have constructed a self that impresses people who can't see beneath the surface.

Longing: A Destructive Force or a Gift?

I am more likely to trust the trembling voice than the self-assured one, the person who speaks with qualifiers rather than with pseudocertainty. The relationship wounds we have endured shape the social self we construct.

We believe that if we project confidence and look good, then we might evade criticism and rejection.

Frustrated longings sear our heart. Rejection, betrayal, and isolation are among the most painful human experiences. Understanding the complexity of human longing—where it comes from, how it gets misdirected, and how to work with it skillfully—is an essential part of any spiritual path designed to reduce suffering and increase joy.

What is the nature of longing? Is it a destructive force or a gift from the gods? Does it divert us from our spiritual quest or lie at the very heart of what moves us toward awakening?

Longing for What Lies Beyond

The spiritual path is born of longing. We are irresistibly drawn toward something beyond our limited self. A quiet passion stirs within our depths for something that will move us toward more love, more life, and more connectedness. Perhaps it is not even *our* longing but simply life's longing to experience more of itself.

The very word *spiritual* derives from a word meaning "breath." Our breath is governed by our autonomic nervous system, which has been hardwired with a longing for life. If you held your breath for twenty seconds, you would quickly become acquainted with a very passionate longing to be filled with life-giving oxygen.

The illusion of self-sufficiency reigns supreme in our ego-driven culture, but our bodies never lie. Just as we need air, water, and food to live, we need to cooperate with our longing for love and connection in order to thrive and be happy. This requires a heart that is accessible and open. No matter our age or condition, the invitation to dance artfully with the fire of our soulful longings never expires.

This exquisite dance requires a heart that is accessible and a body that is relaxed and open. If we reject the sacred life force of our longing, we will be diverted from a truly embodied spiritual life. Our hearts, our bodies, and our minds can become hardened and rigid, and the life force dwindles. Even more ominously, on a larger scale our existence as a species is put at risk. Nature will not hesitate to select us out of the cycle of life if we collectively deny our human vulnerability and interconnectedness. Thriving as individuals and as a species requires wisely accommodating our human yearning for love and connection.

Awaiting Conditions to Thrive

The way we experience longing is influenced by how the significant people in our lives have responded to us. When our yearnings were met with acceptance and mirroring, we relaxed inside; we could be ourselves and move through life freely and openly. When our tender longings were doused with the icy waters of neglect, shame, or abuse, they began to feel unsafe and even dangerous. Our yearnings went into hiding and took the rest of our being with it. We began to view liberation as *freedom from longing* rather than recognize that liberation requires us to flow with the changing rhythm of our longings. However, no matter how stifled or rejected we have felt, our insistent longings never die. Like a seed in the desert, they may hibernate for years, awaiting safe conditions to burst into a beautiful display of color.

The path toward inner freedom includes awakening to the human longings that live within us. If we can understand the mechanisms that drove our sacred yearnings into hiding, we may recognize how they have become distorted parts of our personality that create suffering in our lives and relationships. We may then be able to take the first steps toward reconnecting with the original, untainted purity of our longings, bringing mindfulness to them in ways that support their reawakening and integration.

The Desecration of Human Longing

It would never have occurred to us as an infant to be ashamed of our longing. There was no ambiguity in our desire for warmth, safety, and love.

We reached out for these comforts unabashedly and complained loudly when they were not forthcoming.

Oftentimes, our plaintive cries for food, holding, or a clean diaper went unheard. Even the most attentive parent cannot satisfy every desire. As our longing for blissful gratification was frustrated, we experienced the suffering of separation. We gradually absorbed the unpleasant news that some people still deny: the world doesn't exist to gratify us.

Unfortunately, children are not inclined to muse, "The pain of my frustrated longing is part of a necessary journey toward increased self-consciousness, a capacity for self-soothing, and empathy for others' feelings and needs. This struggle will enable me to outgrow my narcissism, self-regulate to some reasonable extent, and create a foundation for mature love in adult life." Instead, the child tastes the first inklings of a bitter disconnection from the gratifying other. She concludes that something is wrong with these needs and desires, or there is something wrong with her for having them. Thus, human longing shuts down through the birth of shame—the insufferable feeling of being flawed, defective, or inferior. Something in us concludes that the less we feel, the safer we become.

Losing the Thread of Connection with Ourselves

Stumbling into adolescence and adulthood, we may continue to hear the message that we are too selfish, needy, or flawed to be loved. The resulting isolation generates emotional suffering that is often unbearable. This begins the epic journey of scrambling to figure out who we need to be in order to win love and connection. We fabricate a self that is designed to gain acceptance and avoid the scalding pain of rejection, but we pay a hefty price: we disconnect from our authentic being, the very place where longing resides; we choke off the spigot to the deep wellspring of life energy.

In the best of cases, the parents' warm and caring bond with the child provides him or her with an approachable, safe harbor. The child is then blessed with a *gradual* disillusionment. The monumental shift from having the nervous system regulated by the parents' responses to self-regulation then goes relatively smoothly. Later, when he or she pursues love relationships, there is a greater capacity to deal with disappointment and frustration. There is greater ease in taking the risks necessary to love and be loved when we have a back-up ability to take care of ourselves when gratification from another is not forthcoming.

The limbic brain, where our emotional patterning is constructed, does not develop well when the child experiences parental love that is ambivalent or unpredictable.[1] To the extent that there has been abuse, neglect, or trauma—or when parents are frequently anxious or controlling—the child's natural developmental process is disrupted.

As I write these words, which are oversimplified for the sake of brevity, I'm aware that some readers might wonder if they've unintentionally harmed their own children. Well, you can relax because the answer is yes. But rest assured that you're in good company; this is the human condition. Please hold yourself with kindness and realize that it is impossible to be a perfect parent. The best gift you can give your children now, whatever their age, is the gift of your own growing compassion, wisdom, and capacity to listen and connect.

Reacting to Parental Longings

Here is another way that we can lose connection with our natural longing. Well-meaning parents may unwittingly coax children to meet their own longings for recognition, respect, and contact. For example, a child's accomplishments in school, music, or sports may be worn as a badge of honor for *the parent*. This creates what is called a narcissistic injury in the child.

It is natural to feel proud of our children's accomplishments. But when their successes and failures overly influence a parent's well-being or identity, there may occur a type of merging with the child that impairs their development.

Children love their parents and fear losing the connection if they displease them. These inner and outer pressures may prompt them to react to their *parents'* needs rather than notice the ones that whisper within their own being. As their own felt desires are repeatedly redirected, their aliveness and joy diminish. Their awareness of what *they* need to be happy becomes tenuous, a pattern that spells trouble as it extends into their adult relationships.

In a related scenario, parents may excessively cater to their children. Perhaps they don't want them to experience the deprivation that they themselves suffered. They may buy them lots of stuff, help too much with homework, and be quick to bail them out of difficult situations. Such well-intended hovering doesn't allow the child to build resilient emotional muscles that grow only through facing struggle and failure.

Conditioned to have a low frustration tolerance, such children may develop a sense of entitlement that blinds them to the needs of others and makes it difficult to patiently deal with conflicts in their adult lives. This may apply especially in wealthy families, where children may develop a condition aptly labeled "affluenza."[2] It is more difficult to recognize their soul's true desire for love and connection when the latest shiny allurement or entertainment option distracts them.

A lack of empathy toward others has unfortunate social consequences. Self-absorption leads to a lack of support for policies that would demonstrate empathy for the less privileged.

Protecting Ourselves from the Pull of Others' Longings

Another way that longing can become distorted is when children feel a persistent need to rebel against their parents. They may have felt that their survival depended upon fending off their controlling or smothering parents, so they may now feel allergic to anyone who appears to want something from them in their adult life. Their longing for connection gets obscured amidst an anxious struggle to protect themselves against others' real or imagined intrusiveness. One client expressed this habit of fending off intimacy this way: "As soon as she gets close, I go away. It's a sticky and paralyzing feeling. I feel smothered the same way my mother smothered me."

When our parents' longings have wreaked havoc with our own, we may not know whether we are responding to people from our own longing or if we're reacting to the push and pull of *their* needs. One client noted a common response to this dilemma: "I'd tell her I love her because that's what she wanted to hear. It was easy to mouth those words, so I figured, 'Why not make her happy?' But it rarely came from my heart. I wasn't authentic. I wasn't clear about what *I* needed."

Sadly, many of us have not developed a skill that is essential for healthy intimacy: the ability to differentiate ourselves from others, to sense how it is for us, to stay connected to our own experience so we can remain true to ourselves while simultaneously opening to another.

This creates a delicate predicament. We don't want to succumb to another's demands or manipulations, so we hold back for fear of losing our very soul. Conversely, in our dread of being left alone, we may cling to people who are not good for us. Or because we've never found satisfaction in expressing our longings and feelings, we withhold them. We're afraid of horrifying our partner and losing the relationship. This push/pull invariably generates suffering along with the common lament, "I can't live with her, and I can't live without her!"

This internal conflict is not only frustrating for ourselves; it is also torturous for anyone yearning to get close to us. We may alternate between being rageful and submissive, clinging to love with one hand while pushing it away with the other. Our volatile reactions reflect our conflicting desire for autonomy and intimacy, which must dance together harmoniously for love to thrive.

Clinging too tightly to our loved ones smothers intimacy, which requires air to breathe. However, if we don't take our dear ones into our arms, we may signal disinterest. What needs to happen inside us so that we might walk a middle path between clinging and aversion? How can we be there for ourselves in such a way that we can meet others with an engaging and authentic heart?

Separation from Ourselves and Others

If raised in an environment that doesn't support our genuine feelings and longings, we gradually turn against ourselves. We tone ourselves down so we don't feel so exposed and vulnerable. As our desire to be seen and understood becomes associated with rejection and hurt, we distance ourselves from this longing. We have had enough pain and turn to safer abodes.

Unable to find a refuge in our authentic experience as felt inside our bodies, we might build our home in the air. We seek solace and stability through our mental constructs. We find comfort in our *ideas* about things rather than living in our body alongside our feelings, for we have learned not to trust our bodily experience. No longer willing to bear the emotional pain, we retreat to the seemingly safe haven of our mind.

The sad consequence of living in our head rather than in our heart and body is that we lose intimacy with life. We disengage from where the juice is. We default into our defense mechanisms, which while walling us off from pain also disconnect us from the exhilarating sense of being alive. We take solace in our judgments about people that separate us from each other and ourselves. A self-comforting ideology cushions us from the agony and ecstasy of being alive.

This disconnection from ourselves is the silent crisis of our time, which has ramifications that extend from the bedroom to the boardroom while also gravely infecting our political system and social policies. The foundation for a healthy society rests upon the mental and spiritual health of its citizenry. As we learn to embrace our authentic longings and feelings— and cultivate self-empathy and the corresponding compassion toward others—our society will gradually evolve in a direction that is more tolerant, humane, and enlightened.

The good news is that longing, like life itself, is a flame that cannot be extinguished. It only awaits suitable conditions that would allow it to flare into a brilliant and sacred intimacy.

The Birth of Defense Mechanisms

If we conclude that our longings *cause* suffering, as some religions would have it, something inside us mobilizes to eliminate this perceived impediment to our liberation. This can lead us to become wary of any inner prompting whatsoever that is tinged with longing. Responding to this perceived hazard generates a split between our experience as it is and how we'd like it to be.

This division in our psyche is sustained by defense mechanisms that are artfully designed to cut off awareness from any unpleasant aspect of experience. We view longing as dangerous or illusory, and our defenses kick into high gear to numb us to these unwelcome parts of ourselves. We become cynical about relationships and tell ourselves not to get too attached. Or we linger in a partnership that offers companionship but does not provide real intimacy, which sets the stage for betrayal when someone comes along who activates the fire of our dormant longing.

Equating desire with weakness or trouble, we may be filled with ambiguity around it. We may sneak moments of pleasure, perhaps through Internet sex or shallow affairs, which may leave an aftertaste of shame or regret. Or our desires may manifest through pursuits that do not bring real happiness, such as chasing after wealth or status.

Some people make the nefarious bargain of trading pleasure for power. Seeking to control their uncomfortable emotions, they lose the capacity to feel pleasure, as they have become thoroughly armored. Joy and peace do not visit people who have numbed their capacity to feel.

You might find this situation rather bleak. But the good news is that understanding the anatomy of human longing and its anesthetization can allow a reawakening to this source of life that is always trying to burst through. My hope is to create a context that invites you to extend a hearty welcome to this sacred longing for life and love.

When Longings Get Sidetracked

Longings denied do not disappear; they get sidetracked into activities that harm us and others. The way forward is to listen closely to our soulful desires and honor where they are trying to move us.

Spirituality may fortify our defenses if it reinforces judgments of our longing as sinful or as a source of suffering. Any attempt to smother the flame of our longing suppresses our life energy, thereby sliding us into a state of depression.

We can observe the ill effects of suppressed longing among those fallen preachers who gained popularity by touting morality and who then fell into notoriety when Biblical injunctions and willpower were not enough to contain the tsunami of their passions. The news media gobbles up stories about "family values" pastors and politicians having salacious affairs. Newscasters highlight the hypocrisy factor, but the downfall really resulted from a lack of introspection and self-integration. They sought simplistic moral solutions for complex psychological and neurological issues, but their rigid moral values were inevitably obliterated by a gathering tide propelled by unmet needs and a lack of self-awareness.

This is not to suggest that the intimacy-seeking limbic brain made them do it. Nor can we allow Satan to take the hit for human shortcomings. Without introspection, dark forces appear to come out of nowhere, but they actually arise from unexplored areas of the psyche.

Sex scandals have also been commonplace among Eastern gurus coming to America preaching abstinence and renunciation. Suddenly exposed to adoring students, many spiritual teachers have discovered the hard way that human passions often override noble intentions.

Honoring Longing/Living Spirituality

The allure of transcendent experiences presents a potent temptation to deny important parts of ourselves. As much as I admire Brother Francis of Assisi, I cringe when he refers to his body as "Brother Ass." And when speaking to God, he exclaims, "What am I, thy unprofitable servant and vilest of worms?" A denigration of the body doesn't bring us closer to God; it leads to a fractured soul.

I've met many Buddhists and other spiritual seekers who maintain rather chilly relationships. They may believe that it's okay to have friends but are not comfortable getting too close and displaying too much affection. In the guise of being non-attached, they become aloof and unapproachable.

The Buddhist view of non-attachment is that we don't become so identified with something or someone that it controls us. It doesn't mean that we dissociate from our yearning for connection. A middle way that leads to secure connections is to bring mindfulness to what is happening inside us as we interact. Are we relaxed, open, and available to relish a moment of connection? Or are we protecting ourselves and reacting based on fear, past wounding, or a misinterpretation of spiritual teachings?

The path toward freedom lies in inhabiting the living moment. Authentic spirituality invites self-transformation through mindfully riding the current of our lived experience. Our release from suffering is not achieved through the impossible mission of eliminating longing but by finding our balance amidst the pushes and pulls of our longings. This high-wire act means honoring our longing exactly as we're experiencing it, which allows our next step forward to unfold.

Sacred Possibilities

Whatever our childhood legacy, our sacred longings never die. During a soulful reverie, we may have an intuition of beautiful possibilities, the love for which our heart longs and the connection we desire. Dare we open ourselves to such opportunities?

Our longing to connect is at the core of being human. We see it in the grasping arms of infants and among lovers gazing into each other's eyes. We touch it when we feel the delicious ache of desire for another person. These shimmering moments tease us with a taste of something deeper and richer—a love, joy, and freedom that often seems just out of reach.

As our inclination toward intimacy becomes part of our spiritual quest, we increasingly recognize that our attraction toward what we call spirituality is simultaneously a longing for connection. An authentic spiritual life coaxes us beyond the boundaries of our own skin. Opening our heart to a felt sense of something larger than ourselves frees us from a prison of isolation. Life touches us in tender, surprising ways as we befriend our sacred longing.

Avoiding Feelings—Avoiding Intimacy

Most of us were conceived as a product of our parents' longing. Since our parents' longing had the power to create life, how could it be anything but sacred? When our pursuit of spirituality becomes disconnected from our longing for intimacy, we perpetuate a dissonance between our spiritual views and our human experience. When conflict arises between our spiritual ideals and our lived experience, we may opt for the spiritual ideas. We may believe that we are being expansive when we are actually stuffing ourselves into a cramped box of how we think a spiritual person is suppose to think, feel, and act. We reduce our life to a small bubble of "spiritual shoulds" rather than embrace a spirituality that includes our humanity. "Be in the now," we tell ourselves. "I shouldn't get so attached to my feelings or my story!" But as the title of a poem by Muriel Rukeyser goes, "The universe is made of stories, not of atoms."

There is value in cultivating more spaciousness around our feelings and stories about who we are so that we don't get lost in them. But we increase our suffering if we engage in what has been called "process skipping" by Catholic priests Ed McMahon and Peter Campbell[3] and "spiritual bypassing" by psychotherapist John Welwood.[4] Ignoring feelings fuels them, though we may not witness the explosion or implosion until sometime later.

Without realizing it, we become attached to a different story: being an "evolved" person who has transcended his or her story. We wrap ourselves in the cloak of a spiritualized self-image rather than wrestle with our human predicament. Instead of extending compassion for people's painful situations, we share our evaluations and tout our beliefs about how liberated they *could* be if they would only meditate more, wake up, or realize who they really are. We may dispense this unsolicited advice as though human sorrows and heartache no longer touch *us*.

"If you meet the Buddha on the road, kill him," goes the popular Zen saying. We are continually invited to slay our idealized image of what it means to be liberated. We are encouraged to look anew at our staid ways of sidestepping human suffering rather than meeting it with kindness.

Affirming Longings Is Pro-Life

World religions urge us to be pro-life. But we cannot be life-affirming and desire-denying at the same time. Although their youthful renderings may be coarse and clumsy, our longings are how life speaks to and through us. It is the octane in our gas tank. Draining out the fuel might seem like a simple solution, but it is not a very elegant one, as it would devitalize the engine that moves us toward love and awakening.

Maturity is about developing a relationship with our desires and longings, along with the swarm of inconvenient feelings associated with them. If we can hear their quiet voice, we can discover how to dance with them in ways that don't harm ourselves or others. If we seek liberation by deporting longing to a dark corner of our psyche, it will return to haunt us. Admonitions to rid ourselves of longing are tantamount to proposing that we delete our sympathetic nervous system and its associated emotions.

Through our experience of what leads to suffering and what supports joyful living, we can learn to listen to our longings while consulting with other parts of ourselves that may offer caution or clarity. Would it be wise to act on a particular desire or allow it to incubate longer so that we don't proceed clumsily or foolishly? Creating a climate of equanimity around our longings allows them to settle. Living with less suffering and more freedom means noticing our impulses and mindfully weighing them until they either pass, offer greater self-understanding, or move us toward some skillful action.

Healthy spirituality includes thinking clearly and living according to beneficial moral values and principles. But more challengingly, spirituality is about living and loving with a fullness of being. Our longings and emotions add juiciness to our lives. The difficult feelings associated with our longings are the grit in the oyster that transforms into a beautiful pearl as we embrace life's irritations with grace and wisdom.

In Zen Buddhism, intimacy is a very important word. In the early Chinese literature of Zen . . . it was used as a synonym for the . . . breakthrough that's more commonly called realization or enlightenment. When you are intimate, you are one with. When you are not intimate, you are in your head.

—Aitken Rōshi

All real living is meeting.

—Martin Buber

Chapter Three

We Exist in Relationship

Before becoming the Buddha, the naïve prince Gautama was so shocked at his first exposure to the ravages of disease, old age, and death that he felt compelled to search for a release from suffering. If he had lived in Western society, where the quest for love is sacrosanct, he might well have added divorce, rejection, and betrayal to this list of afflictions.

If we listen closely, we will make our acquaintance with a deep inner yearning, a longing for love and connection. If we are single, we may sense it as we scan the room at a party or event. As our eyes meet an interesting person, our heart is kindled; we feel alive with fresh possibilities. If we're in a partnership, we might notice our mind searching for ways to deepen or refresh the connection.

Part of the Web of Life

We exist in a vast, complex web of life. We live in relationship. To be human is to want to be met and seen, to have our inner beauty and goodness reflected back to us, and to relish a nurturing resonance with others. An essential aspect of awakening is discovering the thread that connects us heart to heart, being to being.

We may feel too vulnerable to acknowledge that we are not self-sufficient, that there is something inside us that invites us to move toward each other. Call it a longing, a desire, a need, a want, an ache for something more. Just as a tree needs sunlight and water, we need other people in order to thrive. It might be a pleasant fantasy to live in a cave with visits from Meals on Wheels, but after a while, we would ache for human connection. Even Thoreau while at Walden Pond had regular contact with his neighbors. Like a lone wolf on a starry night, we might howl from a deep place within our soul on a lonely weekend, longing to be soothed by another wolf's reassuring cry.

One longtime meditator expressed the denial of her longing this way: "I thought I didn't need relationships. I am terrified of my own longing for love. I fight it all the time by pretending that I don't need anybody. I thought that I should be able to do everything for myself. But this only makes me more miserable. I'm realizing that I actually feel more free when I allow myself to need people and let them in!" We are freer when our longing for contact is met, just as we are no longer preoccupied by hunger pangs after a satisfying meal.

Our need for human connection is hardwired into our nervous system. Child development research confirms that our relational limbic brain doesn't develop well without strong bonding. Failed connections may trigger an active depression in which the child loses interest in life, or a masked depression expressed through aggression or combativeness.

Our need for connection doesn't evaporate upon reaching adulthood. When our primary longings are denied or frustrated, we may become driven by substitute desires for power, wealth, or recognition, which do not lend themselves to being satisfied. The blind pursuit of such secondary desires disconnects us from ourselves and separates us from each other, which accounts for much of the personal and collective misery we see around us.

Our yearning to connect becomes more urgent when it is unfulfilled. We become ripe for exploitation by seductive people whose charm outfoxes our wisdom. We are easy prey for religious leaders who promise instant salvation or politicians who promise to return us to the glory days. We are susceptible to advertisers who persuade us that buying their product will bring us love, respect, and pleasure. What it often brings instead is addictive shopping, financial debt, and obesity.

Our Romantic Tradition

The twelfth-century French troubadours, who celebrated longing as the very ground of existence, sparked the Western romantic tradition. An idealized form of sexual passion and romantic rapture was seen as the ultimate meaning of life.

As I discussed in *The Authentic Heart*, the code of the troubadours was that a true lover is constantly obsessed with his beloved. Today's profusion of love songs and romantic Hollywood movies are legacies of this tradition.

If the Buddha were to share a meal with the troubadours, he might gently suggest that they exemplified his second Noble Truth, that feverish cravings generate suffering. Few would deny that they often do. However, not sharing our love with a special person can create a different kind of anguish. How can we resolve this apparent contradiction?

We may be inclined to dismiss romantic love as a passionate delusion. Indeed, the romantic messages that commandeer the airwaves are painfully naïve and destined to disappoint us with some version of "I'm a big nothing without you; life isn't worth living without your amazing love." These sentiments bestow awesome power on the other person to make our lives a glorious heaven or living hell.

While religions extol love, they tend to be wary of romantic love, fearful that the firestorm of our passions will annihilate others or damage our fragile soul. Indeed, caution is well advised: untamed longing can become a wildfire that destroys lives. Betrayal, domestic violence, and broken families are a small sampling of the ravaging progeny of unbridled passions. The freedom to love invokes a responsibility to love wisely and deal skillfully with love's emotional aftermath.

Longing for Sacred Resonance

Romantic yearnings evoke a passion that wants to move forward in some way—toward more love, more connection, more pleasure, more . . . something. Like a plant beguilingly drawn toward sunlight, we gravitate toward what helps us open and thrive. A holy restlessness born of longing irresistibly draws us toward greater aliveness.

Our longing to connect with something larger than ourselves through intimate relationships opens us to the mystery of being alive. Perhaps this ever more poignant sense of being alive is what we really want—to become more fully ourselves by being together and staying open to these luminous possibilities and following where they lead us. Allowing ourselves to be drawn toward this expansive love is at the heart of what it means to be a human and a spiritual being.

Life is dry and empty without human connections. We long to share moments of wonder and awe as we gaze at a sunset or view an eye-catching flower. We ache to be held by tender arms and touched by kind eyes. We yearn to share the playfulness of the child and the vibrant intimacy that arises when our minds are still and our hearts open. We long to be held by another's compassionate understanding and to bask in mutual kindness flowing from hearts seasoned by wounds and wisdom.

Honoring Sexuality

Inhabiting our body invites us to honor its need for a felt connection with people and life. For many of us, regular sexual intimacy enhances our emotional and spiritual well-being. Such intimacy includes touching, cuddling, and kissing, which can be deeply fulfilling if we are present for it.

You may be pleased to learn that sex appears to be good for your health! Studies at Wilkes University in Pennsylvania found that men and women who had sex once or twice a week had higher levels of the antibody immunoglobulin than those who had sex less frequently or not at all. Other research suggests that being sexual reduces our stress and sensitivity to pain, thanks to a surge in the love hormone oxytocin, which bonds us to each other.[1]

It would be shortsighted to seize upon such research to justify recklessly indulging our passions or violating our values. It is prudent to find some middle way between hapless indulgence and fearful recoiling from our sexuality.

Suppressed Longing as Self-Betrayal

Emotional and sexual longings are much more potent than our naïve moralizing about rising above them. We may believe that we are done with these passions, but they may not be done with us! A despotic mentality applied to emotions—brandishing a club and battering them or badgering ourselves for having intense longings—only makes us feel more ashamed and defeated when they gain the upper hand. When longing becomes a spurned lover, it will relentlessly beseech us for attention. Our ignored yearnings become painfully distorted, like metal twisted by the fires of denial and hardened in the icy water of repression.

There is a story about God knocking on a man's door. Opening it, the man mutters impatiently, "Go away, I'm busy looking for God." Perhaps the very longings and feelings we shun are the ones that would open a gateway to the sacred.

If we are convinced that our longing for intimacy contradicts our longing for liberation, we will recoil from one or the other path. Pushing away our yearning for intimacy is a rejection of how life's sacred fire is trying to express itself through us; this is the ultimate self-betrayal. At the same time, recoiling from the possibilities of awakening because we believe it means detaching from relationships is to misunderstand how these two paths support each other.

The Shame of Failing Holds Us Back

Distancing from relationships may protect us from the shame of feeling flawed or unlovable. As one meditator described his struggle, "It's liberating to see that those parts of myself that I've judged as ugly might actually be beautiful! It's freeing to acknowledge that there's a part of me that wants or needs things, and that's okay. I've never been allowed to have longings. I've been too sensible for that. It's too messy. If you long for something and don't get it, you're a loser, you're worthless, so you better not long for something you can't get! It would prove I'm undeserving. . . . That's pretty sad, right? I need to learn how to risk being turned down and then deal with the feelings that come up." Rather than being run by the shame of failing at love, this man began reaching out to people as a part of his spiritual practice.

By distilling out the shame from our wants and desires, we can more readily embrace them—that is, notice how they live in our bodies, welcome them, be gentle toward them, and hear what they might be trying to tell us.

Allowing ourselves to simply be where we are emotionally instead of where we think we should be spiritually creates the foundation for being intimate with ourselves and others. Our desires and feelings have an opportunity to settle and reveal themselves when our spiritual practice includes being gently disposed toward them. When we skillfully befriend our longings and feelings, they are less liable to overwhelm us and more likely to show us our own unique way forward.

Acknowledging that our longing to connect is essential to human and spiritual development, we find the salve that will heal the apparent split between spiritual practice and our humanity, between renunciation and the joys of living an embodied life, between individual liberation and the ability to embrace intimate relationships and the human community.

Can you feel your body? Stop for a moment. Feel your body. One septillion activities going on simultaneously, and your body does this so well you are free to ignore it. . . . You can feel it. Life is creating the conditions that are conducive to life inside you, just as in all of nature. Our innate nature is to create the conditions that are conducive to life.

—Paul Hawken

Convictions are more dangerous enemies of truth than lies.

—Friedrich Nietzsche

Chapter Four

Clinging to What Disconnects Us: The Root of Suffering

❦

Many of us have become disillusioned with outward-looking religions and the single-minded pursuit of affluence. It is no wonder that Eastern spiritual teachings have found fertile ground in the hearts of spiritually restless Western seekers. Like depth psychology, Buddhism invites us to inquire deeply into what makes us tick.

Trickling into the west, Buddhism has influenced everything from Christianity to New Age philosophy to tennis. Mindfulness-based approaches to psychotherapy and stress reduction have been gaining popularity as research confirms their effectiveness. Meditation has been shown to relieve a variety of medical conditions, strengthen the immune system, and improve psychological functioning.[1]

Unlike religions that are allergic to science, Buddhism is keen to interface with scientific research and discoveries in areas as diverse as neuroscience and quantum physics. Einstein stated that if there were any religion that could respond to the needs of modern science, it would be Buddhism.

However, while Buddhism is interacting beautifully with some domains and disciplines, there are ways in which common interpretations of Buddhism can have an undermining effect on our relationships. My attempt here is to discover the thread that connects the core teachings of the Buddha with research-based findings on what makes relationships thrive.

The Heart of the Buddha's Teaching

Twenty-five hundred years before the emergence of existential philosophy and psychology, the Buddha observed that being alive means experiencing *dukkha*, which has been translated as suffering, stress, anguish, angst, dissatisfaction, or imperfection. This became his First Noble Truth: a pervasive discomfort and unease permeates our lives like the air we breathe. This insight led to forty years of teachings about a path that would ease our suffering.

Similar to modern-day psychotherapists, the Buddha was pragmatic. The Dalai Lama has noted that "from one viewpoint, Buddhism is a religion; from another viewpoint Buddhism is a science of mind and not a religion."[2] Like Freud, the Buddha encouraged us to face unpleasant truths. But going beyond ego-based psychology, he offered a psychology of liberation, suggesting that we can experience the ultimate peace and freedom by attending to our experience in a particular way.

The Buddha's Second and Third Noble Truths describe the origin and cessation of suffering. He identifies the cause of suffering as *tanha*, literally meaning "thirst," which is often translated as desire, craving, hunger, or the fever of unsatisfied longing.

How tanha is translated makes a crucial difference in how we understand important nuances of Buddhist philosophy. Unfortunately, many authors and teachers have translated tanha as "desire." This questionable translation perpetuates the belief that simple longings and desires are decidedly undesirable, which is not the Buddha's teaching and which creates a psychological quandary.

If our innermost yearning is a sacred fire that springs from the basic life force that animates existence, then perceiving it as an obstacle to liberation may turn us against ourselves. By viewing this fundamental longing as the source of suffering, we may come to view this basic life force—indeed, the energy of life itself—as dangerous or harmful. It is then a short step to feeling shame or disgust about our innate desire for human connection.

Embracing Desire

The Buddha encouraged us to welcome whatever arises in our experience with compassion rather than judgment. Welcoming and "being with" our experience is not the same as "being for it" or "being against it." It does not mean gratifying every whim and indulging every desire, but rather cultivating a mindful awareness of how we are experiencing life, what we're wanting in a particular moment, and applying wisdom to discern whether it actually serves us or not.

The belief that desire causes suffering can trigger a battle between the natural part of us that yearns and the part of us that wants to be liberated. We may engage in a misguided effort to transcend desire, which numbs us to the inner promptings that can lead to inner and outer connections. Sadly, this reinforces what attachment theory—a research-based school of psychology—calls avoidant attachment or ambivalent attachment; we don't feel safely and securely connected in our relationships.

There is a skillful way to be present to what arises in our minds, our hearts, and our bodies as a result of our natural experience as living beings. By welcoming rather than pathologizing desire, we allow it space to be. A gentle, mindful inquiry allows us to greet our longings with kindness rather than dismiss them as troublemakers. Desire arises, and it is *how we relate to what arises within us* that can lead us either to suffering or to liberation.

We will never awaken or enjoy a spontaneously arising intimacy when we fend off unwanted experiences. By not embracing our experience as it is, we take a path that strays far afield from what the Buddha taught.

Desire Versus Craving

A growing chorus of Buddhist voices are suggesting that suffering is not generated by desire itself, but rather when desire curdles into the extremes of *craving*, *clinging*, and *grasping*, which are better translations for the Pali word tanha. The slippery slope into grasping happens so swiftly that we may barely notice how we get caught up in it and swept away.

In the Buddhist view, grasping for gratification and pleasure creates a chronically agitated state of dissatisfaction. However, it is often difficult to catch the distinction between a wholesome desire and an obsessive craving, or to notice when the shift from one to the other takes place. And so we may throw the baby out with the bathwater and judge every passing desire as "bad." Can we recognize that clinging leads to suffering while being gentle toward our very human instinct to move toward what we desire?

We might be gentler toward ourselves by realizing that when we move from simple desire to craving something, we have disconnected from our body in a certain way. We have stopped being mindful of what is really happening inside us and gotten stuck. And it is this very *disconnection from ourselves* that causes our suffering. As we notice and befriend our authentic feelings and longings, we learn to distinguish desire from grasping and become more connected with ourselves; it is then that we find greater equanimity.

How often do we find ourselves reaching for comfort food or pouring another glass of wine before even noticing the desire that gave rise to it? How often do we reflexively grab the remote control without considering whether there is something else that we *really* desire to do instead of zoning out in front of the television? If we can pause a moment and turn our attention within, we might notice quiet stirrings beneath our habitual grasping. Probing more deeply, we may feel a vague sense of sorrow or a gnawing loneliness that reveals a desire for companionship. Identifying this tender longing leads to a choice: we can engage with the longing internally or we can do something about it (or some combination of both).

Mindful of our sorrow or isolation, we might sense a tugging feeling in our abdomen or tightness in our chest. The simple act of being mindfully aware of our experience can lead to a shift in how our body holds it. A loosening or letting go may occur by simply allowing our feelings to be just as they are. Tenderly welcoming our sorrow or loneliness without exaggeration or minimization might gradually yield to a sweet sense of connection *with ourselves.*

But if this lonely feeling keeps recurring, perhaps we are being prompted not only to be mindful of it, but also to notice if it is urging us to act.

Perhaps the feeling is telling us, "You need people!" This may prompt what Buddhism calls "Right Action" or "Skillful Action," which could mean calling a friend, attending a social event, or joining a dating website. Our feelings are trying to deliver a message in the best and most natural way they know how: through the medium of our direct, bodily felt experience.

Whether we notice desire or craving, the way forward is not to judge it, sending it to the corner like a naughty child chided and shamed. Neither is it to continually indulge our immediate appetites. Allowing ourselves to be led by unexamined feelings and impulses, we may never uncover what we really desire. We immediately slip into craving or grasping in a desperate attempt to fill an inner emptiness or numb our pain without even noticing the longing that gave rise to it.

It takes courageous mindfulness to discover what we are actually longing for. Perhaps we need nurturing contact, a walk in nature, or a warm hug to soothe frazzled nerves. A desire to make money might reflect a longing for safety. This is not unreasonable but may swing us out of balance if we pursue a career so single-mindedly that it distracts us from our interpersonal needs.

An Example of Grasping and Clinging

When baseball superstar Barry Bonds hit his record-breaking 756th home run, a fan reflexively pounced on the ball, which was said to be worth a half million dollars. Here is how the local paper described the ensuing frenzy:

> Some people pushed others to get to him. There was shoving, elbowing, and possibly worse. Security and cops showed up and began pulling children away from the grown-ups who were doing battle. . . . One woman . . . admitted that she tried to pull the ball from the guy. . . . "I was holding on to his arm; I was trying to get the ball," she said. After falling, she was thrown back in the scuffle and bumped her head, leaving her with a headache. She was one of about half a dozen fans injured in the scuffle.[3]

We might like to believe we are above the fray, but this scene is an apt description of the human condition, of the clinging and craving that create suffering. We claw our way toward what we think will bring happiness—wealth, power, possessions, fame, sex—oftentimes bumping more than our head in the process. Even when what we desire brings misery, we may maintain the frenzy of pursuit.

The dictionary defines clinging as a refusal to give up something, or remaining emotionally or intellectually attached. The felt quality is a sense of being driven, obsessed, or stuck, such as when we pursue a relationship with someone who is unavailable. Or we might cling to habitual criticisms of our partner or unflattering opinions about other people without turning the mirror toward ourselves.

Clinging is the futile attempt to grasp the ungraspable and control the uncontrollable. It is like the popular definition of insanity: doing the same thing over and over again and expecting different results. We keep pursuing a person, object, or experience that we hope will satisfy us, but it never quite does. Like a Chinese finger trap, the harder we try to pull our fingers free, the tighter the trap becomes.

Clinging and craving reflect our common human condition. Being mindful and accepting of where we are right now is the starting point for change.

Clinging to Our Fantasies

Our experience with love, loss, and betrayal may help us appreciate how desire may quickly segue into craving and suffering. Here are some ways it might operate in some heterosexual married men.

We see a lovely woman at a party (visual pleasure and attraction). We enjoy chatting with her and relish a sense of delight; we leave it at that. So far, so good. But then something within us cannot let go of this woman. Perhaps we are dissatisfied in our current partnership or we're gripped by the allure of a new adventure. Whatever the reason, we feel an impulse to connect more deeply with her (desire and longing). If we can stay connected to ourselves, we become mindful of this desire alongside a sense of our boundaries and life's limits. Perhaps we glance at our wedding ring and soberly remind ourselves that we are in a committed relationship and that we can't have every woman who fascinates us. By honoring our feelings while knowing our limits, the desire passes. Mindfulness and wisdom prevail. No harm, no foul.

If we are gently mindful of the pleasant feeling that accompanies our desire, we can avoid trouble. A warm feeling lingers for a short while, and we welcome it as a reminder that we're still alive and kicking. We walk a fine line between acknowledging our pleasure and prolonging it through our fantasies. Our mild desire is innocent and enjoyable; it doesn't hurt anyone, and we're grateful for the lighthearted banter. But it is a short stride from desire to grasping.

A less benign path opens if we allow our pleasure to lead to runaway fantasies. Bursting with a giddy pride as we receive the attention of a pretty woman, we may luxuriate in imagining how it would feel to be intimate with her (the beginning of craving). Instead of simply noticing these feelings and fantasies without taking them so seriously, we may start to *believe* in them; we begin to crave the pleasant sensations she arouses within us. We ask for her card and then later call her.

If our appetite is whetted by further contact, we may want her even more (craving). We can't stop thinking about her (clinging). We persuade ourselves that she's a better match for us and that she will really make us happy (our delusory idealization fuels more and more clinging and grasping). Finding ourselves in an intimate setting with her, we rudely discover that reality fails to match our fantasy. We are deeply disappointed (anguish, misery). Sadly, we have just created a big mess in our current partnership and generated suffering for several people.

The Cycle that Leads to Clinging and Craving

Our senses, including our mind, receive the world around us. This contact inevitably leads to pleasant, unpleasant, or neutral feelings. Wanting more pleasure may lead to clinging, which proceeds to craving and greed.

Thus, the cycle of suffering is perpetuated, which Buddhism refers to as the cycle of dependent origination.

Since human beings are wired to seek pleasure and avoid pain, one thing leads quickly to another. We chase after gratification without being inconvenienced by reality or consulting with the wise parts of ourselves that reflect upon the well-being of self and others. We react automatically, losing sight of what we really need to be happy.

As we observe this cycle—desire/longing leading to craving/clinging leading to anguish/suffering—we begin to understand the eastern notion of karma (the logical consequences of our thoughts and actions). We may then also appreciate what Freud meant by the repetition compulsion, the roller-coaster ride that never seems to end, the bad dream from which we never awaken. The good news is that we can learn to work with this cycle so that we can enjoy what is pleasurable without craving more, which often brings misery to ourselves and others.

Many Buddhists attempt to break the causal cycle of suffering by bringing awareness to the very first instance of contact of an object with the senses. Their practice is aimed at totally eliminating the arising of desire. This is a tall order and a questionable one in my view because it tends to disconnect us from feelings and intimate relationships. This appears to have been the Chinese monk's practice in the earlier story, which ultimately led to his benefactor destroying his hut. She apparently believed that he was getting too attached to his spiritual practice and losing touch with his humanity. If he had brought mindfulness to how he felt when the young woman caressed him rather than stiffening against the pleasant sensations, he might have declined her invitation with more grace and kindness.

If the old woman had been practicing mindfulness, she could have brought attention to her rage rather than act it out violently. Finding calm rather than clinging to her anger, she could have discussed her concerns with the monk, demonstrating the compassion that she had expected him to show the young woman. But in a reflection of our common humanity, their mutual limitations fueled a cycle of suffering born of different forms of clinging.

A path that is integral with our lives in the world is to bring a spacious awareness to the joys and sorrows of being alive, embracing the pleasant and unpleasant experiences that arise from living our lives. By bringing mindfulness and wisdom to the full range of our experience, including our feelings, longings, and cravings, we may break the cycle that leads to suffering. Staying connected with our felt experience, we can enjoy a greater sense of intimate engagement with our world and relish the fulfillment that life offers without craving more.

Differentiating Desire from Craving and Clinging

The transition from desire to craving often happens under the radar. If we pay close attention, we may notice an intense, driven quality to our feelings. We are in hot pursuit of something that we're convinced will gratify us. Our body may register this craving as a sense of burning, edginess, or pulling. If we attend to its felt quality, it is painful, a tight fist, not an open hand; our stomach is knotted, our breathing taut.

Craving has a twitchy, agitated quality that stirs up emotional mud. It may be associated with restlessness, anxiety, or being out of control. Like consuming a drug or alcohol, indulging the craving may release tension, followed by feelings of shame or a deeper sense of dissatisfaction. One Buddhist representation of this state is the realm of the hungry ghosts, which teems with pitiful creatures who have huge stomachs and pinprick mouths. They live out their lives in continual dissatisfaction, trying to fill themselves but not quite able to get enough.

Clinging and grasping are similar to craving. They have a quality of holding on. There is the single-minded pursuit of self-gratification without awareness of the unsavory consequences. We try to fill ourselves with things that don't really provide fulfillment. We may lose awareness of what we really long for as we pursue substitute gratifications. We may even lose touch with longing itself as we spin more and more out of control.

Not only are clinging and grasping a hindrance to spiritual practice, they also make intimacy more difficult as they spawn fiery emotions in our relationships. Clinging has a suffocating property. By smothering people with cling wrap, we don't allow them space to be and breathe.

Preoccupied with hauling in what we want, we don't see what others need to be whole and happy. Craving comforting and connection, we might resort to raging protests that spew searing sparks of criticism and contempt. Something in us may even want to punish others so they feel some of the pain we are experiencing.

Rather than judge ourselves, it is important to recognize that underneath our impassioned pleas and heated conflicts we are legitimately seeking love, connection, and caring. But if we pursue connection by attacking, shaming, or controlling people (acts of clinging and craving) rather than revealing our authentic heart, we push away the love we want, thereby fueling a cycle that leads to mounting despair.

Clinging and craving might show up in quieter, less-obvious ways. Craving stability, we may avoid conflict entirely. Our intention may be to preserve the peace and protect love, but by not taking the risk to address tricky issues, we may bottle up emotions until they seep out destructively.

Unlike Craving, Longing Can Be Fulfilled

Our longings carry an implicit wish to move our life forward. Craving and grasping attempt to "stop the world." We attempt to latch on to people or objects in order to freeze a situation so it doesn't go away or change, but there is a quality of compulsivity or desperation that moves us away from ourselves and others. Not knowing how to attract love and connection, we may cling to our familiar attacks or stonewalling, which ensure that our longing for love remains unrealized.

The fears and wounds that lubricate the engine of craving distort how we reach out to people. Craving and clinging are often expressed through the toxic language of criticism, demands, and denigration. Jabbing people with our agitated discontent bruises the gentle shoots of love. Trying to grab onto loved ones sucks the oxygen from the room. By pursuing people through aggressive pushing and pulling rather than inviting them toward us by revealing our tender heart, we fuel a cycle of disconnection that shackles us to the wheel of suffering.

As we gently hold our soulful longings, we can reach out to connect instead of frantically trying to merge. When we stay close to our tender yearnings, a softening happens in which we are better positioned to *reveal* our feelings and wants, as well as let in nurturing and comfort when they visit. The place in us that clings and craves does not have the porous receptors that can let love in; but a sweet and satisfying connection can flow between two people who share their soulful longings in ways that invite contact. It is not an embarrassing lack of spiritual progress to beckon someone toward us with a glance, gesture, or words that say, "I want you," "I miss you," "I need you."

Underlying Longings

By creating an inner climate that allows a space for craving, we may uncover underlying longings that have wandered into craving's territory. Discovering and then inhabiting these unmet longings can be painful, but if we embrace them with loving-kindness, it may be experienced as a sweet kind of pain. The sweet ache of desire orients us toward what we need to be whole and happy.

Making a space for longing means finding the strength to be tender, open, and accessible. Society often judges such vulnerability as weakness, not recognizing that these qualities require enormous courage.

Our longings for connection, understanding, or touch reveal a heart prepared to be met. Moved by the gentle whisper of our longing rather than the loud screams of craving, we reveal our humanity and invite contact.

Consistency requires you be as ignorant today as you were a year ago.

—Bernard Berenson

Happiness is a butterfly, which when pursued, is always just beyond our grasp, but which, if you will sit quietly, may alight upon you.

—Nathaniel Hawthorne

Chapter Five

The Anatomy of Clinging

I f we spot a tiger in the jungle, how will we respond? If we luxuriate in analyzing whether we are safe, we may soon become a tasty meal. But if we react without thinking, we're more apt to save our hide. Our reptilian brain (also called the "lizard brain" or "old brain"), which lives at the base of the skull, has been brilliantly designed over millions of years of evolution to protect us through rapid deployment when danger lurks.

Whether a tiger is stalking us or our partner's unkind words pierce our tender heart, there is an activation of the amygdala, the old part of our brain that is hardwired to take over when danger is sensed. Within milliseconds, the fight, flight, or freeze response kicks into high gear, protecting us from real or imagined threats to our safety and well-being.

When old wounds get poked or fears activated, our heart races. Blood flows to the large muscles of our body. Just as lizards are poised to protect themselves in a millisecond, we have mechanisms that are similarly prepared to protect us from physical danger or, more commonly in the modern-day jungle, emotional peril. Flooded with anger, we hurl a spear, a dinner plate, or an unkind word. Or terrified of making a bigger mess, we freeze up and disconnect, which may drive our partner into an escalating frenzy. We retreat to the computer room, plugging our synapses into the comforting world of cyberspace, but this abandonment of ourselves and others leaves us emotionally and spiritually bereft.

Reactive Emotions Perpetuate Disconnection

Defensive reactivity is our body's default mode of operation that protects our vulnerability. These reactions become problematic, as often they kick in automatically when they are not really necessary. Our high-alert system has ensured our survival as a species, but it doesn't do wonders for us as a fallback mechanism in our intimate relationships.

For example, we might attack our partner for returning home late before we even hear what happened. Or we misconstrue an innocent remark. A compliment such as "you look good today" might be heard through the filter of our fears and insecurities as "are you suggesting that I didn't look good yesterday?"

She attacks (fights) and he withdraws (flight). She longs for the validation, warmth, and caring she never got from her neglectful parents. When her present-day longing is not met, it transforms into frantic clinging. He longs to be appreciated and valued. His family environment was chaotic; he yearns for peace and harmony. When strong emotions are expressed, he feels unsafe and clings to the computer and television for comfort. Each of their reactions is totally understandable when seen through the lens of their frustrated longing for love. A volatile brew is concocted as the raw spots related to their heart's yearnings interact.

Hearing a real or imagined attack, something inside us screams, "It's intolerable to feel this hurt, shame, and fear. I've had enough pain!" Rather than feeling into it, exploring where it is coming from, or seeking clarification, we instantly attack: "How can you be so insensitive, selfish, oblivious to my needs?"

We bypass threatening feelings of hurt or loneliness and convert them directly into anger and blame before we know what whacked us. We interpret the other's actions in the worst possible way. What happens next is the opposite of our intention: we trigger our partner into either attacking us back or retreating, thereby perpetuating a painful cycle. Our mutual longings crash and burn in the inferno of mutual contempt and disgust.

Attacking and blaming are propelled by instinctual habits of self-preservation so that we are not eaten alive. But our reactivity perpetuates a chronic disconnection from the more tender parts of our being.

Embracing these delicate feelings allows us to soften, thereby signaling to others that we are safe to approach.

Personal and spiritual growth means noticing and working with our reactivity, whether we call it self-protection and defensiveness (psychological language) or clinging and craving (Buddhist language). Mindfully recognizing that we are being reactive or defensive, or that a scary or painful place just got activated, is the first step toward noticing our more vulnerable underlying feelings and longings.

The emotions we have the most aversion to—all the ones that we don't want to face and feel—can fertilize a beautiful love between two people who learn to dance artfully with these unnerving emotions rather than trample them underfoot. Sharing tender feelings of hurt, fear, or loneliness can invite a blossoming of love and connection like nothing else can.

Uncovering Our Felt Experience

As we bring gentle awareness to our reactive emotions, we begin to uncover our more deeply authentic feelings. We pause and say hello to the tender nuances of this moment's lived experience. This includes welcoming and sometimes expressing feelings linked to our longing for intimacy.

Contacting and conveying our tender yearnings is like a prayer for connection. By holding our longings with loving-kindness, we are better able to reveal what is in our heart without shutting down or resorting to aggressive demands, harsh words, or exasperated body language. We are able to make a gentle request or offer a tender glance or playful gesture. By allowing self-expression to come from a place of intimacy with ourselves, we are more likely to invite intimacy toward us.

Clinging might sound like a bizarre term to the Western ear. We are more familiar with related words like addiction and compulsion, in which we're driven by something that seems to have control over us. Whatever we call it, bringing the light of mindfulness to how we cling to any kind of static security allows it to soften and open up. Something within us is then freed to find a path toward the comforting, enlivening, and meaningful connections that we long for.

Clinging to Beliefs About Ourselves

Being biologically wired for connection, our body informs us when we are disengaged from our fellow humans. We may experience a depressive emotional numbing or an anxiety that reflects the push/pull of wanting connection while at the same time fearing it. Rather than embrace this loneliness or angst as a normal part of being human, our neocortex often exacerbates our plight by ascribing negative meanings to our feelings.

A cycle of suffering is generated when we meet our longing for connection with critical judgment rather than compassion. If we have been frequently shamed or criticized, we might have internalized the conviction that we're flawed or unlovable. Clinging to this painful narrative locks in our misery.

Believing that we are not attractive enough, smart enough, or good enough to be loved, we lock down and frustrate others by not opening to the caring that is freely available. Clinging to shame—the felt aspect of our critical inner voice—prevents us from spreading our wings and soaring when a loving breeze wafts toward us.

Clinging to Fixed Positions

A common form of clinging is to take fixed positions about people and situations. Becoming more attached to our viewpoints than connected with each other, we try to help others see the light through self-aggrandizing advice.

Clinging to being right can become a delicious addiction because it activates the pleasure centers of the brain. But it also isolates us and offers only a fleeting flash of satisfaction. Intimacy requires mutual respect, admiration, and humility, and the ability to monitor and relinquish our critical judgments.

If we have a low tolerance for uncertainty, we will neatly order our world by putting people in fixed categories. People are good or bad, they're either with us or against us, they're "saved" or infidels. Clinging to these self-comforting beliefs creates intolerance, which on a larger scale ultimately undermines democracy.

We may favor politicians who prey upon our fears, exploit our discontents, and rely on our ignorance and gullibility. Unfortunately, these are often the very politicians whose message gets splashed across the airwaves by an industry that thrives on controversy. With their difficulty tolerating ambiguity, they take hardened positions on complicated issues and speak with a conviction that activates our angst and preys on our psychological vulnerabilities, such as for acceptance and belonging.

Taking this concept to an extreme, we might observe such tactics in Hitler's horrifying rise to power. He seemed to be amused by it all when he famously exclaimed, "What luck for rulers that men do not think!"[1] And Joseph Goebbels, Hitler's minister of propaganda, is credited with popularizing this familiar political maneuver: "Make the lie big, make it simple, keep saying it, and eventually they will believe it." We are here reminded of dark, fear-spreading tactics that are immune to the truth, including Joseph McCarthy infecting American politics with unsubstantiated claims of widespread communist infiltration in the 1950s, and more recently (though with less-horrific consequences), a dogged, unfounded insistence from some bastions of power that President Obama is a Muslim or was not born in the United States.

Sadly, we often elect officials who remain committed to their fears and dissociate from the complexity and ambiguity that is part of life. As the philosopher Voltaire warned us, "Doubt is not a pleasant state of mind, but certainty is absurd."

Clinging to a Spiritual Self-Image

Spiritual folks often repeat the mantra, "Don't get too attached!" We might appreciate how clinging and attachment are associated with pain and then make a virtue out of shutting down our feelings. We might also try to narrowly live out the popular dictate that being in the now is "where it's at."

Unfortunately, such brilliant formulas do little to actually help us. Reducing suffering is largely a matter of accessing the non-rational structures of our brain rather than clinging to clichés. These parts of our being need gentle tending; they are not going to just lie down and die. The key to happiness and awakening is finding a way to accommodate our limbic brain, not lobotomize it.

One enticing pitfall along the spiritual path is to become firmly attached to an *image* of being non-attached. Preoccupied with being spiritually correct and self-contained, we may minimize our need for connection. Shackled to a *self-image* of tranquility, we may fail to notice that our blood is boiling when our nervous system gets lit up, such as when we are unfairly criticized.

Through some clever mental gymnastics, we may appear calm on the outside while seething underneath. We may think we are being unconditionally loving when our combative in-laws want to extend their visit, but perhaps we've dissociated from our feelings and our body. What we deem to be spiritual non-attachment may be emotional shutdown.

We may try to hold our longing for connection at bay, but this fire cannot be contained by denying its power; it will quietly scream for attention until it is finally heard, perhaps through a psychological crisis or physical symptoms, such as headaches or back pain. We can find freedom only by hearing what our longing requires from us and dancing gracefully to its music.

Clinging to Non-Clinging

A helpful image for our attempt to abolish clinging is the mythological Hydra, the many-headed monster. The moment we lop off one head, two more appear. Our attempts to practice non-clinging usually spawn more subtle forms of clinging. For example, we might think that we are spiritually advanced by maintaining a cool distance from people. However, we might actually be clinging to:

- A desire to stay safe by not taking risks
- The shame of failing
- A fear of being rejected, getting hurt, or being smothered

More accurately, these emotions may cling to us, which freezes the flow of our experiencing.

By holding too tightly to the principle of non-clinging, we may not fully engage with people, pulling away at the first sign of conflict. We may be clinging to something difficult to identify, such as:

- Judgments about a person
- A desire to find someone who is perfect
- A beatific dream that relationships should be trouble-free
- A conviction that we are not contributing to a conflict
- A belief that we are more evolved than other people

Ideological Clinging

Ideological clinging is often so pervasive that we don't recognize it. Our beliefs shape our worldview and set us up for heartache when reality fails to match it. As the popular bumper sticker says, "Don't believe everything you think."

Our beliefs are only approximations of reality; they never fully capture what is real and true, so clinging to them keeps us caged in a dim reality. To avoid solitary confinement, we may try to lasso people into the same shadowy prison to keep us company. We may attempt to convert people to our religious or political viewpoint so that we don't feel so alone.

World history is driven by conflicting intellectual, political, and spiritual ideologies, which perpetuate endless conflict and misery. Modern-day politics in America, including the speech of some prominent talk show hosts and politicians who spread fear and thrive on divisiveness, exemplifies a self-righteous clinging to ideology and a subsequent strangling of the freedoms these pundits claim to promote.

Fixating on any limited identity removes us from the present moment and deposits us firmly in our heads. We usually don't notice how we restrict ourselves by clinging to fixed images and limiting stories. Jim Dreaver, a non-dual teacher who understands the importance of embracing feelings, offers a compassionate alternative: "Instead of living out of some myth or story about who you are . . . live in a state of openness, of welcoming everything that comes into your awareness."[2]

Clinging in Relationships

Recognizing how subtle forms of clinging show up in our relationships might offer a fresh perspective on how we keep spinning our wheels. Some examples of how this can manifest include the following:

Clinging to a desire to change people rather than accept them as they are

We have little power to change others. In fact, it is primarily our consistent caring and acceptance that enables people to relax enough to grow and change. It often requires some experimentation to discover what we can and cannot accept in a relationship. It is helpful to get clear about this so that we don't perpetuate our (and others') suffering.

Holding tightly to our perceptions and negative interpretations

When we are hurting or frustrated in a relationship, we tend to ascribe meanings to others' behavior that may not be true. For example, if our partner is irritated with us, we might insist that they are really angry with their father or too needy. Clinging to our analysis might ease an uncomfortable sense of powerlessness, but it shuts down curiosity and conversation. It diverts us from taking responsibility for how we may be contributing to their discontent. Did we do or say something that was hurtful? Perhaps they're reacting to a shaming comment, sarcastic glance, or lack of responsiveness.

Holding on to a person who is continually abusive or unavailable

We might cling to someone who evokes a deep-seated feeling of familiarity. Perhaps they remind us of a parent who was elusive or unavailable. If we could only get him or her to love us, then we would finally be okay. If we have become sexual with them, our brain may trigger powerful chemicals, including dopamine and oxytocin, which intensify bonding and may override our good judgment.

Clinging to what disconnects us

Dr. John Gottman's pioneering research on marriage has identified four factors that disrupt intimate engagement and predict marital failure: contempt (sarcasm), stonewalling (shutting down), criticism, and defensiveness.[3]

From a Buddhist perspective, we might view these slayers of intimacy as manifestations of clinging. We desire connection but we are so consumed by old hurts or fear of rejection that we resort to sarcastic comments and hurtful criticisms. We're so convinced that love won't be forthcoming that we scratch and claw for it. We cling so tightly to the shame of feeling wrong or undeserving of love that we get defensive or shut down.

For example, Tom would often attack his partner, Julie, with comments such as these:

"You spend too much time with your friends!"

"I'm not important to you!"

"You never listen to me!"

Not surprisingly, such comments did not exactly inspire Julie's receptivity. As Tom uncovered and expressed the feelings beneath these accusations, he helped Julie understand him and move toward him. Notice how different it feels to hear Tom's feelings rather than his accusations:

"When you see your friends, I feel lonely."

"When we don't spend much time together, it brings up old feelings that I don't deserve love."

"I really need you to hear that I miss you when you see your friends."

Whereas before, Julie was getting the message that she was doing something wrong and she was bad, now she hears that Tom is hurting, which prompted a more affectionate response.

When our soulful longings are entangled with fear, shame, and old wounds, we may push and poke our partner to try to get what we want. Unmet longings can bring a harsh edge to our words, voice, and body language. We try to sell our viewpoint so our partner sees the light and behaves properly. We plow on, unmindful of how we are treading on their delicate heart.

When we cling to criticism, resentment, and self-protection, we are usually not aware that we're hurting inside. Our partner may also be unaware that we are hurting, lonely, or afraid, even if we think they should know.

Scorching our partner with declarations of their deficiency injures trust. Intimacy is obscured by the rising smoke of our analysis and accusations. Our partner may respond in kind, deeming us to be clingy, desperate, or mean. A cycle of attack and self-protective countermeasures creates an increasing sense of distance and despair.

One aspect of the Buddhist view of Right Speech is allowing our words to flow from the rich tapestry of our feelings and longings. We are invited to stay inside ourselves long enough to contact and reveal what we're actually experiencing without hurtful attacks or attributing dubious motives to another's actions. Speaking from the felt experience that underlies our automatic reactions of fight or flight invites a conversation that connects us.

Uncovering Felt Experience Beneath Clinging

It bears repeating that it is not desire itself but rather the frenzied way we try to satisfy it that furthers isolation and spreads suffering. Rather than attend to our longing and find ways to express it, we act it out, perhaps by scolding others or trying to reform them.

Later, we will explore practices that connect us to our bodily felt experience, which creates a framework for embracing and expressing our longings from a more mindful place. As we learn to steady our inner flame by attending to ourselves in a particular way, we're better prepared to speak directly from the place inside us that desires contact without burning people with the fire of our longing or immolating ourselves. We also find a refuge within our quiet depths when what we desire is not forthcoming.

Being mindful of how we attach to beliefs and behaviors that separate us is a step toward returning to ourselves. What is most crucial is not to itemize the myriad ways we cling but rather to attend to our underlying felt experience. Psychotherapists and non-dual teachers John Prendergast and Kenneth Bradford offer this encouragement: "There is a natural ability to be spaciously intimate with our lived experience, however roughly or smoothly it arises."[4] Whatever we are clinging to loosens its grip as we turn toward our lived experience with a spacious intimacy and allow life to unfold as it will.

Embracing Our Dissatisfactions

The Buddha's declaration that life is saturated with suffering might reinforce our preexisting tendency to avoid *experiencing* suffering or deepen our aversion toward it by judging it as bad. We perpetuate inner turmoil by not pausing long enough to notice our discontent. We cannot heal what we refuse to feel. Most suffering is created by our very effort to deflect it. Buddhist teacher David Brazier encourages an attitude of acceptance: "The Buddha's teaching starts with an assault upon the shame we feel about our suffering."[5]

By welcoming and sorting out the ambiguous and blurry feelings associated with our desires and longings, we open ourselves to life and each other. We move toward awakening as we allow ourselves to experience the felt shades of our desires and dissatisfactions—finding a middle path between resisting them and merging with them. Acknowledging and revealing the pleasant and unpleasant feelings that are part of living enables us to rest in a deeper intimacy with the life that flows within us and between us.

Like what you like and don't like what you don't like. Nonattachment might lead to warfare with the part of you that enjoys the world. In this case, nonattachment would be just another tyrannical belief and itself a source of unhappiness. Not picking and choosing would be the opposite of nonattachment, something more unsettling and demanding.

—John Tarrant

You will not become a saint through other people's sins.

—Anton Chekhov

Chapter Six

Making Friends with Clinging and Craving

❦

A Zen verse attributed to Jianzhi Sengtsan, the third Zen patriarch in China in the sixth century, was a favorite of mine for many years: "The Great Way is not difficult for those who have no preferences. When love and hate are both absent, everything becomes clear and undisguised. Make the smallest distinction, however, and heaven and earth are set infinitely apart."[1]

These verses had a strong impact on the earnest, seeking mind of my youth. Having no preferences sounded like a cool way to live—being totally detached from life's dramas. I was quick to sign up for that!

Years later, it dawned on me that many of the lovely patients I had seen in psychiatric wards seemed to have few desires or preferences. And I'm quite confident that they were not enlightened. I have also observed a curious "stench of enlightenment" (as the Zen folks call it) among people in spiritual communities whose faces feature a glossy, neutral veneer and who appear humorless and disconnected. I often notice an irresistible urge to tease them, to break through their seriousness and self-importance.

Do You Prefer to Have No Preferences?

Being human means having desires and preferences. If we prefer to have no preferences, then *that* becomes a preference. How can we possibly live without having likes and dislikes? Do we prefer clean air or is it equally acceptable to bathe our lungs with hydrocarbons? Do we prefer having close friendships or being alone?

It gets pretty boring to be with people who do not know what they want. It is more engaging to know whether they prefer Chinese or Mexican food tonight. "Whatever *you* want dear" can get pretty old. Preferences add passion and juiciness to our lives.

I believe that Sengtsan's verse is meant to inspire us to cultivate equanimity so that we are not yanked off-center every time an alluring object appears. What brings anguish is clinging too tightly to things that do not bring real satisfaction, as well as not dealing gracefully with disappointments when things do not go our way.

"Having no preferences" makes sense if we define it as taking life as it comes and accepting ourselves as we are instead of struggling to manipulate ourselves and our surroundings to look and be just the way we want. It means experiencing openly whatever comes and maintaining self-honesty about whatever feelings arise from our contact with the world, whether pleasure or pain, elation or repulsion.

Our body and being know our natural likes and dislikes, and constantly send signals to us, although we're not always inclined to listen. As our self-awareness grows, so does our ability to give a welcoming nod to our preferences without being thrown off-balance by them. Entering the stream of experience, we flow with the myriad joys and sorrows that accompany being alive.

Extinguishing Craving: Not So Easy

Recognizing that the part of us that grasps keeps us disconnected and unhappy led to the Buddha's Third Noble Truth: the alleviation of suffering. Traditionally stated, liberation means the elimination of suffering through extinguishing our craving. But could this suggestion perpetuate the very dilemma it was meant to eradicate?

The Buddha taught in a cultural context appropriate for his time. But consider what machinations can unfold within us when we hear the admonition to extinguish craving. There is so much conditioning in our competitive society to achieve perfection and excellence. If we can excel in everything, no one can criticize or shame us. Eager to win respect and avoid failure, we strive to build and polish a self that will propel us over some imaginary finish line.

If we believe that extinguishing craving is our ticket to freedom, we are inclined to leap into battle mode. We are on it! We become totally oriented toward fixing and changing ourselves. Sadly, we may then foment an inner war between our mental picture of the blissful possibilities and our actual felt experience, which takes us far afield from what the Buddha actually taught.

Truths Get Lost in Translation

Teaching spiritual truths is a tricky business. We can only imagine the challenges faced by spiritual leaders such as the Buddha and Jesus as they tried to convey subtle experiences in ways that others could "get." It appears that the Buddha not only considered what is true but also how such truth might be heard. Consequently, he taught different things in different ways to different people.

Truth can get lost in translation as it moves from one mind to another and from one culture to another. No doubt there is timeless wisdom, but as times change, the way that those truths are expressed needs to change. The directive to "extinguish craving" has all the earmarks of trouble for our Western culture, which is all about poking, prodding, and fixing ourselves to match our ideal model of how we should think, feel, and act.

The aspiration to eradicate craving can be music to the ears of anyone already inclined to protect themselves from the plethora of uncomfortable emotions that relationships stir up. As one friend told me, "I used Buddhism to avoid relationships. I was afraid that no one would love me. It was difficult to believe that anyone would really be interested in being with me and understanding me." For this longtime meditator, the teachings about clinging and craving supported her tendency to keep her distance from people, which perpetuated her painfully unmet longing for connection.

The shadow side of Buddhism in the West and elsewhere is that it can reinforce an aversion to ordinary feelings, wants, and longings. Unwittingly subverted to serve our defenses, meditation can be used to circumvent the very real ways that life affects us. The sad outcome is that we become distant from our humanity, which leads to more suffering, not to liberation.

Accommodating Our Genetic Wiring

Through a simplistic interpretation of Eastern teachings—one that accommodates our defenses—we may view longing, desiring, and wanting as seductions away from the spiritual path *rather than being an essential part of the path*. We may try to eradicate anything resembling desire or delude ourselves into thinking that we have actually transcended it.

Longing is hardwired into our limbic brain and nervous system. Whether we like it or not, being human means being wedded to desire, which can readily morph into clinging. Millions of years of evolution won't be erased by moralistic thinking or willpower. Nor will meditation provide enough leverage to budge this two-thousand-pound gorilla. But why would we want to? Desire and longing are not something to eradicate but something to befriend and flow with, extracting the enriching energy and aliveness they provide for life's journey.

The Desire to Eliminate Desire

If we believe that our job is to extinguish desire altogether, we may adopt the black-and-white attitude that wanting is bad and letting go is good. This mindset keeps us vigilantly poised for a futile battle against how we are neurologically wired.

Many years ago, when I was a graduate student, I met a meditation teacher at a social gathering. After exchanging pleasantries, he asked how I was doing. Reflecting the pressures of my student life, I replied, "I'm struggling to keep it all together." Hoping for a compassionate response, I received a rather glib one: "Why don't you let it all fall apart and see what happens?"

After further dialogue, it became clear that he was suggesting that my desire to get a degree was creating suffering and that I should suspend my studies and spend more time meditating. He gave this advice without knowing me or inquiring about my struggle or asking what completing my studies meant to me. Fortunately, I didn't follow his simplistic solution, but a potential moment of connection was lost as my authentic sharing was met with subtle shaming rather than empathy.

Contrast that teacher's advice with Shunryu Suzuki's response to a student who often visited the Zen center to meditate and was struggling to complete his doctoral thesis. The student recounts the exchange fondly: "Invariably, Suzuki Roshi would come up and tap me on the shoulder, wrinkle his forehead, point toward my apartment, and whisper, 'Why aren't you over there writing the thesis?'"[2]

The desire to pursue a meaningful life and livelihood is a vital part of living. Wise spiritual teachers know that wanting to eliminate desire may prompt a newly hatched desire to eradicate desire. This perversion of our aspirations takes us on a journey far removed from the purity and goodness of our original longing.

Extending Compassion to Craving

What would it look like to extend compassion to our human desires and the stronger cravings that may arise from them? By attending to whatever we are noticing right now, can we allow ourselves to welcome our cravings, whether for sex, dessert, or admiration, without quickly disowning them? A non-judgmental attitude positions us to attend to the feelings and longings that percolate beneath. We may then uncover what we really desire, which might be intimacy, comforting, or connection. Our craving to be right might reflect how long we have suffered from the shame of being told we are wrong, along with an unmet longing for respect and kindness. Uncovering what we really want allows our inner process and our life in the world to move forward in harmony with each other rather than out of sync.

We become liberated from the chokehold of our cravings as we notice their inherent intelligence and the messages they hold for us. We might then discover that our misery is often a function of clinging so tightly to what we *think* we need that we don't pause long enough to explore what we *really* desire.

An authentic spiritual path includes discerning the longing for freedom and connection that reside deep within our being and differentiating them from more surface desires that lead to repeated suffering. We distinguish between the unavoidable pain that leads us out of our pain, such as the natural grief born of loss, from the pain that results from pursuing pleasures that don't bring real satisfaction and which only compound our suffering. By holding our desires lightly, we can see where they lead and then fine-tune our way forward.

Equanimity Through Opening to Our Experience

Finding equanimity is not possible if we squelch our desires and fight our feelings. If we are sad or hurt and conclude something is wrong with us for feeling this way, then we may become depressed or anxious. If we judge ourselves for feeling angry, we're likely to feel worse. If we think we are wimpy or unspiritual for being fearful, then we compound our suffering by layering shame atop fear.

What Jiddu Krishnamurti calls "choiceless awareness" includes being aware of pleasant and unpleasant emotions. It is very human to want to be somewhere other than where we are right now, especially if it doesn't feel good. But if we try to muscle our way into some preferred experience, we will likely multiply our misery. For example, if we are hurting from a breakup yet refuse to grieve, we might wind up rebounding to a new partner before we're ready.

Being awake includes opening to our experience as it presents itself. Life's ordinary challenges are less likely to devolve into suffering when we embrace our experience as it is. Touched by gentle mindfulness, our turbulent mind and emotions become still. Tensions melt and heartaches soften; problems come into clearer perspective. We are freed to glimpse life with more clarity and less clinging.

The Evolution of Longing

Eastern spirituality is often seen as a path of detachment, of letting go of the self. But it is really about *loosening attachments to some things so that we're freed to connect with others and with what is.* We are invited to notice and relinquish our distorted judgments about ourselves, the shame that blocks us from embracing ourselves, and our hankering to manipulate people. Resting more comfortably within ourselves, we may experience moments of pure presence in which we are neither attached nor non-attached: we're simply here. We are intimate with what is. A sense of fulfillment and connection with people and life dawns naturally without our needing to lunge after it.

As two people gain access to their ever-changing experiencing and share this together, a vibrant intimacy can come alive. By living in ourselves in such a way that luminous, engaging connections arise with more regularity, our desires and cravings tend to diminish. As personal longings are met or soothed, they begin to transform into a more expansive, transpersonal longing for the well-being of all.

The bodhisattva ideal of Mahayana Buddhism is often explained as the postponing of our own liberation in order to help others become free. A more nuanced perspective is that as we pursue our own desires mindfully, fulfilling those that promote well-being and relinquishing those that lead to suffering, we will find that our deepest desire is to awaken. We further discover that we are the most fulfilled when others feel fulfilled, which sparks an inner prompting to promote their happiness.

The desire to help others arises not as a way to stroke our ego, see ourselves as good, or accrue karmic credits. As our spiritual path allows us to find more peace and see things more clearly, we begin to feel in our bones that serving others delivers the deepest joy and meaning.

A Western Middle Way

The Buddha taught "the Middle Way"—a path that lies between the strict asceticism of his time and the path of self-indulgence. In his era, yogis went to mind-boggling extremes of self-mortification in the belief that it would subdue the body and release the spirit to unite with God. So perhaps the Middle Way of the Buddha's time leans too far in the direction of self-denial for Westerners today; the bar for robust spiritual practice was set quite differently back then.

Teachers like the Dalai Lama and Thich Nhat Hanh have encouraged us to adapt the essence of Buddhism to our own culture. As Thich Nhat Hanh put it, "The forms of Buddhism must change so that the essence of Buddhism remains unchanged."[3] The Confucian emphasis on the family, for example, transformed Buddhism into a family-friendly religion in China.

We live in a society where romantic love and intimate friendships are cherished. The search for personal fulfillment and interpersonal pleasures are deeply ingrained in us. As Buddhism enters the West, it is cautiously adapting to our proclivity toward romantic love, which includes embracing the joys and sorrows that accompany our longing to love and be loved.

This adaptation will entail clarifying Buddhist concepts to accommodate our Western psyche, culture, and language. Notions such as emptiness, no-self, impermanence, and non-attachment make many people cringe, often leading to the perception that the spiritual path is a somber journey toward self-denial and depersonalization. Freud believed that Buddhism is life-negating.

Properly understood, Buddhism and other Eastern paths are heartily life-engaging. Rather than being dour and ominous, we become *more fully alive*, available to touch and be touched by life. Many people have remarked on the outrageous sense of humor and hearty appetite for life displayed by Zen masters and Tibetan teachers. Dōgen, who introduced Zen to Japan, spoke of the "samadhi of self-fulfillment."[4] Self-enjoyment—relishing our body and life—is at the very heart of spirituality. Paintings of Zen monks Han-shan and Shih-te during the T'ang dynasty depict two playful men with broad, innocent, contagious smiles and childlike hearts.

Self-Restraint: Pausing to Notice Our Deeper Experience

Enjoying the richness of life is not to deny a place for the healthy self-restraint and discipline that spiritual teachings often encourage. Self-restraint is not a very sexy word; however, it simply means setting boundaries with what doesn't serve us well. Loosening our attachment to things that harm or restrict us frees us to connect with what nourishes and supports us. For example, restraining ourselves from watching scary movies might be appreciated by our heart and nervous system. We have a better chance of being happy if we are not obese, don't smoke, and find the discipline to exercise regularly.

A healthy lifestyle sometimes involves postponing immediate gratifications for the sake of greater future rewards. Sensing inwardly, we can pause and ask ourselves, "Is this what I really want to do; does it really feel right?" We can then notice what comes.

One way to practice restraint in the context of relationships is to gently hold our uncomfortable feelings rather than act them out. If we are angry with our partner, we might crave an immediate discharge of frustration by hurling a sarcastic comment or slamming the door. This is likely to trigger a defensive reaction, which leads to an escalating conflict.

Restraint in this context begins by pausing instead of succumbing to reactions of rage and blame. We may then bring gentle awareness to how the anger feels in our body and notice what might underlie it. By finding some space around these strong feelings rather than acting them out, we might recognize that our anger is a kind of pained protest that reflects a longing for connection. We desire intimacy and are upset that we're not getting it![5]

If we can pause long enough to get our arms around what we are actually experiencing, then rather than rail against our loved one, we might reveal the hurt beneath our anger. We invite people toward us as we express our yearning for closeness that quietly dwells somewhere within the impulse to attack or blame. By revealing our genuine feelings and longings, we're more likely to be heard and share an intimate moment.

Deeper connections spontaneously arise as we connect with the richness that lives inside us. When we mindfully attend to our inner experience, our body and emotions relax. We are then better prepared to bend a receptive ear toward the sacred longings and precious feelings that whisper within. Contacting and expressing our genuinely felt experience nurtures a climate that allows people to feel safe coming toward us. We create a garden where love wants to live.

Part Two

Intimacy with Others

Seeking and maintaining contact with others is a primary motivating principle in human beings. Dependency is an innate part of being human, rather than a childhood trait that we grow out of as we mature.

—Susan M. Johnson

Attachment principles teach us that most people are only as needy as their unmet needs. When their emotional needs are met, and the earlier the better, they usually turn their attention outward.

—Amir Levine and Rachel S. F. Heller

Chapter Seven

Spirituality Meets Attachment Theory: Is Suffering Caused by Attachment or Non-Attachment?

E very few winters, relentless rains batter Northern California. Noticing a flood under my house after a heavy downpour, I opened a small door to air it out. After the flood cleared, I closed the door. Never did it occur to me that any life form would seek refuge in this desolate place. But days later when I reopened the door, an eerie feeling assailed me as I glimpsed two glowing eyes in the dark distance. Was it a possum, a skunk, some dreadful rodent? Using binoculars, I saw that it was a cat! Later I discovered that it was my neighbor's cat, which had been missing for days.

I left the door open and expected Dickens to make a hasty getaway, leaving a nice thank-you note. But like a homeless person clinging to a cozy spot, he refused to leave. He was still there the next day. Peering more closely, I could see that he had scratched down some sheets of insulation to keep himself warm. Apparently, he saw this as his new digs and was settling in; but as he had no food or water, his judgment seemed rather impaired.

I love cats and was concerned about Dickens's well-being. Realizing that bold action was required, I fought past the cobwebs and my claustrophobia, creeping inch by inch through the tiny crawlspace to rescue him. But it quickly became clear that he had little interest in being rescued. I was his sole hope for salvation, but he kept clinging to his deluded sense of safety. I tried reassuring him: "It's okay. I'm here to help you. Let me carry you to safety." But whenever I got close, he would scurry away, as if to say, "Yeah, right, that's what everyone says! Why should I trust you? I can take care of myself and don't need your help, thank you very much!"

Though his survival depended upon me, I couldn't win his trust. Like a spurned lover, I found myself feeling powerless, frustrated, and even angry that he did not recognize my noble intentions. My neighbor finally had the bright idea of taking a less-gentle approach; we would make aggressive gestures toward him that would chase him out.

This "tough love" approach worked, and I was delighted. But I've had to let go of any desire for appreciation. I often see Dickens sunbathing in my yard, but do you think he'd be grateful? No way. Whenever I get close, he scurries away. His "owner" reassures me that he is suspicious of everyone, so I've learned not to take his rejection so personally.

Dickens is a feral cat with no inner template for trusting. I can imagine that he never had a chance to bond with his mother and that he endured multiple traumas before my neighbor generously adopted him. Dickens has an avoidant-attachment style, in contrast with my deceased cat, Blossom, who seized every opportunity to crawl into my welcoming lap. Blossom experienced good bonding with her mother, which led to a secure attachment style.

Many of us have a lot in common with Dickens. Old trauma and abandonment have imprinted a core belief that trusting is dangerous. Our lower brain prompts us to escape danger by reacting through fight, flight, or freeze. Like Dickens, our habits of self-protection may now run on automatic pilot, even when someone wants to adopt us as a friend or partner.

Clinging to caution reflects our body's learned survival mechanism. Lacking the secure internal base that develops from warm bonding, our capacity to discern whether a person is safe becomes impaired. We hold back from taking sensible risks to pursue connections and taste life fully. We revert to the black-and-white world of our primitive brain—better be safe than sorry. But similar to other mammals, when we are disconnected, we are really not safe at all. Tigers prey on animals that have strayed from the herd. Isolated seniors are easy prey for scammers. Lonely individuals are more prone to depression and having compromised immune functioning.

When It Is Hard to Let in Love

In some Buddhist circles, it is sacrilegious to question the teaching that suffering is spawned through our attachments. But with abundant research pouring in about child development and human attachment needs, we must consider whether the opposite could be true. Is misery actually created by the lack of attachment—that is, the lack of connection and healthy human bonding?

However strong our intention to live with an open heart, it is not so easy, especially if we didn't have strong connections growing up. Poor early attachment has been shown to impair our emotional development and neural integration. When our love receptors have withered due to lack of nutrients, we find it difficult to receive love and feel connected.

Wounded trust due to unreliable bonding or abuse prompts our young psyches to don a self-protective armor. When people reach out to us later in life, we may notice an uncomfortable neural squirming and emotional shutdown. Our antennae quiver at the slightest sign of being shamed, criticized, or unwelcomed. Our belly tightens, our breath constricts, our eyes divert. The reactivation of fear and our bodily memory of being hurt override our ability to trust and connect.

Attachment Theory

I am not usually captivated by the latest fads in psychology, but attachment theory is popular right now for good reason. It was not enthusiastically embraced when psychoanalyst John Bowlby developed it back in the 1950s. His observation that humans share the bonding behavior of mammals and don't thrive when mother love is not forthcoming was sacrilegious to psychoanalysts at the time. They reduced most human behavior to intrapsychic causes and didn't put much store in what happens between mother and child, or between people in general.

It is difficult for us humans to acknowledge our powerlessness and vulnerability. We get befuddled to consider that neither the earth nor the human ego is at the center of the universe and that our existence is a gift that rests upon a delicate balance with nature and other human beings. But our distaste for acknowledging our interdependence not only isolates us, it also has devastating effects on our planet.

The Need for Bonding

Bowlby's central observation was that we need love and connection to be healthy and happy. He suggested that infants are endowed with a brain and nervous system that propel them toward safety and growth by establishing a secure attachment with the mother. The audacious view that mother and child follow their natural instinct to bond and that mothers embrace their impulse to comfort their infants was scandalous at the time.

Coddling children was repulsive to mainstream behavioral therapists in the 1950s, who argued that indulging children with hugs and holding would spoil them. "Mother love is a dangerous instrument," warned behaviorist John Watson, who was convinced that responding to a child's cry for attention would create a perilous dependency.[1] He believed that children should never be kissed or allowed to sit on a parent's lap, and he warned that the Boy Scouts, the YMCA, and pajama parties could lead to homosexuality—a horrifying prospect back in those days.

Watson's belief that too much attachment in childhood leads to misery has been soundly supplanted by the recognition that it is a *lack* of attachment that leads to a failure to thrive. A persuasive flood of research suggests that children need the reliable presence of an emotionally available, responsive caregiver in order to experience a secure base from which to explore the world and take intelligent risks.

The Myth of Self-Sufficiency

We might like to inflate how powerful we are by believing that we can transcend the need for connection. But, alas, it is hardwired into our brain. As University of California–San Francisco medical professor Thomas Lewis puts it, "Total self-sufficiency turns out to be a daydream whose bubble is burst by the sharp edge of the limbic brain."[2] The desire for a fulfilling closeness is not some immature or unspiritual thing we would do well to outgrow. We need intimacy throughout our lifespan for healthy psychological development and to maintain a healthy brain and heart.

Without connections with a partner, family, or community, our immune system fails to function robustly. Cancer survivors who enter support groups live longer than those who have no social support network. People with pets not only feel better but often live longer, as do those who have a network of good friends. The scientific evidence supporting attachment theory is very compelling: lack of healthy attachment causes suffering.

Eastern religions and their New Age offshoots are gradually coming to terms with what science now knows about human development. It is difficult to maintain the view that attachment is something to eschew when it is clear that the lack of supportive bonds is at the root of much of our suffering, generating agonizing anxiety, depression, and isolation.

Some may wonder about those Taoist hermits who lived in caves or monks who practice in isolation. Both in ancient times and, to a limited extent, today, there appear to be a very small number of people who have achieved interesting states of consciousness through extreme isolation. But most monastics do not practice in isolation; they might practice non-attachment to things of the world, but they usually form strong bonds with their monastic communities.

Poor Attachment Leads to Clinging or Withdrawal

If we lacked a safe bond as a child, we tend to orient ourselves in one of three ways as an adult:

1. We cling to people to secure connections and evade an inner emptiness.
2. We isolate ourselves through avoidance and self-protection; we give up on love.
3. We bounce between the extremes of clinging and distancing. We become ambivalent about love. We engage in push-pull; we demand connection, but when it is offered, we pull away.

A string of disappointments may leave us feeling powerlessness to create satisfying relations; something in us collapses. Sadly, we may simplistically conclude that desire is the problem, not realizing that it is impaired bonding that has soured us on love.

Susan Johnson, whose remarkable work with couples is based upon attachment theory, describes the anguish that results when our need for connection is endangered: "When the security of a bond is threatened, attachment behaviors are activated. If these behaviors fail to evoke responsiveness from the attachment figure, a prototypical process of angry protest, clinging, despair, and finally, detachment occurs."[3] It may seem paradoxical, but the failure to bond underlies much of our clinging and suffering, whether as an infant or an adult.

Without healthy bonding, we are more vulnerable to loss and rejection. If we enjoyed reliable connections as a child, we tend to feel more secure and trusting in our adult relationships. Having internalized a sense of safety and trust, we're less defended; our heart is more open and available, and we reach out to people with relative ease. Relationships become a source of satisfaction. We are less clingy and demanding when our attachment needs have been met and continue to be met.

This doesn't mean we are damaged goods if we didn't have adequate bonding. If our parents were unavailable, perhaps we connected with a grandparent, teacher, friend, or friend's parents. Even if not, old wounds can heal by attending to them gently, perhaps with the help of a skilled therapist, and by developing the supportive bonds we need to feel whole and connected.

Clinging as a Reaction to Failed Attachment

As we have seen, clinging is often viewed as a source of suffering that is best eliminated. But if we deconstruct clinging, that is, understand what comprises it, we may welcome it as a doorway to awakening.

From the standpoint of attachment theory, interpersonal clinging is merely an outsized attempt to secure the nurturing and contact that have eluded us. Blessedly, we haven't given up on life and love. We haven't collapsed into despair and depression. Unashamed of our needs, we pursue them unapologetically and protest loudly when our needs are unmet.

The shadow side of seeking contact is that our manner of pursuit is often frustratingly ineffective. When we approach others with a dramatic sense of urgency or entitlement, our tone of voice may be critical, contemptuous, or shaming. We may look for love in all the wrong places. Our nervous system may become jangled based upon the slightest sign of inattentiveness: a belated phone call, a straying eye, a differing viewpoint, or the minor irritability in another's voice. Our frustrated longing for safety and comfort often shows up in reactive ways, pushing away the intimacy we desire.

Holding Our Wanting

Research confirming the viability of attachment theory has put a final nail in the coffin of the popular belief that desire and longing cause suffering. A vital step toward inner peace, fulfilling relationships, and happiness is realizing that the problem lies not in our wanting, but rather in *how we hold our wanting*. The unconscious, indirect, or compulsive ways we pursue our desires get us into trouble, as does our inability to gently hold the unwieldy feelings associated with our longings.

Telling others or ourselves that clinging creates suffering is not helpful, even if there is some truth to it. If our beloved leaves us and we are devastated, we're not likely to be soothed by a friend's simplistic advice to "let her go" or "don't cling to her!" We might reply, "Thanks for the thought, but that makes me feel more pain and shame because I can't do it!"

What moves us toward letting go is our friend's comforting presence and heartfelt listening. As they extend caring and hold our pain with us, our anxiety and anguish ease. Feeling more connected and less isolated frees us, as opposed to adhering to some spiritual half-truth. A taste of liberation can come through with a little help from our friends.

The Complexity of Clinging

Buddhists may casually refer to clinging as a source of suffering, over-looking the fact that this word represents a larger realm of psychological complexity. Clinging is a multifaceted molecule comprised of emotions such as fear, shame, anxiety, and anger that bind to the purity of our longing, born of real or imagined threats to our well-being—or even our emotional survival.

For example, we may yearn for closeness with our partner. Before we know it, we are overflowing with sexual desire and we push at our partner to be sexual with us. If our partner wants to go slower rather than respond immediately, we might bark back, "What's wrong with you? You're not in the mood *again!*" Of course, such indictments push our partner further away. As the fear of rejection, old hurts, and anger begin to infect our longing, we withdraw even further into an isolated burrow of craving.

What we are actually longing for is more than just sex. We want to experience a deeper emotional and spiritual intimacy. But it is difficult to stay present with our subtle, perhaps pain-tinged longing, so the craving for sex takes over. If we can stay with the delightful ache of bodily desire, embracing its sweet and sour texture, then we are right there in the luscious moment. Perhaps we can convey our feelings by saying something like, "I'm feeling a very sweet ache for you right now." As we become aware of and reveal our mutual experience, we may ride the sacred wave of longing right into each other's welcoming hearts.

When we are driven by cravings that are split off from our heartfelt longings, we are swept into distractions that end up creating suffering. Mindfulness of our true yearnings drains the energy from runaway cravings. If we can allow our nervous system to settle enough to notice our true longings, we're poised to take a step toward authentic relating.

Any hint of judging ourselves for clinging paralyzes our ability to uncover our deeper felt experience. Our suffering is softened when we explore its experiential components. What is really happening in our interior world when we are pulling on or attacking our partner? What feelings arise and how do they live in our tissues? What are they trying to tell us? What needs to happen so that a tight or anxious place inside us might shift and our process move forward? What we call "clinging" may then reconstitute itself in ways that connect us with ourselves and others and ultimately free us.

Abandoning Longing

If our desire for connection has been repeatedly defeated, there may follow a denial of our need for contact. We may turn against our longings and evict the tender feelings associated with them. Demeaning or ignoring our need for contact, we may become the rugged, unruffled individual who claims to not need anyone.

Susan Johnson explains how this pattern develops: "Attachment theory suggests that the only way some children have to maintain relationships with unavailable parents is to minimize their awareness of attachment needs and block out any longing for intimate contact."[4] If we have become invested in not needing anyone, then even when people come along who would love us, we may not be emotionally accessible. It takes rigorous self-honesty to recognize that our longings haven't disappeared; they have simply gone into hiding.

Threatened by longing, we may denigrate not only ourselves but also judge those who are more forthright about their longings as "too needy" or "overly sensitive." Just as we have become numb to our own needs, we may become tone-deaf to others' pleas for contact and understanding. This insensitivity is inherently shaming, as it invalidates another's experience. However spiritually savvy or psychologically aware we may be, when we're triggered, our communication skills may go out the window, overridden by the urgent press of unmet needs.

Bringing Mindfulness to Longings

We are encoded by life with a choiceless longing. We may recognize its signature as a vague, background discontent that stems from an unremitting sense of disconnection. If we're interested in awakening, how could it not include recognizing our longings, dancing skillfully with them, and tracking where they take us?

Unacknowledged longings often animate us, but they may come out roughly, indirectly, or diffusely. We may become aggressive or desperate in trying to fulfill them (clinging and craving). They may operate in a split-off way, that is, without our being aware of them. In other words, our unmet needs hijack our lives.

In some half-conscious way, we may try to shuffle our uncomfortable feelings onto others. We hurl hurtful words or do nasty things to make them taste some of our pain, shame, or fear. Creating spaciousness around our longing can safeguard us from sliding down the chute of craving immediate gratification or subtly punishing others. How sweet love can be as we learn to hold our yearnings and feelings gently and allow contact to arise from this more equanimous place within ourselves.

How Wounds Contaminate Our Longing

Our fears play out in painfully familiar ways in the arena of relationships. For example, my longing for more contact might prompt me to implore my partner to spend time with me. But instead of simply revealing my longing by saying, "I'd love to spend time with you on Saturday, sweetie; how would you feel about that?" I might blurt, "Are you busy again Saturday? You never have time for me anymore! You're so self-centered!"

Experiencing the situation as a threat, my activated amygdala goads me to attack and defend. The urgency of my unmet longings leaps out through hostile criticisms and shaming accusations about her character. Underlying my angry attempt to control her is a desire for connection and an utter sense of helplessness to satisfy my longing.

Given my hostile manner of communication, it is little wonder that my partner doesn't relish the prospect of my company, and so my shrill communication fuels a cycle that perpetuates my isolation and anguish. The more I attack, the more she pulls away. The more she distances, the more aggressive I become.

Becoming mindful of my deeper experience, I notice that my criticism and contempt come from a tight, anxious place. In Buddhist language, they reflect my clinging to old hurts and anger around rejection. I am clinging to the assumption or conviction that she doesn't want to spend time with me. I am clinging to mistrust and, perhaps, also to fear and insecurity around my lovability. Perhaps more accurately, my old hurts and fears are clinging to me. I am fused with ancient wounds that are heavily charged, which prompts me to resort to familiar, yet impotent weaponry.

Clinging Fuels a Cycle of Hopelessness

The charge around my unmet needs is voiced in a way that sends shudders of anxiety and disquiet through my partner's tender heart. I am provoking her rather than inviting her to relax toward me. Her defensiveness and distancing may stir up additional pressure in my chest that finds relief by venting additional accusations. As I get more out of control, the conflict keeps escalating, adding hopelessness atop heartache.

Of course, my partner has no clue that I am feeling afraid, sad, or lonely. My aggressive language offers little evidence that I enjoy her company and want to be with her. After all, I've basically accused her of being a despicable creature! Unless she is rather saintly and, realizing that I'm hurting, moves gingerly toward me, she will probably conclude, "I don't feel safe being with such a nasty brute."

Viewed through one lens, my clinging is being voiced in cruel ways that push her away and increase my anguish. But viewed through another lens, my aggressive display is a plea for connection prompted by a legitimate longing. Sadly, my yearning is expressed in a twisted way due to earlier wounds of rejection and isolation and because I lack the skills to express feelings and longings in a skillful way.

De-Clinging Through Self-Soothing

If I can find a way to discharge some of the energy around my wound-based resentment and blame, then I have an opportunity to uncover my deeper longings. De-clinging means finding a way to soothe myself and then approaching my partner from a softer place. Neither my desire nor my clinging are problematic if I can allow them space, bring calm awareness to the feelings and meanings implicit in them, and express what is really going on in a self-revealing, openhearted way.

Sitting in the center of my tender longing, I might say soulfully, "I'm missing you" or "I feel sad that we haven't spent much time together lately" or "I'd like to be held by you." These tender offerings from my authentic heart invite love and intimacy to come into being. This language of intimacy is one aspect of what Buddhism calls "Right Speech," where kind and gentle words foster closeness and caring.

There is an intimate linkage between how we relate to ourselves and our capacity to connect with others. If I can steady myself by gently holding my sadness, fear, and loneliness, and then tenderly express what I am feeling and wanting, I'll increase my chances of being heard. My partner is more apt to soften and respond compassionately as she hears my heart's desire.

The Poetry of Our Longing

The heart's poetry takes time to incubate. As the fire of yearning is contained within the holding environment of self-compassion, it transforms into a kind of prayer or plea for contact. We tenderly voice our heart's longing for the nourishment of an affectionate touch, loving gaze, or supportive understanding, while surrendering control over the outcome.

Right Speech means taking time to attend gently to our gnarly feelings before voicing them. As we embrace the fear, shame, and anger associated with our longings, the sludge settles, and we can see more clearly what we really want. We can then reach out in a more gentle, inviting way as we touch the purity and beauty of our longings.

Responding from Our Longing

Embracing our feelings and longings means relating to them with an intimate loving-kindness. As we reside within the sanctuary of our heart and soul, we develop inner resources that enable us to be *in* our longing and respond *from* it rather than get caught up in the knee-jerk reactions of our fear-based reptilian brain. As we distill from clinging to our innocent, tender longing, we can interrelate with more equanimity and less fragmentation. Gradually, we learn to give and receive love without the grasping that contaminates our longing to love and be loved.

It is no small task to hold our feelings and longings gently enough to *directly communicate* rather than *react* from them. As we will explore later, meditation, Focusing, and mindfulness-based practices can help fashion a foundation for love and intimacy by creating an inner holding environment for the emotional fires that rage or smolder within us.

Focusing on Your Deeper Longing

The next time you feel angry or frustrated with a loved one, take some time to sit quietly with yourself. Notice what you are feeling beneath your frustration or disappointment. Is there some longing that is painfully unmet—perhaps a yearning for kindness, closeness, or caring? If so, take some time to hold this tender longing within yourself. See what happens as you sense it inside your body. Where do you feel it? What does it feel like? Is there a tight place in your chest, a squirmy feeling in your stomach, or a sweet ache in your heart? Can you let it be there without doing anything about it right now?

By embracing it, you may find that the intensity of your need or longing begins to settle. As you feel calmer and more connected to yourself, you might consider approaching your partner and speaking from the tender place of longing, rather than a place of blame. Instead of attacking with the blunt edge of your longing—without even knowing that the longing is the real thing that is brewing inside you—simply reveal the longing itself. Voice how you miss connecting, how you love being together, how you feel sad about the recent conflicts.

Sadly, we often assume that our partner knows what we feel and long for. Or a destructive pride prevents us from voicing our wants. When a couple can begin sharing their deeper longings and wants, they often enjoy less defensiveness and more intimacy. It takes courage and strength to share tender feelings. If such sharing feels too risky, difficult, or painful, you may consider consulting a qualified couples therapist.

Healing Attachment Wounds

The path toward a spiritually rich intimacy involves attending to both our inner and outer worlds. Bringing warm mindfulness into our inner world allows us to connect with ourselves and heal restrictive patterns that lock up our heart. But if we keep our focus exclusively within, we can become overly self-absorbed. I have often heard people declare, "I need to get *myself* together before getting into a relationship." But if we wait until we are perfect, we might be living in a nursing home before we're ready!

We will always be in process. We don't need to be flawlessly whole before pursuing partnerships or friendships. Recognizing that *everyone* is struggling allows us to cultivate compassion as we fumble our way toward intimacy. We have all been hurt or betrayed to varying degrees, and we need each other in order to heal and grow. Insisting that our work is entirely interior is just as shortsighted as the romantic notion that salvation lies in being rescued by another person.

Finding Our Balance

When Henry David Thoreau was living at Walden Pond, he famously said, "I wanted to live deep and suck out all the marrow of life."[5] If we take this approach to our relationships, we may want to seize the moment and pull love and intimacy toward us. But moments cannot be seized; they can only be allowed, which means settling into ourselves and allowing our experience to unfold. We pluck the tree-ripened fruit when the moment is right.

We tend to either look too much outside ourselves for fulfillment or retreat too far within. Fixing our gaze externally, we may have supersized expectations of what others can provide. By withdrawing too far inside, we may have allowed our aspirations to become downsized. The intimacy duet requires a middle way between losing ourselves in another person and submerging ourselves in a sea of solitude.

If we are too avaricious in pursuing connections, we may never pause to consider what we can do *for ourselves* that would create a climate for intimacy to grow. As we develop resources within ourselves, we're more inclined to trust that intimacy will visit us without needing to control its creative dance, without fighting to haul in love and contact. We allow intimacy to unfold by cultivating presence with ourselves—relaxing into what we're experiencing in the moment, and communicating from our deepest-felt sense of what is alive for us right now.

We create a foundation for connection by holding ourselves with loving-kindness. Rather than grasp with devouring eyes, we gaze openly and savor the play of contact between us. We affirm our needs and wants while glimpsing what others need to be happy. We enjoy the fulfillment of increasing others' happiness and making a difference in their lives.

Our capacity to love and be loved expands as we allow our nervous system and mental chatter to settle enough so that our heart becomes freshly available for contact. Meditation and spiritual practices can accelerate this healing and opening, but traditional methods of spiritual practice are not enough. We also need to attend to our emotional life in a gentle and skillful way.

The sea always filled her with longing, though for what she was never sure.

—Cornelia Funke, *Inkheart*

Desire, in its longing for completion, is ultimately in search of being.

—Mark Epstein

A Psychology of Liberation:
Living with Longing

❦

As we have seen, if we believe that our desires and longings cause suffering and that our spiritual work is to extinguish that fire, we're inclined to suppress our experience rather than welcome it. But it takes only a slight adjustment in understanding the Second Noble Truth to make a crucial difference in how we approach spiritual practice—one that could lead to less sorrow and more joy.

We cannot know with absolute certainty what the great spiritual teachers actually said or meant. Similar to the teachings of Jesus, the words of the Buddha were not recorded until hundreds of years after his death. The accuracy of the Buddhist canon is dependent upon flawless human memory. A similar debate exists among Christian scholars about whether key Biblical passages flowed from the mouth of Jesus or the imagination of later scribes.

Making matters even more complex, nuances are easily lost as words are translated from one language to another. The meanings of words also change over time, which further complicates any efforts to ascribe absolute meaning to the human convention of language. It is therefore incumbent upon us to cross-reference sacred texts, however hallowed we may hold them to be, with our personal and collective human experience.

Longings Are Associated with Suffering

If we carefully track our experience, we will realize that our longings and desires are *associated* with suffering. People we love leave us or die, our achievements don't deliver the expected satisfaction, our hopes often fade into disillusionment. But this doesn't mean that our desires, such as for love or a meaningful life, *cause* suffering.

A common interpretation of Buddhism is that having desires inevitably leads to anguish. But from another perspective, thirsts and longings are simply an inevitable part of our existential condition. When we are hungry for food, this hunger doesn't *create* anguish. But if we don't honor what our body needs, that lack of responsiveness creates much suffering, indeed!

The same applies to emotional hungers. What becomes problematic is *how we relate to our desires* and the panoply of feelings they evoke. The good news is that we can learn to hold our desires lightly, pursue them wisely, and be prepared to courageously embrace the inevitable losses and disappointments that life brings.

Being Gentle with Our Longing

A common Buddhist instruction for dealing with desire is to notice it and let it go. But this advice may lead us to reject an essential part of ourselves. A more nuanced understanding invites us to be mindful of where our desires are trying to move us or what they are really about. Whether or not a particular desire leads to misery is a function of how we relate to it.

Poor early attachment can lead to a disconnection from our desires. If we were not emotionally met and understood, we learned to protect ourselves by dissociating from these painfully unmet longings. Our tender heart shut down to shield us from unbearable isolation.

Becoming numb to our wanting anesthetizes our capacity to care and love. One client conveys the experience of many: "Part of me hasn't allowed myself to really care. It's terrifying to care; I'm afraid to care too much. It's been disappointing when I've loved and needed someone. So now I pretend I don't care to protect myself from rejection. But then a part of me really does care, and it bubbles up in intense anger and annoyance, and I end up driving people away. I protect myself from rejection, but now I'm just lonely." Sadly, the price we pay to protect ourselves from the unavoidable hurt of rejection is the suffering of isolation.

Our psycho-spiritual integration is furthered as we accept our desires rather than view them as an adversary. The poet William Blake was aware that longing gets a bad rap when he said, "He who desires but acts not breeds pestilence."[1] However, the appropriate "act" might be one of attention, not an impetuous acting out of these desires. At times, our desires may move us toward some action, such as requesting someone's phone number at a party or asking for a hug. At other times, we might simply notice our longings, such as when we see a gorgeous person at a restaurant. The point is to engage with our desires intelligently, not drive them underground where they may quietly fester.

Dancing with Longing

The shift in attitude from abolition to acceptance of our felt experience is a step toward liberation. By viewing desire as a doorway rather than a roadblock, we can fully welcome it. As we dance with it skillfully, we can tap into the life energy it contains, thereby bringing greater passion into our lives. We can be receptive to where it moves us, delivering us, albeit in a bumpy way, toward an exquisitely nourishing contact with others and life itself.

As we hold our longing with loving-kindness, we learn to ride its unsteady wave toward emotional and spiritual fulfillment rather than be yanked about haphazardly by its wildness. This path includes embracing ourselves gently when our yearnings are frustrated. Bringing gentleness to the feelings that accompany disappointment eases our pain and allows us to learn from our experience.

Dealing with longings skillfully, especially when they are frustrated, is an essential part of "Right Effort," which is part of the Buddha's Eightfold Path. This is not a campaign to eradicate something but rather the effort to gently attend to all aspects of our experience and humanity. Engaging mindfully with the rhythm of our longings, we move gracefully with the dance music of life.

Observing Experience or Being Moved By It?

The various thirsts and hungers that compete for attention are invitations to consider some important aspect of our life. Sometimes the issue is clear and the solution is simple. The ache in our stomach tells us that we crave nutrients; do we want a soyburger or a green salad? If we simply notice the desire without acting upon it, we might notice ourselves fainting from self-neglect!

The same principle applies to the more complex world of our emotional/ spiritual needs. If we repeatedly notice a longing for intimacy, do we just keep watching it, or is there an implicit plea for action inherent in what we are noticing? Should we just sit alone in our room and be mindful of the recurring ache in our lonely heart on a Saturday night? Or is this feeling sending us a message to get more creative and courageous in reaching out to people? Might it feel right to attend a lecture, visit an art opening, or peruse ads on a dating site? Our innate wisdom includes allowing ourselves to act—translating our inner signals into skillful action.

Noticing Versus Acting on Our Longings

The path toward freedom and happiness involves engaging with our desires so that we don't routinely dismiss the ones that merit attention. Sometimes we may simply acknowledge that a particular desire is arising without acting on it. At other times, if we only notice the desire and let it go, we might reject an important message that life is offering.

A desire to remodel our home might be a convenient distraction from an inner emptiness. But it might also reflect a sacred longing to create more beauty in our lives. An inner restlessness might reflect a desire to make a meaningful contribution to our world. A feeling of emptiness might prompt a phone call to an old friend. Our world shrinks if we routinely dismiss our desires without hearing the wise messages they might hold for us.

Is it possible that some portion of our longings arises from something far greater than what we can imagine? Dare we consider that life itself is longing to experience more of its grandeur through us? Are we a vehicle through which the life force is yearning to move toward greater consciousness, love, and beauty? By turning a blind eye to our desires, are we saying no to life?

Honoring the Meaning of Our Longings and Feelings

Whenever an uncomfortable feeling arises, we might want to meditate, read scriptures, or chant away our pain. These practices may succeed in soothing us momentarily, but like a child clamoring for attention, our feelings are likely to return until we attend to them and hear the messages enfolded within them.

The subtle suppression of our feelings shuts us down rather than opens us up. An authentic spiritual life expands us. We become more contactable. We engage life with a tender, open heart.

Feelings are a shorthand word for how life affects us, ranging from intense emotions to more nuanced feelings and sensations. Being open to life means attuning to our felt reactions to it. Being present with our ever-changing felt sense of being bodily alive requires a courageous mindfulness and holding what comes with kindness. This self-compassion creates a foundation for being kindly disposed toward others. As we become tender toward our own humanity, we can more readily extend our caring toward the world.

What Generates Suffering

Rather than desire itself being problematic, what may generate suffering are the following:

- We are unclear about what we really want or need; we pursue secondary desires rather than our primary longings.
- Our desires take us on a wild chase that leads us out of the present moment.
- We are not able to *receive* in a way that might nurture the place in us that experiences longing and wanting.
- We have unrealistic expectations that have us living more in our heads than in the present moment.
- We don't know how to relate wisely to our desires, feelings, and psychological processes.
- We feel shame around our longings and desires and, therefore, deny them or act them out indirectly.
- We can't let go of something that is beyond our reach. We have trouble accepting limitations.

Getting clear about what we really want or need versus pursuing secondary, conditioned desires

Believing that our wants are suspect, we may dismiss them without tracing them to their core. We don't allow ourselves to sense into them directly and patiently explore what they are about. We don't consider whether our desires originate from a deeper intelligence that wants to move us toward something more expansive and joyful.

When we are unclear about what we really desire, we may pursue secondary gratifications while our primary longings remain hidden. For example, we may crave sex when we really long for intimacy. We may overeat to soothe an inner emptiness when we actually need love, holding, and comforting. We may pursue wealth and status when we really long for acceptance and belonging.

When our primary longings have been repeatedly frustrated, we may get fixated on secondary desires that don't really satisfy us. We get more energized by shopping than by having lunch with a friend. Toys and things activate the pleasure centers of the brain until we tire of them. We then proceed to refresh our desire system with a new assortment of alluring objects. But sadly, when we replace our primary need for love and connection with the pursuit of power, possessions, or other distractions, our deeper yearnings go unnoticed.

By becoming fixated on a particular desire, we may overlook other ways to meet our needs. We might overly depend upon our partner while neglecting other sources of nurturing. Cultivating resources, such as friendships, art, music, or a spiritual practice, can broaden the ways we connect with ourselves and life itself, and it has the added advantage of refreshing our partnership with new nutrients.

Our desires remove us from the present moment

Our longings create suffering if they take us on a wild goose chase away from the present moment. The allure of how things might be better can perpetuate a struggle to remodel our lives or reform others. We become lost in fantasies about how we want things to be, and life passes us by.

We increase our suffering by not allowing a friendly space for our true longings to unfold and trusting that they will lead somewhere positive or instructive. This path begins by noticing whatever we are experiencing right now.

Terms like "being present" or "living in the now" are popular nowadays, but they lose their meaning when overused. It is easier to grasp the *concept* of being present than to experience it, yet the spontaneous joy of being alive and intimate with others can be experienced only in the current moment.

Interestingly, the word "current" not only means "existing in the present" but also refers to "the steady flow of water or air in a particular direction." Oceans don't resist the ever-changing current; they are vibrant and alive with continual change. There is nothing to hold on to. As we take a cue from nature and no longer resist the current flow of our experience, we're likely to be less troubled.

Being present means being aware of our present experience as it is, which means being intimate with ourselves. The path toward being present leads us to attend more and more to whatever we are experiencing right now. When we're present with ourselves, rather than trying to figure out what is wrong with us, we're well positioned to be present with others and sense what is meaningful and alive for them in this moment.

Being freshly alive and present as we interact allows rich moments of connection. Instead of attending inwardly, our tendency is to become outer-directed. We evaluate whether a person meets our standards. Rather than share our feelings and longings, we cling to our judgments and evaluations as a misguided way of staying safe or drawing people toward us. Such reactions remove us from the present moment, distance us from others, and perpetuate isolation.

Popular spiritual books encourage us to be in the moment, but they often overlook an important aspect of "being here now"—making room for the feelings and longings that are happening right now. For example, we may experience a sense of being driven to advance professionally. We might fantasize about how it would feel to get an advanced degree or executive title we've been longing for.

Some people might suggest that being in the now means letting go of this drive for advancement, since we are then looking toward the future. But in reality, the now is inseparable from the past and future. Our longing for a better life can produce future "nows" that are more meaningful and fulfilling if we think clearly and plan properly.

Being in the now includes staying with the "feel" of what we notice about "wanting to advance." As we welcome this current desire, we might notice something new. For example, it might occur to us that what is really important is to garner the respect of our friends rather than trying to get everyone to love us by being powerful or renowned. Exploring more deeply, it may dawn on us that what is most important is to respect ourselves and live with integrity whether or not we're respected by others.

Something inside us might release or open up as we uncover what is really motivating us. Being with our presently felt experience allows a gradual unfolding of new meanings and directions. We may still want to advance professionally because it engages more of our talents and increases our income, but we can now do it in a less driven, more relaxed way.

We move toward liberation as we allow the emergence of our natural inner process and learn to track it and trust it while noticing how it changes and evolves. This is different from a purely mental self-exploration that is disconnected from feelings. Our process takes a natural direction as we open to it experientially. The quality of longing or craving loosens as we hold it more lightly.

Obstacles to receiving and allowing contact

I have heard many Buddhist teachers suggest something like this: "We have an insatiable desire to fill ourselves from the outside, but our longing for love and intimacy can never be satisfied." The implication is, "Don't torture yourself by looking to relationships for happiness. You're looking in the wrong direction!"

But what if relationships don't satisfy us because we don't *let in* love and caring when it visits us? Our longings are only associated with suffering to the extent that we're unable to receive graciously. When love shines upon us, we don't absorb its warmth. Our body/mind stiffens rather than becoming porous to love. We don't allow another's caring and presence to touch the spot that desires connection. As John Welwood puts it, "We cannot receive love . . . if we are not open to the raw and tender experience of wanting it."[2]

Who among us doesn't appreciate knowing that we are cared about or valued? Yet when someone offers a compliment, expresses gratitude, or reaches out to touch us, do we allow it to seep deeply into our body and being? Are we mindful of how we are touched by it? Perhaps our stomach relaxes or we notice a warmth in our heart. Can we permit ourselves to savor that precious moment? Or do we dismiss a compliment by telling ourselves, "Don't get a swelled head." Or do we wonder, "What will they expect from me in return?" Or, clinging to shame, we may think, "Wait until they really get to know me!"

Suffering results from not relishing the good things in our lives. Perhaps we have internalized the Sunday-school belief that it is nobler to give than to receive, better to love than to be loved. But if everyone specialized in giving, then who would be available to receive all that good stuff? The parched earth can't let in a life-giving rain if it is covered by plastic tarp. Offerings of love and gratitude bounce off us if our clinging to a misguided non-attachment or independence disables us from soaking it in.

Without the capacity to be touched by caring and appreciation, we render these gifts less meaningful. Sacred receiving, letting things in with heartfelt gratitude, is a gift to the giver! When we are visibly moved, it conveys that they've made a difference in our lives. We may then bask together in a non-dual moment in which there is no distinction between the giver and the receiver. Both people are giving and receiving in their own unique ways. This shared experience can be profoundly sacred and intimate—a moment of delectable grace.

There are many reasons we don't let in nurturing. Our childhood legacy may lead us to believe that we don't deserve love. We may feel insecure about being loved or feel shame and anxiety around sexual love, especially if we have endured sexual abuse. We may fear that if we let in love we will be rejected once again. We may be afraid of letting go of control. But our heart beseeches us to selectively loosen the reigns of control and let people in.

Receiving can be especially difficult when our early attachment needs have not been met. Insecure bonding with our mother disrupts our ability to self-regulate our nervous system, which goes on high arousal when people come near us. We mistrust their motives or fear that we will be smothered or become too attached. As a result, we push people away.

More commonly, we are ambivalent about letting people in. Part of us longs for contact while another part is wary. Our resulting ambivalence and mixed message keep love away, generating suffering for ourselves and others.

By finding a pathway to healing our blocks to receiving, we become more available to let in love and nurturing. Something within us softens and smiles as we lower our guard and allow a person entry into that sacred place within us that longs for a kind word, a tender touch, or some sweet gesture of love.

We may be concerned that if we bask in appreciation or a delectable moment of contact, our ego will swell. But, in fact, the very opposite is true. *Receiving requires us to be non-egotistical.* Letting life and love *in* happens naturally when we are simply present. When we're full of ourselves—that is, overly self-conscious—we are not available to receive. Instead, we are preoccupied with looking good, being cool, or behaving according to some spiritual or moralistic belief system, such as the conviction that receiving will feed our ego.

The Buddhist notion of emptiness is instructive here. By emptying ourselves of limited self-identities and misguided beliefs about what it means to be spiritual, we become more empathically attuned to what is around us. As Stephen Batchelor puts it, "Contrary to expectations, an empty self turns out to be a relational self."[3] Opening ourselves to life, we regain the child's propensity to receive openly, blended with the adult's capacity for gratitude. Such innocent receiving can become a holy moment insofar as it makes both giver and receiver more whole and connected.

Receiving occurs as we simply learn how to be, free of trying to control and manipulate ourselves or others into being ideal people. A lovely flow of giving and receiving happens naturally as we empty ourselves of rigid expectations, pretense, and judgments.

Unrealistic expectations

A common view in Buddhist communities is that no matter how satisfying an experience may be there will always be a residue of dis-satisfaction. The implication is that since everything is impermanent, if we get too thrilled by something, we will feel an inevitable pang of dissatisfaction.

No doubt, many experiences have left us feeling disappointed and frustrated. But perhaps disillusionment occurs to the extent that we hold expectations or illusions about what people or things can provide us. For example, if we expect others to fulfill every need and read our mind, we set ourselves up for disenchantment. If we desperately cling to a thrill, we're bound to feel let down. However, if we simply remain open to an encounter, whether pleasant or unpleasant, then there is less likelihood for discontent. Even if we are disappointed, our feelings are likely to shift if we meet them with gentleness.

Obviously, some experiences are very dissatisfying, such as pursuing people who haven't lived up to their advertising or our fantasies. Other experiences may be quite fulfilling: attending a concert, a bike ride in nature, making love, or having tea with a dear friend may warm our heart.

Buddhism wisely emphasizes that nothing will deliver *permanent* happiness. But if we are not prospecting for permanence, then we're free to enjoy each luminous moment with a recognition that it will pass, while remaining open to what comes next. As the poet William Blake understood,

> He who binds to himself a joy
> Does the winged life destroy;
> But he who kisses the joy as it flies
> Lives in eternity's sunrise.[4]

Suffering subsides as we embrace what is alive in each moment. We then simply experience whatever arises without the hopes and expectations that wrench us into the future. If we experience pain, we embrace it, knowing that it will pass. If we experience pleasure, then as Tibetan Buddhist teacher Pema Chödrön suggests, "The trick is to enjoy it fully but without clinging."[5] Suffering subsides as we stay current with experience just as it is.

Relating wisely to desire, feelings, and our psychological process

It bears repeating that it is not desire itself but rather *our inability to deal with it wisely* that makes the crucial difference between liberation and dissatisfaction. Trying to extinguish desire only intensifies it. Suffering diminishes as we develop a skillful and harmonious relationship with our changing desires.

By welcoming and allowing our longings to be and breathe, we allow them to loosen up and transform. More space is created in our psyche as we give them ample room. As Zen master Shunryu Suzuki said, "To give your sheep or cow a large, spacious meadow is the way to control him."[6] We invite trouble by squelching our desires or acting upon every impulse rather than uncovering what we really want and weighing whether or not to act upon it in a particular situation.

The path toward liberation involves a warm sort of mindfulness—gently embracing our felt longings, feelings, and wants, and learning how to deal with our psychological process rather than trying to fix, escape, or extinguish it. This acknowledgement of our human desire for connectedness means thoroughly accepting ourselves as we are rather than striving for some kind of impersonal enlightenment.

During the time of the Buddha, the art and science of psychology didn't exist as we know it. There doesn't seem to have been much understanding about how contacting and expressing feelings can help us connect with each other. There wasn't much guidance about working with emotions in a somatic way. In Buddhist doctrine, what we call "feelings" are lumped together with many different mental phenomena in a category called "mental states," all to be treated in the same way: let them pass and let them go by invoking detached observation. A Western-influenced Buddhism would be more inclined to guide us to attend to our feelings and then allow them to unfold.

No doubt, there is value in finding some distance from feelings that overwhelm us. We may become so identified with particular emotions that we believe that this is who we are or *all* that we are. Every spiritual path wisely reminds us that we are much more than our feelings.

Suffering is not *created* by our feelings. But it is perpetuated when the same painful feelings recur over and over again because we don't have the skills and savvy to deal with them. Just as children demand attention until they are heard, our feelings will relentlessly beseech us until we gently turn toward them and compassionately listen to the messages that they are trying to convey. As we will explore later, practices like meditation and Focusing help us find the right relationship with overwhelming feelings so that we can work with them more skillfully. As psychologist Eugene Gendlin often says, "If you want to know what the soup smells like, it's better not to stick your head in it."[7]

Feeling shame around our longings and desires

During the Buddha's time, shame was probably not discussed during teatime or dharma talks; there was little awareness of its etiology or psychological effects. Yet understanding the life-suppressing effects of shame may transform the way Buddhism and other spiritual paths are practiced.

Shame is that sinking feeling in our gut that tells us we are flawed or defective. It is the recognition that we're being perceived negatively. It is the painful sense of being suddenly exposed and seen as defective, inadequate, or unworthy. Gershen Kaufman explains that "to feel shame is to feel *seen* in a painfully diminished sense."[8] Neither liberation nor intimacy flourishes in the soil of self-contempt.

Many of us were raised in families where our feelings and wants were criticized or ignored. Consequently, we may see them as insignificant or even dangerous rather than valid and important. It is frightening to show vulnerability when we have been repeatedly ridiculed. Sadly, the life energy contained in our desires is then rejected, which is a subtle but potent form of self-violence.

When we were children, if our longings and emotions were not met with kindness, then something in us began to feel unwelcomed and unwanted. Limping into adulthood, we may then withhold our authenticity from others, fearful that we will be shamed for being ourselves. As a result, our tender feelings become submerged, leaving us cut off from ourselves and others.

Shame prompts us to seek affirmation and approval rather than connection and intimacy. We look outside ourselves to sense whether we're emotionally safe. As one meditator recognized, "I'm always looking for clues about what others need from me. I've been tainting my authenticity with the constant refrain of 'how will this play?'"

Craving acceptance, we lose connection with our own wanting in favor of what we think others want from us. Continually testing the waters to check how we are being perceived, *we lose touch with our own experiencing.* Rich connections are possible only as we stay connected to ourselves and allow our actions to unfold from what resonates deeply within us.

As one client articulated this common quandary, "As a child, I wasn't allowed to want anything. I always tried to figure out what others wanted. I still look to others to orient myself. As my shame heals, I'm taking some power back that I wasn't allowed to have: my feelings, my opinions, my desires." As he learned to dance with the fire of his authentic desires and feelings, he experienced more vitality in his relationships.

Shame conditions us to look good and seek perfection. We want to succeed at something . . . finally. We may also unwittingly transfer this need to excel to our spiritual path. We may pursue a spiritual practice to establish ourselves as better than others or promote a sense of being special, which compensates for feeling inferior.

We can't let go of something beyond our reach

Sorrow is generated by holding on to what is unattainable, clinging so tightly to our hopes and desires that we refuse to accept what is. Perhaps we keep fantasizing about reuniting with a former partner who is unavailable.

Or we want to shape our lover into the ideal mate we have always dreamed about. We may continue to seek understanding from parents who are incapable of giving it, or we can't let go of our oversized expectations for our children.

The simplicity of the phrase "letting go" doesn't match the complexity of the task. As the Buddhist teacher Stephen Batchelor explains, "'Letting go' is not a euphemism for stamping out craving . . . letting go begins with understanding: a calm and clear acceptance of what is happening."[9] Many Buddhist teachers suggest that what we most need to let go of is this: wanting our experience to be different from how it is.

It is often difficult to assess what is attainable versus what is unrealistically rosy. Are we needlessly limiting ourselves or overreaching? There is a learning curve here that requires allowing ourselves a generous palette of mistakes and regularly basking in the healing waters of self-forgiveness.

We only create more shame if we believe that our positive intentions alone or an athletic burst of willpower is enough to release stubborn compulsions. Letting go involves uncovering beliefs and feelings that are keeping us stuck. For example, underlying our difficulty in letting go of a failed relationship may be a fear of being alone or the shame of being a loser. Equating relationship failure with personal failure, we get submerged in a quagmire of self-doubt.

Noticing and letting go of dysfunctional beliefs (that we are flawed or defective) may begin to ease our pain. But we often need to gently meet the deeper feelings that are keeping us stuck before they are inclined to shift.

Letting go proceeds by "letting into." We open to our current experience and hold it gently, while being curious about its ever-changing nature. We experience our experience without inflating it or denying it, while remaining open to the forward movement that is inherent within it. For example, if we are angry about an impending divorce, we might turn toward our underlying fear or shame and hold these feelings with loving-kindness. Expanding our tolerance for these uncomfortable feelings provides space for something more to come, perhaps a sense of grief and loss, and a kind of sweet recognition that this is part of the human condition. The suffering generated by being in conflict with ourselves subsides as we allow our feelings to unfold in their own way. The good news is that they will let themselves go when they're ready.

Emotion is the messenger of love; it is the vehicle that carries every signal from one brimming heart to another. For human beings, feeling deeply is synonymous with being alive.

—Thomas Lewis, Fari Amini, Richard Lannon

What we're really seeking is an experience of being alive, so that our life experiences on the purely physical plane will have resonances within our innermost being and reality, so that we can actually feel the rapture of being alive.

—Joseph Campbell

Embracing the Pleasures
of Relating

I am very fond of my teeth. Over the years, I've grown quite attached to them. For a long time the relationship was mutual. But lately my teeth haven't been so attached to me.

You see, some of my teeth are letting go more and more while I try harder and harder to persuade them to stay just a little longer. As each year passes, my dentist fights to keep my teeth intact. Although he claims to be a Buddhist, he decimates countless colonies of bacteria every four months. That's more frequently than most people get their teeth cleaned. But like I said, I'm very attached to them.

My teeth have been hanging in there despite my years of being persuaded by Tony the Tiger to eat sugary cereal for breakfast when I was a kid in Brooklyn, not to mention other sweet delights. Now I crave dental floss more than sweets.

Savoring Versus Craving

One way that Eastern paths are commonly understood is that we need to release our attachments. Someday we will lose much more than our teeth. Loss is inevitable; death is inescapable. The more we hold on, the more suffering we create for ourselves. But just because we understand that things are impermanent doesn't mean we shouldn't take care of our teeth and other body parts.

Knowing that life's pleasures will one day pass doesn't mean I'm spiritually bereft if I enjoy the full flavor and richness of a whole-wheat New York–style pizza while I can. In fact, an awareness of its ephemeral nature can make each bite more scrumptious and precious, at least when I remember to be present and awake. It is only problematic if

- I'm allergic to wheat or dairy;
- I don't balance it with other nutritious foods;
- I keep eating once I'm full;
- I get seriously bummed out if I can't have a pizza;
- I'm preoccupied thinking about and craving pizza; or
- I believe that my happiness depends on continually filling myself with things from the outside.

It is similar with intimate relationships. Someday we will lose the people we love, so why set ourselves up for heartache? Enjoying the lushness of what is available now will mean grieving later when it passes. Won't we suffer less if we stay safely detached?

Embracing the Ephemeral

Life is ephemeral, but it is also precious. Can we savor a good meal or meeting with an old friend? Can we share love with people we care about? Can we live in the immediacy and intimacy of the moment, welcoming the mix of pain and pleasure, joy and sorrow that is part of being alive?

There is a Buddhist story in which a man is being chased by a tiger. He runs furiously until he meets a precipice. There is nowhere to go. He spots a vine and begins climbing down to escape the tiger's claws. A mouse comes along and starts nibbling at the vine. As his fate becomes more precarious, he notices a luscious strawberry within his grasp. He plucks it and eats it—absolutely delicious!

This story is not meant to be taken too literally. We cannot ignore the reptilian brain and its instinctual reactions when danger lurks. Yet it is an apt metaphor for our lives. Danger stalks us. Someday we will die, perhaps sooner than we realize. But in the meantime, can we savor life's simple pleasures? Can we live in the present moment and relish a strawberry, a warm caress, a stroll in the woods, a gentle rain without craving more than what is here right now—knowing full well this too shall pass?

We awaken to a beautiful spring day. The air is fresh, the birds are singing their lovely tunes, and we notice an inner stirring to take a stroll in the park. How should we handle this desire?

One option is to recognize that this lovely day will soon yield to a dark, cold evening. The birds' melodic tunes will fall silent. We will be exhausted from our hike. So why get so excited? Why get seduced by passing pleasures? Well, why not relish life's transient gifts? The sun will set but is likely to rise again!

Pema Chödrön reminds us that our beautiful sandcastle will inevitably be swept away. Nevertheless, "The trick is to enjoy it fully but without clinging, and when the time comes, let it dissolve back into the sea.... When you fall in love, recognize it as impermanence, and let that intensify the preciousness."[1] The luscious and creative aspects of life are here to be enjoyed. If not now, when? Today's pleasures will pass; but if we stay open, there will be more wonderful surprises later. And perhaps some part of what we have relished will live on.

As we become acquainted with the pitfalls of loving, we may be dissuaded from seeking the pleasures it offers. But it would be tragic to deprive ourselves of life's joys just because they will pass. The next trial, the next sorrow, the next heartache awaits us. But so does the next belly laugh, the next heart connection, the next playful banter with a friend. This is life. A meaningful spirituality means tasting life fully, moving gracefully from one experience to another with as much equanimity as possible.

The Quandary of Fulfillment

A question that often generates hot debate among Buddhist practitioners is whether the spiritual path is supposed to bring joy and fulfillment. If we pursue personal happiness, aren't we aggrandizing the self? Aren't we feeding the ego by chasing after things that are impermanent and cause suffering? Others suggest that if Buddhism doesn't offer joy, then why pursue it? Isn't fulfillment one of the fruits of spiritual practice?

The word "fulfillment" carries enormous complexity. Deriving from the root words meaning "full" and "fill," fulfillment means to "fill full." This poses an interesting question. Where are we filled from? Do we actualize our potential by filling up on things from the outside or by finding it within ourselves?

We can't dispute the fact that we need things from outside ourselves. Even the most enlightened among us will never be liberated from the need to be nourished by food, water, and sunlight—and by people as well. Intimacy opens up something inside us that nothing else can.

Fulfillment and Vulnerability

Fulfillment doesn't alight through grabbing things for ourselves and being oblivious to the world. Happiness doesn't visit isolated egos. Instead, we are nourished through interactions with the world. To be is to interact.

From the macro to the micro, everything exists in relationship. Ocean currents shape our weather, which in turn affects the oceans, which then influence us.

An atom consists of protons, neutrons, and electrons. On one level, these particles need each other in order to exist. But their nature is simply to live in a harmonious, cooperative relationship. They have no desire to exist separately, which is quite fortunate for the stability of the world.

Our "advanced" brains give us the capacity to think that we can find fulfillment through pursuing our own private agendas. Unlike many societies that we label as "primitive," we have lost our natural capacity to live in harmony with ourselves and each other, which is apparent if we observe the state of our world.

The human ego has been on a roll for the past thirty-five thousand years. Perhaps this has been a necessary evolutionary phase. We have domesticated animals, tilled the soil, demolished rainforests, carved dams, built massive transportation arteries, and we've multiplied to mind-boggling numbers.

It is time to reel ourselves in a bit now, to take a deep breath, look around, and realize that our well-being and survival depend on living in harmony with each other and our environment.

We will never find ultimate satisfaction through gratifying ourselves with more objects of beauty and comfort. Countless millionaires are utterly miserable. Our challenge is not to accumulate more things that gratify us, but to discover what brings genuine fulfillment. A tender touch, giving and receiving gratitude, and lighthearted banter with a friend are priceless gifts that warm our heart. Mindfulness practices that connect us with our quiet depths can support us in relishing these precious moments.

The Freedom of Interdependence

The Eastern notion of liberation lies in stark contrast with the popular Western notion that freedom results from ratcheting up our independence. Our Western concept of freedom evolved from a rebellion against political, social, and economic restrictions imposed by authoritarian societies: "I'm free to think and act how I want; nobody will tell me what to do!" This adolescent view of freedom has become the new religion in Western countries and, increasingly, around the globe. Yet it fosters an attitude that impedes our spiritual liberation. As Johann Wolfgang von Goethe wisely saw, "None are more hopelessly enslaved than those who falsely believe they are free."[2]

The fashionable view of liberation is to do it all for ourselves and not need anything or get attached to anyone. But the latest discoveries about how our brain is wired, not to mention common sense, suggest that our well-being depends on harmonious connections. Any hope of genuine freedom must include liberation from the anxiety of disconnection.

As the defenses that perpetuate the illusion of separateness melt, we open to the life and love cherished by all spiritual traditions. We become more sensitive to how our choices affect others. We recognize that rights come with responsibilities, and that nurturing our friends, neighbors, and community nurtures ourselves. We then taste a different kind of freedom; we are liberated from expending energy resisting our interdependence, or what Thich Nhat Hanh calls "interbeing," the reality that everything is connected with everything else.

Interestingly, many political and religious leaders vaunt freedom, except when it comes to the holiest aspects of our humanity: love, sex, and death. Gay marriage, sex between consenting adults, and the right to die when facing terminal illness are sacred decisions that they feel compelled to control. What does freedom mean if it doesn't extend to how we decide to relate to our loved ones and what we do with our bodies?

Embracing Fulfillment

A healthy spiritual life means allowing space for our natural desires and inclinations while noticing the overreaching that can tilt us toward suffering. Can we enjoy the warmth of a cozy fire but stop adding fuel when it rages out of control? Can we rest in ourselves in a way that allows interpersonal squabbles to cool down rather than escalate?

On the road to awakening—and even as we are awake—we will experience longing and wanting. The important questions are "how do we *hold* our wants and longings" and "how do we relate to the pleasure and pain that flow from their fulfillment or frustration?"

The more we find fulfillment in a well-balanced lifestyle, the less we need to seek it. The more we trust the natural rhythms of our organism, the more we live at peace with ourselves and with life. There are paths we need to follow within and paths we need to follow in our outer environment. There are some things we can *do* to find interpersonal fulfillment, such as polishing our communication skills and attending gatherings where we might meet people. But a great deal of what we need to *do* is simply get out of our own way and just let it happen. As Buber put it, "The *Thou* meets me through Grace—it is not found by seeking."[3]

Being awake means living more and more in the flow of a nourishing give and take with our environment. The ecstasy of being alive can happen in any moment when our anxious strivings yield to settling back and opening to life. Fulfillment happens; chasing after happiness pushes it further away. The Venerable Lama Gendun Rinpoche, a Kagyu lama, says it well: "Happiness cannot be found through great effort and willpower, but is already present, in open relaxation and letting go."[4]

If we scoop a handful of sand and clench it tightly, it will slip from our grasping hand. But if we hold the sand with an open, cupped hand without clinging, then we can keep it for a moment. The openness, presence, and letting be that are cultivated through spiritual practice allow us to dwell in a place where we can experience intimacy. This experiencing is the opposite of possession. Any effort to possess or control intimacy stifles its radiance. Intimacy means dancing with fire, not smothering it.

Love and intimacy require openness, but this doesn't mean collapsing into passivity. Intimacy is nourished as we continually reveal what we are experiencing: how we feel, what we want, and how we're affected by each other. We can have fulfilling relationships to the extent that we notice how we are being affected by life and each other, while being similarly curious about others' experiences, and conversing skillfully when our wants or views collide.

Being Fulfilled

Liberation is not a numbed state of neutrality; it is accompanied by a vibrant peace and joy. There is nothing more to seek when we are filled with a luminous presence and connection with life. There is no need to keep searching for satisfaction when we're *experiencing* it.

When our needs are met from within and from without, we are no longer needy. We can enjoy the satiation of a good meal or a good conversation. If we find ourselves wanting more, we can be mindful of this desire and weigh whether to act upon it or just settle back into ourselves. Do we want another delicious kiss or to savor the one we just had? Do we want a piece of cake after a satisfying meal or can we enjoy the satisfaction of feeling full? Will another bite offer enjoyment or indigestion? If we listen closely, our body will signal when we are satisfied and don't need more. We can then notice the desire without being hijacked by it.

The Hazards of Seeking Fulfillment

Fulfillment eludes us if we lean too far toward gratifying ourselves from the outside. Rather than lose our balance and merge with a desired person or activity, can we tend the quiet flame that glows within our own being? Fulfillment evades us when we seek it too purposefully. It arises naturally as we are present to life; it ensues from living a wisely balanced life, neither too far in nor too far out.

The expression "far out" is instructive here. During the seventies, my friends and I would robotically say "far out" whenever we heard something interesting or non-ordinary. "Far out, you met the perfect woman!" or "Far out, the ice cream shop has a new flavor!" Exciting things seem "far out" exactly because they take us outside ourselves; they are not our common, everyday experience. We don't yet have words to express how these experiences feel inside or what is meaningful about them.

What if we were to go "far in" when we experience something enlivening or extraordinary? What is the felt experience of a special kiss, a completed painting, or a touching movie?

Going "far in" means relaxing into our bodies. What do we notice inside as we glimpse a beautiful butterfly, hear about a friend's success, or are mesmerized by a cat playing with a string? What is happening in our stomach or heart as we gaze into our lover's eyes? Do we experience delicious warmth or expansiveness or a fear of being seen or losing ourselves? Can we stay with our bodily felt experience rather than leap out of ourselves as we notice a delightful or threatening feeling?

A Dynamic Balance

There is something here that points toward a middle way for Westerners, a path between looking too far outside for fulfillment and diving so far inside that we overlook the simple pleasures offered by life. We don't exist apart from our intimate interactions with the world. Likewise, we will never find happiness if we are too dependent on being fed from the outside.

This middle way involves a dance between being intimate with what is inside and allowing fresh waters to replenish us. We gradually come to inhabit an inner space that is seamlessly connected with the life outside ourselves. This is the formula for intimacy with life. We receive the world as we rest comfortably (and sometimes uncomfortably) within.

The source of happiness cannot be said to exist solely within or without. There's nothing we can solidly cling to and claim as our own. The spiritual path is a dance that includes self and other, and fulfillment is found somewhere within the flow of this ever-changing dynamic balance.

Awakening Together

The more that humanity becomes personally, socially, and politically conscious, the happier and freer we will all be. As more people awaken, we'll have more opportunities to relish loving, intimate, and playful connections with them. The more we recognize that our own freedom and happiness are enhanced as others feel secure and fulfilled, the more we will work together to uplift them rather than perpetuate a system in which the gap between the rich and poor, the powerful and disenfranchised, keeps growing. The ancient Greek philosopher Aristotle wisely proposed a system in which the richest person could be only a certain number of times richer than the poorest, which cleverly gives the wealthy an incentive to raise up the bottom.

Our fullest awakening is forever entwined with the awakening of others. We wake up together or hold each other back. We are truly stuck with each other. As my bumper sticker puts it, "Everybody does better when everybody does better." The Dalai Lama expresses a similar sentiment: "If you want others to be happy, practice compassion. If you want to be happy, practice compassion."[5] By creating conditions for others to be happy, we serve ourselves.

God guard me from those thoughts men think
In the mind alone;
He that sings a lasting song
Thinks in the marrow bone.

—W. B. Yeats

Don't be afraid of me. Come closer to me. Bring me your gentle spirit. Speak more slowly. Enunciate more clearly. Again! Please, try again! S-l-o-w down. Be kind to me. Be a safe place for me. See that I am a wounded animal, not a stupid animal. I am vulnerable and confused. Whatever my age, whatever my credentials, reach for me. Respect me. I am in here. Come find me.

—Jill Bolte Taylor

Chapter Ten

The Perils of Positive Thinking: Embracing the Non-Rational Forces within Us

❦

M odern neuroscience is confirming what spiritual folks have been claiming for centuries: our thoughts and intentions have potent effects on our health and happiness. Consider the placebo effect. If we believe that a certain pill will cure us, it often does, even if it turns out to be sugar. The New Age airwaves have seized upon this convergence of metaphysics and science to promote the power of positive thinking and visualization.

Honoring the Non-Rational Forces Within Us

Some branches of the school of positive thinking have gone so far as to propose that we create every painful event or feeling. In short, bad things happen because we have bad thoughts. But do we really have such power over life?

The Buddha's teachings are often selectively borrowed to reinforce our penchant to control life. In the Dhammapada, the Buddha is quoted as saying, "We are what we think, having become what we thought."[1] Simplistically clinging to these words, we might conclude that if we can modify all our thoughts to happy ones, we will find bliss.

The Buddha's teachings cannot be reduced to one-dimensional sound bites. The Buddha also said that life is characterized by suffering, and that the path toward liberation involves an Eightfold Path that is more complex than simply changing our mindset. It is true that a good life is more probable if we believe that we deserve it and don't cling to unhelpful and false beliefs, such as insisting we are a permanent victim of a difficult childhood. But we need other insights and resources in order to move forward.

It takes more than positive intentions and upbeat thinking to move toward a spiritual life rich in intimacy. It is not simply a *choice* to move toward love, as many New Age proponents profess. It certainly doesn't hurt to believe that good things are possible, but clinging too tightly to such beliefs overlooks the power of the non-rational forces within us. We need to engage with our feelings so that the reptilian instinct to freeze, attack, or retreat doesn't hijack our spiritual intentions.

That Pesky Inner Reptile

The viewpoint that we are spiritual beings who can overcome any adversity by holding the "proper" thoughts and intentions is tricky to practice because our pesky biology is always ready to mess with our lofty spiritual ideas. Our beliefs cannot override the fact that our brain and nervous system contain the stuff of reptiles. Our lizard brain is poised to ensure not only our physical survival but our emotional survival as well.

Our ancient ancestors who worried the most were rewarded with survival, and they passed their genes on to us. Neuropsychologist Rick Hanson explains it well:

> We are their great-grandchildren, sitting atop the food chain. Consequently, multiple hair-trigger systems in your brain continually scan for threats. At the least whiff of danger—which these days comes mainly in the form of social hazards like indifference, criticism, rejection, or disrespect—alarm bells start ringing. See a frown across a dinner table, hear a cold tone from a supervisor, get interrupted repeatedly, receive an indifferent shrug from a partner . . . and your heart starts beating faster, stress hormones course through your

veins, emotions well up, thoughts race, and the machinery of fighting, fleeing, freezing, or appeasing kicks into high gear.[2]

Our nervous system remembers a trauma as if it were yesterday. It saves files of agonizing memories of being punished for imperfections, shamed for crying, humiliated for dropping the ball, and much worse. Our body and brain store unbearable moments of embarrassment and fear, even if our mind can't recall the gory details and vow "never again!"

Imprinted with dire threats to our need for affiliation and belonging, our lizard brain now springs into action to protect us: "Tell her you feel hurt, and she'll think you're a wimp and leave you. Tell him you miss him, and he'll think you're too needy and withdraw. Don't take a swing at life's opportunities because you might strike out again."

The lizard brain is not known for assessing nuances or considering our spiritual values. Its message is unambiguous: this situation resembles something so painful that I am injecting a biochemical salve into your body to protect you from danger.

We can access the limbic brain and reptilian brain through body sensations, such as noticing when our heart is racing or throat tightening. A gentle scanning of our visceral sensations can help relax our body and enable us to see more clearly what is really happening. Somatic approaches, such as Focusing (discussed later), help us attune to the language of our body. We may then move more fluidly between our sensations, thoughts, and feelings so that our spiritual intentions are not sabotaged by the less rational parts of our psyche.

Transcendence or Dissociation?

You might remember the Buddhist story I told earlier about a man being chased by a tiger who ate a delectable strawberry while clinging to a vine for dear life. I suppose that he was thinking positively and not dwelling on the negative! For him, the cup was half full rather than half empty. He could savor his tasty snack without being distracted by his regrettable circumstances.

These stories can leave the impression that it is possible to transcend our reptilian brain through spiritual practice or positive thinking alone. Indeed, meditation research suggests that monks who practice meditation have altered their brain chemistry in remarkable ways. But we are still subject to the limits imposed by our biology. Perhaps this unfortunate chap enjoyed the strawberry not because of any spiritual attainment, but because he dissociated from his body and the terror he was experiencing!

The Dalai Lama exemplifies a spiritual seeker who has no pretenses about transcending his humanity. When asked by an interviewer if there was anything in his life he regretted, he recounted the story of an older monk interested in an advanced esoteric practice. The Dalai Lama responded that such a practice would perhaps be more appropriate for a younger person. He later learned that the man had killed himself, wanting to be reborn in a younger body so that he could undertake this practice.

When asked by the interviewer how he got rid of his feelings of regret, he paused a long time. He then responded, "I didn't get rid of it. It's still there."[3]

I find it refreshing that the Dalai Lama *paused* before responding. He searched inside to notice what he felt in relation to the question. How much deeper and richer could our relationships become if we all remembered to adopt a pregnant pause before responding?

Also, note that the Dalai Lama didn't offer rationalizations to minimize the pain of this traumatic event, such as "It was his decision to kill himself; it's not my responsibility" or "He created his own reality for himself." While there may be elements of truth in these beliefs, our own choices, words, and actions affect others' hearts and contribute to their decisions. We are in this life together; we affect each other.

Dissociation is a well-known mechanism in the psychology of trauma. Disconnecting from our bodies provides a kind of anesthesia, such as during an assault or traffic accident. I remember this clearly when I was mugged in my twenties while walking in a rough neighborhood in San Francisco. I spotted two unsavory characters walking toward me and figured that this was a great opportunity to practice what the New Age people were preaching. I surrounded myself with white light, contacted my spirit guides, and headed straight toward the potential trouble.

I firmly intended to walk fearlessly past these gentlemen, but apparently they failed to notice the protective light around me, or perhaps my light-generating capacity was deficient or my spirit guides had more pressing business at hand. In any case, it just took one solid blow to my head to launch me into a state of shock. Blessedly, I didn't feel a thing until whatever anesthesia my body produced faded after an hour or so. They got away with the $5 in my pocket and my bus pass. Fortunately, I was left with only minor bruises. It was a vivid experience of how we're wired to cope with an overwhelming assault to our nervous system by blotting out devastating terror and pain.

Even the most spiritually conscious person would not want to be fully present when such shocking events are happening, just as we wouldn't want to undergo root canal surgery without Novocain. But the problem is that our trauma-detector may get stuck in the "on" position without our being aware of it. Daunted by the prospect of another physical or emotional blow, something within us may become hypervigilant in defending against potential pain. Urgently scanning our environment to detect whether we are vulnerable, we may become disinclined to take the risk to love. Our trauma-based "no trespassing" sign keeps people safely distant from our heart.

Trauma Can Damage Intimacy

Our body's mechanisms for ensuring our security can unwittingly shield us from intimacy. Habitually protecting ourselves, we may not extend welcoming vibes that broadcast the message that we are safe to approach. Greeting people, we may display a stiffness and caution that is uninviting. Or there may be a syrupy, less-than-authentic sweetness that comes with the hidden plea "please be nice to me and don't go away!"

Unbeknownst to us, people can sense our distance or coyness or when we are not permeable to love. Without a clear signal, they may surmise that we're either distant or inauthentic. They may not feel welcomed and, therefore, pull back. Once again, we have pushed away the love we want, thereby reinforcing our hopelessness and reconvincing ourselves that intimate relationships are not for us.

Healing Trauma

Meditation can provide a context for healing trauma by cultivating the equanimity that allows us to face our experience as it is. Unresolved trauma and grief can be healed only as we gently attend to how these feelings are being held in our body. This can be supported by working with a skilled and caring therapist who can provide a safe holding environment for us to release old traumas and hurts that block us from giving and receiving love. As psychotherapist and meditation teacher Harvey Aronson wisely recognizes, "If these sources of pain are not adequately addressed, they will motivate a sequence of behaviors that can lead us to crash and burn spiritually."[4]

By bringing mindfulness to our bodily felt sense of our life issues, we have an opportunity to heal the traumatic messages emblazoned on our lizard brain. Approaches such as Focusing, Somatic Experiencing, and Emotionally Focused Therapy (EFT) for couples address this felt dimension of our being and are a helpful complement to spiritual practice.

To stay with that shakiness—to stay with a broken heart, with a rumbling stomach, with the feeling of hopelessness and wanting revenge—that is the path of true awakening. Sticking with that uncertainty, getting the knack of relaxing in the midst of chaos, learning not to panic—this is the spiritual path.

—Pema Chödrön

When we feel heard a silence falls.
In that silence more may come.
Often it is something deeper: we can feel it
Just now forming at the edge of being.

—Rob Foxcroft

Chapter Eleven

Relishing Life's Pleasures and Embracing Our Humanity

❦

Our tendency to shut down as we face painful experiences is understandable; we are creatures who are wired to seek pleasure and avoid pain. But dare we consider how in the subtlest of ways we might not fully let in pleasant feelings when they saunter our way?

The wounding experiences that trigger a self-protective numbing to pain simultaneously deaden our nerve endings to pleasure. Basking too long in enjoyable feelings can be potentially perilous because, historically, if we lowered our guard, we might become dinner for a hungry carnivore. Vigilance has a survival advantage; savoring pleasure does not. Such an inglorious fate is improbable these days, but our self-protective instincts have been rerouted toward protecting ourselves from other unpleasant assaults, like being blindsided by emotional attacks or rejection.

The Egotism of Resisting Pleasure

Some spiritually inclined people view pleasant experiences as dangerously seductive. They fret about getting too attached or facing eventual disappointment. However, pleasure is almost unavoidable if we are present to life. Because we have taste buds, most of us would enjoy a good pumpkin pie or my mother's lasagna. Viewing a gorgeous sunset or a field ablaze in wildflowers, we're likely to experience awe and beauty. Similarly, something in us relishes compliments and appreciation. Can we allow ourselves to shimmer with delight as we let them in? Or do we quickly turn away, fearful that relishing the pleasure of praise will activate clinging or expose us to some ill-defined danger?

It actually takes more work to push pleasure away than to receive it. Maintaining defenses takes work; awakening means being less defended—allowing ourselves to savor a good meal, a warm hug, a stranger's kindness.

Many of us are actually egotistical when it comes to receiving. We are so preoccupied with ourselves, so distracted by fear-based considerations, that we're not available to receive. If we are concerned that a compliment or gift might trigger our ego, it just did! If we simply receive it without our mind's interference, then there is a lovely moment of connection. Our awkward self-consciousness blocks a natural, innocent openness.

When offered a compliment, do you wonder,

- Is it okay to receive this?
- Do I deserve it?
- Are they trying to manipulate me?
- Will I be obligated to give something in return?

These kinds of considerations keep us spinning in our thoughts and create distance. A non-egotistical option is simply to receive with humility and appreciation: "Thanks for the compliment. It feels good to hear that." Or perhaps a glowing smile that conveys that we were touched is enough.

Life offers abundant pleasures. Few would disagree that sex is pleasurable unless we have a medical condition that interferes. Dancing, hiking, massage, music, gardening, and conversing with a friend may also offer healthy pleasure. Availing ourselves of resources that bring delight also keeps our immune system robust.

Nature appears to want us to enjoy the pleasure of intimate connections. Being in love triggers a neurochemical cascade in which oxytocin and other hormones spill into our bloodstream, creating a sense of euphoria. Urging ourselves to "let go" of our longing for love is not likely to persuade our brain and neurotransmitters to cooperate. The path of least resistance is to learn how to dance with our longing for love and intimacy rather than sit on the sidelines and battle the emptiness of a non-intimate life.

The Joy of Savoring Life

Awakening allows us to dwell in the exquisite spiritual ecstasy of being alive. Joy and fulfillment beyond belief is what spiritual life is all about. And within the very heart of spirituality is a longing for happiness for ourselves and all beings.

Loving-kindness meditation, sending love and good wishes to others, begins with wanting good things for ourselves. The traditional refrain is "May I be peaceful, may I be free of sorrow, may I be happy." Here are some alternative, self-affirming phrases:[1]

- May I accept and affirm myself just as I am.
- May I meet all of my feelings with a kind, calm, and loving awareness.
- May I find the strength to be with difficult experiences.
- May I have the wisdom to pause and be gentle with what I'm feeling before reacting.
- May I be clearer about what I want and find a way to express it without hurting others.

Loving ourselves creates a foundation for loving others. One client expressed a common confusion about this: "I always thought that if I had love and compassion for myself, I wouldn't have it for others. I was using Buddhism to support my codependency." She came to realize that having compassion for herself and others are equally important and work together quite handily.

Being happy means savoring life. As we cultivate a calm heart and spacious awareness, we become more mindful of the difference between enjoying and clinging. We come to experience the pleasure of a pizza, a beautiful sunset, or lovemaking without craving more.

Non-Aversion Toward Our Humanity

One of my favorite Zen stories affirms our humanity as we grow spiritually:

> One day it was announced that the young monk Kyogen had reached an enlightened state. Much impressed by this news, several of his peers went to speak with him. "We have heard that you are enlightened. Is this true?" his fellow students inquired. "It is," Kyogen answered. "Tell us," said a friend, "how do you feel?" "As miserable as ever," replied the enlightened Kyogen.[2]

No matter how profound our spiritual openings, we remain forever subject to the human condition. Kyogen continues to experience misery. But perhaps what defines his attainment is that he is no longer miserable because of his misery. He no longer craves being somewhere he is not. He accepts his experience as it is, with gentleness and good humor.

We multiply our suffering by trying to transcend our humanity. Before any inner state can shift, it must first be noticed, accepted, and felt into. Accepting our desires and emotions means treating them kindly rather than carrying self-judgments that suppress our aliveness.

Embracing Our Story

Spiritual teachings invite us to live free of dualities that perpetuate suffering. This means embracing *all* of who we are without pushing anything away. But without intending to, some spiritual teachings foster a split between our experience as it is and how we would like it to be. They may do this by encouraging a "letting go" of feelings or by suggesting that they aren't real or relevant. They might persuade us that past traumas and dramas are just a "story" that diverts us from the spiritual path.

The positive aspect of this viewpoint is that we are not destined to remain a victim of our past, however horrible it may have been. Rather than torture ourselves with old narratives that we're not good enough or worthy of love, we can affirm ourselves and live in the vibrancy of the present moment. However, urging us to let go of our story can make us feel like a failure if we can't quickly accomplish such a feat.

Admonishing ourselves to "live in the present" might actually divert us from the present. Being present can only mean present to what we are experiencing right now. If we're trying to ignore, disallow, or relinquish a feeling that has arisen, we're no longer here.

Being "a person who has let go of stories" might become just another story. There may also be the unintended consequence of developing an aversion toward the feelings related to our stories, which are beseeching us for attention. True freedom is not found by trying to free ourselves from feelings or desires; it can only be found by opening to our felt experience with a compassionate heart. As Jack Kornfield explains it, "'Free' is not free from feelings. But free to feel each one and let it move on, unafraid of the movement of life."[3] Pushing away feelings disconnects us from ourselves and prevents us from developing a deeply felt compassion for our own and others' suffering.

Being present with life means allowing ourselves to be touched by another's pain. Dismissing their sorrows as a mere illusion or story may bespeak a lack of emotional depth. We may feel a sweet connection gazing into people's eyes, but can we continue holding them in our compassionate gaze when they talk about their intrusive in-laws or physical ailments? Avalokiteshvara, the bodhisattva of compassion, is often depicted as being so touched by the world's suffering that a tear flows from her saddened eye.

Accepting Versus Finessing Our Experience

Spiritual teachers often agree that liberation is always available if we are present enough to notice it. But the subtext is often, "Being present shouldn't include being in too much pain—you're supposed to be calm or in bliss." Or worse, "If you have emotional stuff that's too painful, it means you're not very evolved. Just shift your perception, and you'll discover who you really are: a being of pure light and unsullied awareness." As a friend steeped in Buddhism put it, "The subtle implication was that if you have persistent, tangled, old feelings, it's kind of shameful, especially if you can't banish them quickly through spiritual practice."

It would be wonderful if through some sleight of hand we could instantly connect with our spiritual essence and realize that we're having an unhelpful thought or ill-advised feeling that is causing suffering. Indeed, if we're caught up in a destructive thought loop, remembering the beauty of who we really are may sometimes help. But it is usually more complex than that. We also need to find a way to *be with* feelings that are gripping us before a tight or anxious place can shift inside our body.

A vibrant spirituality involves a natural movement between honoring our feelings and then basking in the luminous openness that comes when the feelings shift. We neither cling to emotions nor push them away. We allow our attention to move fluidly between content and process—that is, what is happening in our lives and our feelings about what is happening. We find freedom not by clinging to any particular state of being (including the ultimate trap, clinging to awareness itself), but by becoming more adept at living in this moment and welcoming what flows toward us—if not with a smile, then with a wise acceptance of what is.

Just as many forms of dance involve a rhythm of coming together and moving apart, relationships need varying amounts of space for intimacy to flourish. A vibrant intimacy is created when we are so connected to our own being that we're simultaneously connected to everything around us.

Does Attention to Feelings Amplify Them?

No doubt, you have felt frustrated by people who voice the same complaints and emotions over and over again. Feeling powerless to nudge them off their hamster wheel, you are chomping at the bit to get off the phone or change the subject.

Spiritual teachers often warn us about the futility of getting stuck in the same familiar feelings. They may even suggest that *any* attention to feelings reinforces them and increases our attachment to a "limited self." But this conviction contradicts the prevailing psychological view that we should get in touch with our feelings. What is really going on here?

I am persuaded by over thirty years of experience as a psychotherapist that attending to authentic feelings isn't the culprit. What creates a rigid or inflated self is our tendency to cling to *certain* feelings while exiling others from awareness. We continue to recycle the same emotions when we fail to unearth our *underlying* feelings and longings.

For example, venting anger might lie squarely within our comfort zone while more unpleasant feelings, such as fear, hurt, or shame, might lurk below the threshold of our awareness. We might complain bitterly about a physical ailment or our partner's unavailability but have little appetite for exploring deeper feelings of powerlessness or sadness. We may brood in angry withdrawal when our partner visits her friends but not touch the loneliness or anxiety underneath.

Anger is not antithetical to a spiritual life. It is an essential part of our life force and allows an empowered response to abuse or injustice. Drawing upon the energy of anger can make us more sturdy and allow us to be tender without being fragile. But anger is often reactive; discovering our authentic feelings that underlie reactive anger or frustration can allow our process to move forward.[4] When we uncover our actual felt experience, something inside us loosens up. We invite others toward us as we stroll gently toward ourselves.

Honoring Anger and Our Boundaries

Another reason troubling feelings recur is that we are not listening to what they are telegraphing about our lives. For example, we might repeatedly recoil from being shamed or attacked in a relationship but we don't set appropriate and effective boundaries. Our spiritual beliefs might prompt us to extend a smile of forgiveness when what is really needed is a clear expression of our hurt or anger and giving voice to what we need.

In Tibetan Buddhism, Manjushri is the bodhisattva of wisdom. His Sanskrit name means "He Who is Noble and Gentle." He wields a flaming sword in his right hand, cutting through the bonds of ignorance that hamper him.

It is not helpful to sit repeatedly with painful feelings resulting from our boundaries or rights being violated; we sometimes need assertive action. If there is a splinter in our finger, our pain is a message to remove it rather than endure discomfort. Distilling the message implicit in our feelings allows our lives to move forward.

A growing number of meditation teachers are realizing that if uncomfortable feelings such as anger or sorrow arise in meditation, it is helpful to grant them ample space. As Milarepa, a Tibetan teacher, said to the devils trying to disturb him in his cave, "It is wonderful you demons came today. You must come again tomorrow. From time to time we should converse."[5] A nonviolent, welcoming attitude toward even the most difficult feelings enables them to shift in their own time while making it less likely that they will recur.

Listening from Our Humanity

How we relate to people is an extension of how we relate to ourselves. Encountering a friend who is hurting from a relationship breakup, we might offer the standard spiritual fare: "You're too attached!" or "Move on!" Although our intention is to help, our comment may be experienced as critical and shaming. "What's wrong with me, why can't I move on?" Our friend is more likely to feel comforted and less isolated on hearing a more human response: "I know how you feel" or "That's a big loss."

Viewing a friend's suffering as problematic might mirror a tendency to reject these aspects of ourselves. As we become more comfortable embracing our own sorrow and hurt, it becomes easier to offer our compassionate presence when others are hurting.

If instead of prodding from our head we extend compassion and understanding from our heart, we might help our friend feel safe and cared for. As Quaker writer Douglas Steere puts it, "Holy listening—to 'listen' another's soul into life, into a condition of disclosure and discovery, may be almost the greatest service that any human being ever performs for another."[6]

We are more apt to soothe people when we enter their emotional world and sense the felt texture of their sorrows and concerns rather than just hear their words. A Delaware Native American chief expressed it well: "I love to feel where words come from."[7]

In the Thai language, *khao jai* means "I understand." *Jai* means "heart" and *khao* means "to enter." When we truly understand another, we enter their heart. Living a relational life means hearing, seeing, and entering each other's hearts and relishing their precious presence. We can do this more readily as we cultivate the nourishing practice of being connected and intimate with ourselves.

Part Three

Intimacy with Ourselves

It is the feeling level that controls most of our inner life . . . bringing consciousness to feelings is critical for awakening.

—Jack Kornfield

In the coming world, they will not ask me, "Why were you not Moses?" They will ask me, "Why were you not Zusya?"

—Rabbi Zusya

Chapter Twelve

Turning Toward Ourselves

❦

A s we have seen, we're hardwired with a longing for intimacy. We want to feel heard, understood, and connected with our fellow humans, however much they may annoy us sometimes. Yet there is another kind of intimacy that awaits us if we learn how to look for it. In fact, it lies right before our eyes. While pursuing the connections we want, we may overlook our capacity to be intimate with ourselves.

This is not to suggest that we don't need people. Rather, we are invited to dance with complexity. We can learn how to turn toward ourselves by holding our heart with the tenderness that we want from others. This self-caring will never substitute for the nourishment and enchantment that come from sharing hearts and souls, but there is something crucial that we can do for ourselves. By cultivating loving-kindness toward ourselves, we build a secure internal base (attachment theory language) and an inner refuge (Buddhist language) that no one can take from us.

Self-Love Versus Self-Intimacy

We sometimes hear the expression, "You need to love yourself." It is hard to argue with such sage advice, but it's not so easily implemented, especially if love and connection were not forthcoming in childhood. When our neural pathways are not accustomed to being soothed by others, it is difficult to soothe ourselves. We might feel especially irritated to be told to love ourselves when we're hurting, when, as Shakespeare put it, "I am bound upon a wheel of fire, that mine own tears do scald like molten lead."[1]

Our capacity for self-care cannot be manufactured out of thin air. Child development research confirms that we need to extract steady nutrients of care and affection from early caregivers in order to build a robust neural network and secure internal base. Without this foundation, we may develop an attachment style in which we anxiously cling to love when it saunters our way, or in which we push love away or become ambivalent about it.

On a good day, something in me smiles when I am told to love myself. But when I'm feeling down and someone utters these words, I often feel annoyed, musing, "Easier said than done, buddy!" I usually trust that their intentions are good, but I suspect that some people recite the simplistic mantra of self-love because they don't know how to relate to my feelings— and don't have much appetite for dealing with their own.

What does it actually mean to love ourselves? Does it mean affirming that we deserve love and kindness? Does it include honoring our rights by setting good boundaries—affirming our "yes" and declaring our "no" without feeling guilty? Might we demonstrate it by preparing a healthy meal, taking a warm bath, exercising, or splurging for a massage?

These attitudes and behaviors may embody a portion of what is meant by "self-love." But perhaps what's more deeply needed is a sacred path of self-intimacy that invites us to be with our experience in a particular way.

Does Familiarity Help or Hurt Intimacy?

"Intimacy" derives from the word "innermost." It is defined as "familiarity" and "pertaining to the inmost character of a thing." Being intimate includes being familiar with a person in the usual sense, knowing their likes and dislikes, recognizing what makes them happy or sad. But in another sense, if we become too familiar with a person, we may get bored, become distant, or lose our sense of curiosity.

Looking deeper, what may create a steady slog toward the dissolution of intimacy is not that we become too familiar with people, but that we become comfortably familiar with our *perceptions* about them. We size them up as insensitive, self-centered, or arrogant. We put them in a mental box of being selfish, distant, or angry. But living in our perceptions and judgments removes us from a spontaneous and alive connection.

Intimacy with others is more likely as we steer clear of analyzing people and reside in the spaciousness of our heart. Instead of clinging to our familiar ideas about others, can we see them freshly and open to their world of subtlety and nuance? Even more challenging, can we break free of the rigid perceptions and judgments we hold toward ourselves and gently embrace our actual experience rather than shame and condemn ourselves?

It is an extraordinary undertaking to extend attention beyond ourselves to see and embrace people as they actually are. It is an act of love to genuinely care about how life is affecting others—being curious about their feelings and longings and allowing ourselves to be touched by what makes their heart heavy and their spirit soar. Extending ourselves in this generous way becomes more possible as we find a measure of peace, comfort, and connection within.

The rocky emotions associated with our own frustrated longings blunt our sensitivity to others' yearnings and feelings. Reeling in the frenzy of our own neglected needs, we are not able to be attentive to their inner world. Struggling to steady ourselves as we ride the rapids of our own longings and frustrations, we may be unresponsive when they express anger or hurt; we may not notice how their emotional flare-ups reflect a burning desire to connect with us.

It takes a calm and generous heart to see the sweet essence of another person, to tenderly hold their precious longings, being affected by how life is touching them and registering their inner beauty. But seeing others as they are is especially difficult when their needs clash with our own. "Hear me first! Be there for me," we silently scream through our nippy pleas and sarcasm. "If you can hear me just right, then maybe I can extend a sympathetic ear toward you!"

Aspects of Self-Intimacy

Intimacy with ourselves means being awake to our felt experience of the moment. We bring calm awareness to the tender feelings and longings that visit us. We touch the pulse of life as it courses through us. We courageously face our feelings without trying to fix or change ourselves.

Self-intimacy includes shining a light on the shadowy zones within us. We acknowledge and even welcome whatever we are experiencing rather than clinging to some feelings and pushing others away. Rather than get too attached to how we want things to be, we notice our actual felt experience. Rather than hold on to self-comforting beliefs, we find more peace with life's unknowns. Rather than try to figure out our partner and itemize what we think is wrong with him or her, we try to figure out ourselves. We get clearer about our feelings and wants and express them in ways that invite contact.

Connections flow more naturally as we learn how to rest in our own being. Intimacy with ourselves allows love to grow. As our yearning for connection and affection is held tenderly, it is less prone to flare out in blame when hopes morph into disappointment. Intimacy flows more readily as we dance artfully with the inevitable sparks that fly from being together.

The availability to love and be loved grows as we cultivate mindfulness. Gently attending to our breath, our body, and how feelings live within us from moment to moment positions us for connection. By holding our own feelings and others' hearts gently, we create a space for people to come toward us. We remain awake for special moments of delicious connection and rapture that arise between two people whose minds are still and hearts open. Living with a heart that is intimacy-ready is the ultimate creative art, the blessing of being available to love and be loved.

Pushing Love Away by Pushing Ourselves Away

We long to be seen, understood, and cherished. But so often we have felt betrayed, hurt, and devalued. As a result, we may carry a rawness that we don't want people to see or touch. We may not even allow ourselves to notice this place when a protective scab has numbed its presence. Confusion and conflict reign when we pull on people to soothe an inner place that we have abandoned.

Trying to avoid the bitter taste of rejection, we may pursue relationships with an edge of wariness. We divert our eyes to avoid contact or make only glancing contact. Or our hardened eyes meet others' eyes, but we stare *through* them rather than really see them. Our antenna anxiously scans for danger. Our shields are up. As we are getting to know a person, our fear of being burned may prompt preemptive criticism and contempt. Even if we try to be kind, our tone of voice may betray deeply held suspicions. We yearn for soft and safe contact, yet something inside us screams, "I can't trust you! Stay away!"

Lowering our shields means finding a way to hold fears and hurts in a tender embrace. As these tight and vulnerable places are held and heard, they tend to loosen and heal. We breathe more freely into a relaxed gut; we feel more inwardly resourced. This self-connection makes it easier to show ourselves. Our longing to be seen, heard, and met is more likely to be satisfied as we express ourselves with calm openness.

Sadly, we often perpetuate a loop in which our fear of rejection or failure or our continued isolation creates a desperation that drives us to attack and shame people to get what we want. We hurl hurtful words such as, "You have a problem with commitment!" or "You're so self-centered; everything revolves around you!" Rather than extend a fragrant flower infused with the sweet aroma of our feelings and longings, we wield a sharp hatchet honed with steely contempt and sarcasm. Beneath this display of hostility, we are hurting or afraid. But instead of sweetly revealing these tender feelings, we're on the warpath, although we're often punching the shadows that linger from our past.

Painful impasses in relationships are perpetuated by our inability to gently hold our own shame, fear, and loneliness. Rather than embrace these uncomfortable feelings, we may shove this undifferentiated mass of muddled emotions onto the lap of our unsuspecting beloved. We become irate or rageful. Feeling besieged or overwhelmed, our partner may shut down, get defensive, or retaliate. Sadly, we may have little inkling about how we're contributing to a cycle that pushes away the love we want.

Allowing our feelings and longings to settle down by being mindful of how they feel inside, we may convey them more clearly and effectively. I am always delighted to see the magic that happens in couples sessions when two people slow down, go inside themselves, and reveal what is in their hearts. Mindfully noticing and revealing our authentic experience melts the armor that creates the suffering of separation from ourselves and others.

Dancing with Emotional Fire

Oftentimes during couples therapy, I see two lovely people passionately trying to convey their sacred longings. I witness them shooting emotional flares that bespeak their frustrated longings. The flame of their discontent may rage so strongly that they interrupt, talk over each other, and insist, "You're not hearing me!"

Oftentimes they are right. Their partner may be so consumed with his or her own burning needs that there is no spare attention remaining. But what they often miss is common to the human condition: they're not really hearing *themselves*. They are not present with themselves in a way that might allow their emotions to settle. They're not skilled at being mindful of the feelings that relationships bring up in them, especially the quieter, more vulnerable ones. They haven't opened a channel to a wellspring that flows within. In short, they haven't pursued a path that parallels their quest for intimacy with others by nurturing a tender intimacy with themselves.

By connecting with ourselves in a gentle, caring way, we are better positioned to recognize and expose our most tender longings and feelings. Rather than maul people with the sharp edges of our needs, as expressed through demands and indictments, we may then express what we are experiencing in a manner that is unguarded, tender, and dignified.

Speaking in a way that is congruent with what we're experiencing can actually feel good, while also dramatically improving our chances of being heard.

Rather than stifle our passionate longings, meditation can cool us down so that we are not overwhelmed or controlled by our desires. Rather than seek to merge with another, we stay connected to ourselves in a way in which true intimacy is possible. Or, more realistically, we dance gracefully between the hot passion that seeks to merge and a quiet connection with our own being so that we don't get too lost.

Taming the Fire

Intimacy is furthered by finding a way to tame our emotional fires before they alight upon others in the form of searing accusations, rage, and blame. This fire dance with ourselves takes a lifetime of practice. Just as we cannot be perfectly attuned to our dance partner in every moment, we cannot expect ourselves to be continually attuned to ourselves. Demanding self-perfection is a setup for shame when we inevitably slip.

As we fumble our way toward holding our own experience with compassion, we become more tolerant of others' missteps. Recognizing that their jabs, like our own, are reactions to their frustration longings, we may take them in stride without reacting so muscularly. Being aware that our beloved is hurting even while we are hurting, we're more inclined to hear their longings and needs, even if expressed indirectly or reactively.

This is not to suggest that we give our partner a pass for abusive behavior that wounds us. But we have the option of gently holding our momentary pain rather than crying "foul" every time we feel stung. We sap the oxygen from conflicts by soothing ourselves while glimpsing the deeper feelings and longings that our partner may not have the wherewithal to verbalize. This is no easy task. But gradually, through this kind of relational mindfulness practice, we can get more adept at gently holding and revealing what we are experiencing while also staying connected to what our partner feels and desires.

Listening to Ourselves

Hearing ourselves and others with a receptive heart has a way of releasing micronutrients that allow intimacy and love to leaven. As we cultivate practices that connect us with ourselves, we are better positioned to replace cycles of emotional escalation and distancing with a habit of mutual nurturing.

Just as a chain is as strong as its weakest link, our spiritual journey is precarious if it rests upon a frayed connection with our feelings and longings. By being present to our breath and body, we rest more cozily within our own being. Staying connected inside as we peer out, we can delight in the play of contact without abandoning ourselves or overpowering others.

If anyone, therefore, will not learn from Christianity to love himself in the right way, then neither can he love his neighbor. . . . To love one's self in the right way and to love one's neighbor are absolutely analogous concepts, are at bottom one and the same. . . . Hence the law is: You shall love yourself as you love your neighbor when you love him as yourself.

—Søren Kierkegaard

Intimacy is a song of spirit inviting two people to come and share their spirit together. It is a song which no one can resist.

—Sobonfu Somé

Chapter Thirteen

Intimacy as a Sacred Experience

〘

An embodied spiritual path integrates the sacred with the personal.
We are drawn toward the liberation of a spiritual path, yet we also
long for a rich and vibrant intimacy. What is the nature of this
mysterious and elusive intimacy for which we long? And how does it relate
to the spiritual path?

Spirituality Opens Us to Intimacy

Spiritual practice promotes qualities that create a fertile climate for love
and intimacy:

- Presence
- Equanimity
- Compassion
- Loving-kindness toward ourselves and others
- Mindfulness/self-awareness
- Right Speech / kind communication

According to Zen master Dōgen, Buddhism is all about relationship.
According to one translation of his vision, "To be enlightened is to be
intimate with all things."[1] This is a lovely statement about where spiritual

practice takes us, a place where we feel so connected that we no longer experience ourselves as separate. We become so open and tender with our world that we enjoy an exquisite intimacy with life.

The non-dual teachings of Advaita-Vedanta philosophy describes what this state is *not*. We are *not* separate, we don't exist apart from life. I prefer the term "intimacy" to affirm the warm felt sense of this awareness. A resplendent intimacy with life is the natural maturation of spiritual practice and mindful living.

Meditation and mindfulness practice are not about withdrawing from the world. In fact, it is just the opposite. Mindfulness helps us disidentify with limiting self-images and preoccupations so that something more deeply alive may emerge into being. As our mind settles and nervous system relaxes, we perceive things more freshly and connect with the world more wholeheartedly.

Connecting with Something Larger Than Ourselves

Like the term "spirituality," the word "intimacy" points toward a richly felt experience that our mind cannot fully wrap itself around. Intimacy ensues when our innermost selves interact. When we relate openly and non-defensively with someone who is similarly open, intimacy happens.

When I have asked workshop participants to find words that resonate with the felt sense of intimacy, I hear responses such as closeness, beauty, love, tenderness, warmth, safety, acceptance, rapture, and ease of being. These words offer nuances of what we experience when we open to the vastness that exists beyond our limited self. These words also convey sentiments that resonate with qualities we might consider spiritual.

Intimacy qualifies as a spiritual experience insofar as it connects us with something larger than ourselves. Moments of deep connection deliver us beyond our separate self into something more vibrantly alive. A warmth comes to our heart, a radiance to our face, a smile to our eyes. We enter into wordless wonder and mystery. We bask in the ecstasy of being alive.

Similar to spiritual openings, intimacy has a numinous quality—it can evoke fear and trembling. As much as we are drawn toward it, we might shrink from its awesome power. Lowering the drawbridge and inviting someone toward us has the awesome potential to transform us as we learn to trust it and go with it. But it might also raise the fearful specter of losing control as something unknown comes into being.

Like life itself, intimacy cannot be commanded or engineered, which explains why relationships can be so maddening. But although we cannot control the flow of a wonder-filled intimacy, we have the power to create conditions in which a luminous intimacy is more likely to spring into being. We can learn to rest in ourselves in a way in which people feel comfortable approaching us. We can express our feelings and longings in a kind and congruent way. As we reside in our undefended heart and show ourselves to others, we send signals that help them feel safer coming toward us. Our availability for intimacy is a sacred aspect of who we are. Beautiful things unfold as we get out of our own way, connect with our tender heart, and stay present to life.

Control Versus Trust

Close relationships are especially frustrating for people who have a penchant for controlling things, which includes most of us! Our longing for connection is so overpowering that we may find ourselves scrambling to secure it. The most precious things in life come as gifts. Intimacy and control are antagonistic. The feeling of connection arises indirectly; it is a consequence of showing who we really are and being present as others show themselves.

How many times have we heard, "You're trying to control me!" This accusation may feel exasperating; it is usually not our intention. Yet, we may so desperately want the pain of powerlessness and disconnection to stop that we will do or say anything to persuade our beloved to bend toward our will. *We try to overpower others when we feel overpowered by difficult or uncomfortable feelings within us.* We exhibit controlling behavior when we feel inwardly out of control.

We cannot control the dance of intimacy, but *we can create conditions in which it is more likely to occur.* We are less inclined to manipulate people as we're mindful of our wants and longings and find ways to communicate them. We are less liable to poke and push people as we become aware of the unwieldy feelings that prompt us to overpower them. As we attend mindfully to our feelings and yearnings rather than be controlled by them, we can communicate our experience in a way that invites contact. *Trust grows between us as we befriend what is happening inside us.*

Intimacy means trusting another person with our heart. But more fundamentally, our capacity for intimacy requires trusting ourselves and trusting life. We need to trust that we can be with whatever experience arises within us before we can really open ourselves to another person, although we sometimes need a little help from our friends in order to stay with ourselves. Trusting that we have inner resources to face what life delivers bestows a gentle, resilient strength.

Reporting Our Inner Experience

A telltale sign that we have moved away from intimacy with our own vulnerability—and abandoned our spiritual core—is when our words or tone of voice are tinged with demands or accusations. When we feel overwhelmed by our tender feelings and longings, we find it difficult to *report* them. Instead, we may *declare* them with an edge. When our words and body language are aggressively critical or accusatory, we are no longer connected with our felt longing. Unable to embody it and express it transparently, we may vent the frustration of not having our longings seen and met.

When the emotional inferno spewing from our unmet longings rages out of control, our partner's instinct is to flee from this wildfire. Their distancing may further fuel the flames of our discontent. A painful cycle spins more and more out of control: the more aggressively we pursue our partner, the more she pulls away. The more she shuts down, the more combative we become. This pursuer-distancer dynamic is a reliable formula for mutual suffering.

Just as berating ourselves doesn't further our spiritual path, intimacy, whether with ourselves or others, doesn't arise through coercion or pressure. *Intimacy is an "invitation only" event.* Gently stated requests, not punishing criticism, allow trust to grow. As we meet our own heart with gentleness, our mutual hearts are more inclined to find their way toward each other.

We create a climate for trust by conveying our felt experience and allowing others to come toward us if they feel so inclined. Staying close to ourselves and conveying our tender feelings and desires allows grace a chance to work its wondrous magic.

Pursuing Love Versus Letting It Ensue

No doubt we have all felt frustrated trying to renovate people in order to wrest a deeper connection. But intimacy is like a floating soap bubble that explodes in your face the moment you grasp it. The Buddha identified this kind of grasping as a source of suffering. Intimacy becomes elusive when aggressively *pursued* rather than allowed to *ensue* as we cultivate gentle attention toward ourselves.

As we practice attending to ourselves in a tender way, we cultivate a spaciousness that connects us with life and the beauty around us. In this manner, the attitude necessary for mature love is allied with the attitude essential for spiritual development.

The intimacy we seek cannot be grabbed; it must be grappled with. Intimacy asks us to wrestle with aspects of our own shadow, our fears, wounds, and unresolved feelings that cling to us. Creating loving relationships requires a quiet kind of power, the gentle strength to be open. Love is allergic to any hint of control, criticism, or demands. An attitude of gracious allowing invites life and love to flow toward us, through us, and between us.

Underlying the Fear of Intimacy

When people in my workshops voice associations with the term "intimacy," they offer warm and fuzzy words. But they also convey emotions of fear and trembling. One person felt "abject terror" when presented with the word "intimacy."

The prospect of opening ourselves to another person may activate lingering hurts, fears, and traumas. We shudder to consider that when we open our heart for another to hold, they may drop it on the ground—leaving us to gather its splattered remains.

Although we may believe that we fear intimacy, it is not intimacy itself that is frightening; we fear the real or imagined consequences of our movement toward intimacy. We dread what it might bring up inside us:

- Painful memories of loss and grief
- The prospect of conflict and the heartache of shattered trust
- Feelings of shame and inadequacy if the relationship flounders
- Losing control and being flooded by unpleasant feelings and sensations—or even pleasurable ones
- Shaking up our familiar sense of self
- Reactivation of pain or trauma from prior relationships

As we have evolved as a species, we've learned increasingly sophisticated ways to avoid pain. As we layer on our armor, our breathing constricts and our muscles tighten. We dissociate from our body and become numb to our longings. We distract ourselves through television, Internet surfing, or shopping.

Seeking further fortification against vulnerable feelings, we may retreat to the refuge of our mind. We find succor in our religious and political ideologies; we cling to judgments about people. These mental machinations separate us further from each other.

Clinging to a Rigid Identity

Relationships often trigger our greatest suffering. What creates much of this anguish is our inability to deal with the shifting feelings that relationships bring up in us and hearing the messages they hold for us, as well as failing to communicate our authentic feelings and longings effectively. Feelings can be a nuisance. They pry us away from our comfort zone and threaten our sense of who we think we are. We try to fabricate a world we can rely on, but there is no real safety when our life is built upon the sinking sands of emotional avoidance.

Intimacy and the feelings it evokes disrupt what is familiar. However, clinging to intimacy is not the culprit but rather hanging on to our familiar identity and sense of self is. Intimate relationships are a spiritual practice insofar as they help us notice how we cling so tightly to what we don't need—our romantic notions of love, our rigidly held beliefs about each other, and embarrassment around our longing—that we overlook what we legitimately want. Our romantic notions of love, our rigidly held beliefs about each other, and being ashamed to have longings push away connection.[2]

Cultivating a spacious mindfulness around our felt experience allows us to embrace how things actually are rather than how we would like them to be. Rather than seek a static shelter, we find a refuge by expanding our tolerance for discomfort. We find peace by dancing gracefully with our experience in the ever-changing moment. Doing so, we build a brain and nervous system that is more resilient and responsive.

As *sentient* beings, we feel life deeply. Intimacy is a celebration of our sentience—feeling what is touched within us through being alive and being together. Another's presence can touch us profoundly if we're open and available. Intimacy awakens us to the vibrant life that flows within us and between us.

The Risk to Love

Stinging from past rejections or betrayals, we may be reluctant to expose our tender heart. Mistrust reigns. A fearful part of us advises caution: "If I show my true feelings and longings, will this go well? Remember what happened last time I trusted someone!" Our reluctance to embrace the risks associated with living and loving keeps us isolated.

Intimacy requires vulnerability. Rather than controlling others, we are invited to trust, just as the spiritual life invites us to place our faith in something greater than ourselves. Intimacy asks us to surrender our usual sense of self, to loosen the tight grip we maintain in an attempt to secure safety, although doing so doesn't really deliver safety. We move toward comfort and connection in relationships by bringing gentleness toward our ever-changing experience and allowing others a portal into our inner world.

By becoming more adept at accommodating feelings that arise on our journey toward another person, we become more confident that we can deal with the multitude of unknowns in relationships. Knowing that we have inner resources to deal with whatever happens, we become more willing to place our heart in the ring, moving forward with courageous tenderness.

Fearing the Loss of Self

The fears brought on by intimacy resemble a major hindrance to spiritual practice: we fear the loss of self. We fear being engulfed, dominated, suffocated, or controlled by another person. In spiritual practice, we may similarly fear the dissolution of our separate sense of self.

What is common to intimate relationships and our spiritual journey is that some part of us must be sacrificed so that something new can be born—a sort of crucifixion before the resurrection. What aspects of ourselves must be held in the crucible so that the alchemical process of transforming lead into gold may proceed? Our self-righteousness, our dreams of perfection, our self-comforting ideologies, and the clinging that reifies a solid, separate ego are invited to yield to a sense of self that lives and breathes in relationship to something much larger than ourselves.

In spiritual practice, we are invited to empty ourselves of whatever perpetuates the illusion that we exist as a self-contained, independent entity. In a similar vein, a key to fulfilling relationships is acknowledging our interdependence. We recognize that we're affected by others and need nourishing interactions to be happy.

The essence of mindfulness practice is to see things as they are. Similarly, our movement toward intimacy eases as we see ourselves and others more clearly. We glimpse our beauty and our beastliness, our own pain and the suffering of others. We recognize our kind and hurtful impulses. We uncover the heartfelt feelings and longings that underlie our impulse to push people away.

In subtle ways, we tend to avoid life rather than trust. We live within a narrow comfort zone. Opening ourselves to what is sacred is anything but safe, just as opening to another involves risk. There is angst and apprehension to be faced on our journey toward a spiritually based relational life that is juicy and alive. We need resources and practices that can help us navigate this bumpy terrain.

Cultivating the Openness that Allows Intimacy

The discovery that the earth is not the center of the universe encountered fierce resistance. Today, we may have similar difficulty perceiving ourselves as multifaceted beings who revolve around something much larger than what we can imagine. In an intimacy-based life, there is no solid "me" at the center, no self-image to cling to and protect. Instead, there is a flow of interactions, an ease of relating to whatever comes our way, an availability to engage wholeheartedly in our daily encounters. As the cult of the individual yields to a celebration of our interconnectedness, we live with a more porous, accessible heart.

Safety is found in change itself, as we welcome the shifting panorama of our feelings and longings and courageously reveal our authentic experience to each other. When two people share their authentic hearts and listen with a kindness and compassion that is central to spiritual growth, a warm relationship may be created. A vibrant and engaging intimacy arises naturally through mutual openness and presence.

As we develop the awareness that expands our capacity for intimacy and love, we are simultaneously walking a spiritual path. What could be more spiritually generous than extending our warm presence toward other human beings and wanting what is best for them? We create a life that is spiritually alive and intimately engaging when we feel so attuned to this precious existence that our own well-being is no longer separate from the well-being of others.

Mindfulness practice is really a love affair with what is so, with what we might call truth, which for me includes beauty, the unknown, and the possible, how things actually are, all embedded here, in this very moment.

—Jon Kabat-Zinn

It was only when I began to truly allow my thoughts and feelings into my meditation sittings and didn't just try to note them or focus on them as sensations or breathe through them that I began to feel sorrow, loss, regret, and my own loneliness. I opened myself up to my anger, hurt, fear, and longing. I no longer believed that I should not have such feelings.

—Jason Siff

Chapter Fourteen

Meditation as Self-Intimacy

I must confess that I'm a romantic at heart. Intimate relationships have provided my deepest joys and deepest sorrows. But I have found more joy and less heartache as I've become clearer about what relationships can and cannot offer. I have set myself up for disappointment when I've looked so longingly to another to make me happy and whole that I've lost touch with my own soul. I have found more steadiness as I stay close to myself while cultivating other sources of connection and creativity.

Integrating Inner and Outer Worlds

Since the intimacy we seek is with another person, it seems obvious that we need to look outside ourselves. But genuine intimacy involves a curious paradox. The path toward another person involves simultaneously walking a path that leads us ever deeper into ourselves.

If we are solely oriented toward looking outward for happiness, then we're at the mercy of how others relate to us. But if our focus is too inward, we condemn ourselves to a lonely existence. Finding fulfillment involves navigating relationships while staying connected to our own soul.

While Buddhism emphasizes the connection with ourselves, the path of relationship invites us to embrace others. It may not be obvious how each path supports the other. But things do go better "out there" when we're "in here" in a wise and skilful way. And things go better "in here" when we're "out there" in a wise and skillful way.

Our spiritual path becomes a desolate journey without nurturing connections. The gnawing ache in our heart may not shift in any meaningful way by simply being with it. We may need to do something *about* it rather than suffer in silence.

Discerning Our Feelings and Needs

Relationships go off track when we are not mindfully attuned to our felt experience. We may hold others responsible for our discomfort—raging, blaming, or shutting down when people fail to gratify us, agree with us, or indulge our requests. We may expect others to alleviate uncomfortable feelings that we need to soothe within ourselves.

For example, if our partner doesn't return our phone call immediately, comes home late, or stares at an alluring creature across the dance floor, we may experience a huge reaction. As we develop the capacity for self-connection and self-soothing, we are less poised to pounce or flee. We're more likely to have a satisfying conversation about these matters as we stay close to ourselves and voice the authentic feelings and concerns beneath our reactivity.

Our fear of abandonment or need for reassurance may loom so large that we may not be able to get our arms around it. An inner conflagration may be triggered by a casual comment or innocuous behavior when we are not aware of our true feelings and longings or when we can't find the inner resources to embrace them.

We may hide our true feelings because we don't want to feel uncomfortably exposed. Consequently, our feelings may come out indirectly. Distancing from what is alive inside us may explain why we feel irritable, moody, or angry sometimes. If we can allow ample room for vulnerable feelings such as shame and fear, we might preface what we say by naming these emotions:

- I feel a little shy to tell you this, but when you didn't call I felt anxious. It really comforts me when you call during the day.
- I'm scared that I might push you away by saying this, but when you came home late, I felt sad. I really missed you.
- I feel embarrassed to say this, but I felt jealous when you looked at that woman on the dance floor.

It takes a quiet inner strength to expose what is vulnerably alive inside us. We can relate to others in a more direct, fulfilling way as we become mindful of what we're really experiencing and show our true feelings and wants without misdirection, games, or shame about who we really are.

Welcoming Experience as It Is

Taisen Deshimaru, who spread Zen throughout Europe in the 1960s, declared that "Zazen is the practice of becoming intimate with oneself."[1] What a refreshingly grounded view of meditation! It is not about attaining some transcendent state or out-of-body experience. It's about having an *in-the-body, self-connecting experience* that is freely available. Bowing to this moment's experience, we make room for whatever we're noticing without trying to change it, alter ourselves, or overcome anything. Buddhist teacher and psychologist Tara Brach calls this "radical acceptance":

> The way out of our cage begins with accepting absolutely everything about ourselves and our lives, by embracing with wakefulness and care our moment-to-moment experience. . . . We are aware of what is happening within our body and mind in any given moment, without trying to control or judge or pull away.[2]

Being totally okay with our experience as it is creates a foundation for seeing and accepting others as they are, which creates a climate for love and intimacy to blossom.

Mindfulness and Meditation

Buddhism may conjure up images of a tranquil Buddha meditating cross-legged with a faint smile on his face. Indeed, sitting meditation is a long-honored tradition that is central to many forms of Buddhist practice. While I have been using the words "meditation" and "mindfulness" interchangeably, I want to highlight their differences.

Being mindful is a fundamental aspect of meditation, but mindfulness is an awareness practice not limited to sitting meditation. In fact, some forms of Buddhism do not encourage sitting meditation at all. In Pure Land Buddhism, for example, the preferred practice is reciting mantras with concentration and chanting with a full heart. Daily mindfulness, being present in heart and mind, is also encouraged.

Some forms of Theravada Buddhism, such as the tradition of Burmese teacher Thynn Thynn, who teaches in Northern California, emphasize the practice of mindfulness in everyday life rather than sitting meditation. She voices a concern that Buddhists sometimes limit their meditation to when they are on the cushion rather than applying mindfulness throughout the day. When you attend a retreat with her, you will bring a calm and clear awareness to the experience of cooking, eating, cleaning, gardening, interacting, and hearing the teachings.

Personally, I find sitting meditation helpful. Just before bedtime is often best for me. I find it calming, renewing, and sometimes even illuminating, and a nice bridge into the mysterious world of sleep. In addition to being present with the breath and body, I do a variety of things during this period that some Buddhists would insist is not meditation, though I would disagree.

For example, I might consider things I am grateful about, not in a purely heady way, but rather allowing space for a felt sense of gratitude to swell regarding various blessings in my life, such as having decent health (at least as of this writing), good friends, and meaningful work. In addition to this gratitude meditation, I might notice personal concerns that are calling, if not screaming, for attention. This may include unpleasant feelings, alluring thoughts, gnawing issues, or even pleasant things that enter into my awareness as I'm attending to my breath.

Sometimes I simply notice these things arising without attachment or aversion. I bring mindfulness to them and allow them to pass. In other instances, especially when they keep recurring, I attend to how I am inwardly experiencing these phenomena in a certain kind of contemplative way, which I'll explore later in the chapter on Focusing.

I maintain receptivity to basking in the deliciously quiet spaces that occasionally arise when thoughts, feelings, and longings are still. Perhaps by my having allowed these more active experiences to live out their life, letting them come and be heard, they become quiescent. At least for now.

Insight Meditation

Methods of meditation abound. Some aim for concentrated or absorbed states of consciousness that deliver us into realms beyond our normal sense of self. One popular approach is the Buddhist practice of *vipassana* (insight) meditation, or "mindfulness" meditation. The Pali word vipassana means "seeing things clearly" or "seeing things precisely."

Most Buddhist approaches maintain an initial focus on the breath. A helpful adaptation by vipassana teacher S. N. Goenke is to engage in body scanning. Bringing gentle awareness from the top of our head to our feet allows us to notice sensations such as jumpiness in our stomach, heaviness in our chest, or tightness in our shoulders. Attending to body sensations often allows a softening of tensions and greater presence. Mindfulness itself has a calming effect, even if what we're noticing is uncomfortable.

Vipassana practice leads awareness to whatever throbs with aliveness in this moment. The practice is extraordinarily ordinary. The most obstinate obstacle we face is trying too hard. Rather than adding anything extra, we are simply being aware of what is. The breath and the body are touchstones to return to when attention wanders.

The traditional aim of meditation is not to relax; it is simply to be present with what arises. Calm often results from being intimate with our currently felt experience, but it is not something to strive for. There is the simple, non-strenuous intention to attend to what is here now and to whatever comes next. The turbulent pool of our mind tends to still as we intimately touch this moment.

As bodily armor melts, we gain more access to what is authentic within us. We are present for whatever happens to arise in the field of awareness from moment to moment. Sounds, body sensations, thoughts, and feelings are noticed and welcomed, not pushed away or judged.

Meditation doesn't offer security. Each time we sit, we risk opening ourselves to uncomfortable places. Sometimes we find the treasures of tranquility and compassion. At other times, pain and struggle await us. Just as intimate relationships require courage, so does meditation. Over time, we cultivate a refuge within ourselves from which we can honestly notice what is actually happening inside us and around us.

Some Benefits of Meditation

State-of-the-art technologies have been used to study meditation and its effects on the brain and body. It has consistently been shown to stabilize blood pressure, lower heart rate, strengthen the immune system, and decrease stress, anxiety, and depression. Studies done at Yale, Harvard, and Massachusetts General Hospital have revealed that meditation increases gray matter in the brain and slows its age-related deterioration.[3]

According to the National Institutes of Health (NIH), "Practicing meditation has been shown to induce some changes in the body. . . . It is thought that some types of meditation might work by reducing activity in the sympathetic nervous system and increasing activity in the parasympathetic nervous system."[4] Meditation helps modulate the fight/flight/freeze response and allows more choice in how we interact with the world.

Mindfulness: The Art of Paying Attention

Jon Kabat-Zinn is known for bringing mindfulness to the mainstream. He founded the Stress Reduction Clinic at the University of Massachusetts Medical Center in 1979. He is a professor emeritus at its medical school and is known for his mindfulness-based stress reduction (MBSR) programs around the world, which use mindfulness to help patients struggling with chronic pain and stress. He defines mindfulness as "paying attention in a particular way, on purpose, in the present moment, and nonjudgmentally."[5] He has stated that his program is not based on Buddhism, although the principles of mindfulness have been most clearly articulated in Buddhist teachings.

Mindfulness practice means gently attending to our experience and inquiring deeply into ourselves. We meet life as it presents itself from moment to moment. We vividly experience what is alive now—the play of breath as it enters the nostrils, the melodic chorus of birds in the distance, a tightness in our stomach as we remember an awkward moment, a shudder of apprehension regarding a health issue. We make space for the full range of what is, rather than how we'd like things to be. We bring a gentle presence to the ever-changing stream of sensations, feelings, thoughts, sounds, sights, or whatever happens to present itself. In short, we become intimate with this ever-changing precious moment.

Meditation Can Help Relationships

Rather than distance us from relationships, mindfulness can help us move toward them in various ways:

- Becoming more still and settled inside positions us to be more attentive to people, including their feelings and needs. Being more sensitized to others' existence allows them to feel recognized, which fosters trust and intimacy.

- When we gently meet and hold our authentic feelings within ourselves, they are less prone to detonate when we're agitated.
- By cultivating equanimity around our feelings and longings, we are better prepared to share them calmly rather than vent them reactively.
- We are better positioned to relish the intimacy that arises as we're present with ourselves and undefended with others. By greeting our own experience with kindness, we are more kindly disposed toward others' experiences.
- Relaxing into the present moment, we are less hobbled by past traumas and ruptures of trust.
- When we uncover deeper layers of our felt experience, our defenses tend to melt and our heart open. Familiarity with what is happening *within* us helps us see more clearly what is happening *between* us.

Meditation helps us become less self-centered in the sense of being less self-preoccupied. Growing into a more comfortable connection with our own experience, we are less concerned about how we're coming across or what image we're projecting. Resting more securely within, we are less consumed by how we appear and thus more inclined to reveal ourselves genuinely. Softening into a tender presence with ourselves, we're more available to love and be loved.

Our awareness of feelings and intimacy are kissing cousins. As we touch our inner world more directly, we are better equipped to reveal the tender textures of that world to people with whom we want to connect. Meditation cultivates a loving, open, contactable presence—in short, it makes us more adorable.

How Spaciousness Supports Intimacy

Meditation cultivates an inner stillness that allows the muddy waters of our mind and emotions to settle. Peering into the quiet depths of our felt experience, we may glimpse emotional stirrings before they kick up the usual sludge that clouds our understanding of what is happening inside us.

As we create spaciousness around our experience, we may hear what it is telling us rather than act out our feelings destructively.

For example, if we feel anger, we can become curious about how it is living in our body before harsh words leap out of our mouth. Giving it space, we might notice how our partner's sarcastic comment sent a shudder of fear or shame down our spine. We may recognize how our anger covers up uncomfortable emotions that overwhelmed our nervous system. We can then share these more vulnerable feelings as a step toward repairing trust and renewing connection.

Not having a handle on what we are experiencing, we're manhandled by the programming of our reptilian brain. We lash out or shut down without even noticing the hurt that prompts these reactions. We try to control others when our inner life feels out of control. Wanting our pain to stop, we become critical or demanding, which triggers reactions in others that only intensify our pain.

It takes a courageous, resilient mindfulness to look beneath the instinctual reactions of fight, flight, or freeze. Cultivating a particular kind of self-focus enables us to attend to the legitimate needs and longings that fuel our self-defeating and hurtful behaviors. As Zen teacher John Tarrant puts it, "Noticing is a practice of love. You don't have to exclude, extinguish, or dislike anything."[6] By cultivating equanimity toward our experience, we're more inclined to reveal our longings as an opening flower, which invites curiosity and connection.

When Meditation Keeps Us Distant

We may be tempted to use meditation to support an aversion to feelings and intimacy. If we limit mindfulness to a narrow zone, perhaps by noting feelings and sensations but never allowing ourselves to feel them, we may find a serenity that teeters on shaky ground. Overlooking the more poorly lit zones of our psyche has an undermining effect on our well-being. A broader mindfulness includes an awareness of feelings and longings that arise from fully engaging with life.

Mindfulness of the body and mindfulness of feelings are two aspects of the Buddha's Four Foundations of Mindfulness. Cultivating a nuanced awareness of how life is affecting us fosters a self-harmony that translates into interactions that are more fluid. Finding more ease with whatever we are experiencing creates a resiliency that enables us to exude calmness and presence, which invites people toward us.

Intimacy Happens in This Moment

Intimacy with ourselves and others can arise only in present time. Absorbed in ruminations about the past or future, we are distracted from the immediacy of this moment. That said, there is a curious way in which our effort to be present may overlook what actually *is* here now.

Regretting the past or worrying about the future may yank us away from ourselves, but our *feelings* about them—since feelings exist only in the present moment—can bring us right back to the here and now. Being present may be as simple as being mindful of our felt sense of worry or regret. Perhaps our stomach is jittery or our chest is constricted. Fearing the future or lamenting the past removes us from the moment only if we don't allow ourselves to experience the felt edges of our fear, sorrow, or whatever is felt from the inside right now. As we bring our whole being to our felt experience of these thoughts or feelings, we return to this moment.

During couples therapy sessions, I notice how referencing the past often perpetuates impasses. For example, as I invite Ted to express his current feelings, he says, "I've told her a million times how I feel!" Amanda exclaims, "He knows he upsets me when he does that! He obviously doesn't like being with me!" Such comments generate defensiveness and move them away from themselves and each other.

Their conversation may return to the present if they can convey the feelings they are noticing with an open heart. For example, Amanda typically says, "You know I hate it when you're on the phone in the evenings." (Ted hears that he's doing something wrong again and gets defensive.)

As she brings mindfulness to her current feelings, she can instead say, "I'm feeling sad about last night when you were on the phone. I was looking forward to being with you." (He hears that she's sad and misses him, which is nice to hear.) Ted responds, "I really hear that you feel sad. I feel frustrated that my work project drags on. I want more time with you, too."

If Amanda suspends her suspicious interpretation that he doesn't value time with her (born of repeated disappointments) and "lets in" his desire to be with her, she may soften. By mindfully communicating what they are experiencing now and mindfully noticing how they feel hearing each other, they take a step toward healing hurts, repairing trust, and feeling connected.

Mindfulness in Psychotherapy

Mindfulness practices have woven their way into various forms of psychotherapy. Mindfulness-based Cognitive Therapy (MBCT) has demonstrated effectiveness for people having repeated bouts of depression.[7] Non-judgmentally noticing moment-to-moment thoughts and feelings allows us to be aware of them without reacting to them.

Mindfulness is also a key aspect of Acceptance and Commitment Therapy (ACT).[8] This helpful approach invites us to acknowledge our feelings and accept ourselves in a mindful, compassionate way, while pursuing what is important for us. Rather than trying to fight our pain or control our feelings, we embrace them but without being controlled by them.

The practice of Emotionally Focused Therapy (EFT) for couples, as taught by Susan M. Johnson, implicitly involves a kind of mindfulness practice.[9] Clients are invited to notice their authentic experience rather than get lost in emotional reactions that generate suffering when dumped upon their unsuspecting partner. Mindfulness applied to relationships includes noticing when we are attacking or withdrawing, uncovering underlying feelings and longings that may trigger these reactions, and noticing how we may be contributing to a cycle of disconnection.

A hundred times every day I remind myself that my inner and outer life depends on the labors of other men, living and dead, and that I must exert myself in order to give in the measure as I have received and am still receiving.

—Albert Einstein

And then the day came when the risk to remain tight in a bud was more painful than the risk it took to blossom.

—Anaïs Nin

Chapter Fifteen

Interdependence with
Others and Nature

❦

M indfulness practice may appear to be narcissistic self-absorption to those unfamiliar with its inner workings. But settling down and connecting with ourselves, being self-centered in one sense, enables us to be less self-centered in another important sense.

It is the nature of attention to want to go somewhere. If we don't ground ourselves by actively attending to what we are actually experiencing, then where will our attention wander? As Benedictine monk Brother David Steindl-Rast explains, "Where else should we be centered, if not in the self?"[1] We become less narcissistic and more responsive to others as we become grounded in our bodily felt experience of the moment.

Paradoxically, becoming less self-centered begins by noticing ourselves. Rather than clinging to how we want things to be, we allow ourselves to embrace whatever we are experiencing. By cultivating a spacious allowing, we're less inclined to insist that things be done our way or that others conform to our will. Seeing *what is* allows us to see others with eyes wide open.

Noticing How We Affect Others

Being human means not only having longings, but also having the capacity to *notice* how pursuing our longings affects others. An essential part of living a spiritual life is paying attention to the consequences of our actions and words. Are we hurting anyone by how we act upon our longings and express ourselves? Are we damaging our environment or other creatures by how we are pursuing our interests—and thereby sabotaging ourselves? The trick is to hold our longings gently, express them deftly, and make adjustments as we notice how we might be hurting others or ourselves.

There is a fine line between the healthy self-regard of validating our longings and the narcissism of pursuing them so one-pointedly that we remove ourselves from the larger web of life. We banish ourselves to a lonely existence when we don't allow ourselves to be affected by people or notice how we affect them. The Buddha's Right Effort in the context of relationships could be seen as an intention to extend ourselves toward others from the vulnerability of our sacred longings rather than aggressively controlling others to satisfy our cravings. We courageously reveal our tender heart rather than veil it.

Mindfulness Cools the Fire

Denying ourselves through some muscular leap into selflessness is incongruous with spiritual life. Complying with a spiritual imperative to love may only reinforce our clinging to a *self-image* of being loving; we dance to the moralistic music but we're only going through the motions. We are not responding from an expansive heart fed by the micronutrients of caring, sensitive attention toward ourselves. The path of love and intimacy involves a middle way that balances our needs with others' needs. The sublime concept of unconditional love is fitting when directed toward our children, but adult relationships require the mutuality of giving and receiving.

Our meditation is misguided if we hope to extinguish the fire of our longings rather than dance with them. But dancing with fire may set us ablaze unless we calm it enough so we enjoy its cozy warmth. Mindfulness allows us to hold our feelings and needs gently. By cultivating a calm, silent attention, we find a comfortable relationship with our longings so that we can enjoy their heat without the fear of getting burned. They are not so overwhelming when cooled just enough by the waters of mindfulness. Gradually, we may notice how feelings and desires come and go, and we warmly welcome them as they pass through. Cultivating spaciousness around our longings gives greater choice about how, when, and whether to act upon them.

Narcissism and Craving

Narcissism has a psychological parallel with the Buddha's notion of craving; our lives are driven by an inflated self-importance with little empathy for others' feelings and wants. Much of our attention goes toward looking good, gathering approval, or wanting to be right, which inflates our sense of power and worth. Or we may lean into the future with an ardent eye toward acquiring more money, possessions, admiration, converts . . . or something. Narcissism may also show up as an unrealistic assessment of how we can change others. If we tune into the actual felt experience of this craving, we will recognize it as an enormous source of suffering.

Religions urge us to love, but this aptitude rests upon our personal and spiritual development. We may believe that we are a caring person, but narcissism and craving are like a colorless, odorless gas. We are often not aware when they are operating and how they limit our capacity to love. Attending to our own growth by uncovering blind spots and being mindful of what is really happening inside us adds a pinch of wisdom to our noble intentions.

We are part of a web of life that preexists any ideas we can muster about it. A felt connection with life, love, or God happens not through our beliefs but through being in ourselves in a way that dissolves the barriers to a connectedness that already exists.

Observing What Is Around Us

As I am writing this, I am sitting in my favorite restaurant in Chiang Mai, Thailand. Sometimes my thoughts flow freely, but oftentimes I struggle to find simple ways to convey things that are not so simple. I then look off into a lovely garden area, waiting for words that might convey what I'm trying to say.

During one such moment, I notice a man and woman standing in the distance. I observe that the restaurant is full and they're waiting for a table. I wonder if I'm being self-indulgent by lingering here writing while two people want their breakfast! I'm at a table for two and I notice a small table for one. I approach them and ask if they'd like my table and say that I'm happy to move. They seem surprised and smile at my gesture; we share a sweet moment of contact as I move my things to the new table.

I'd be thrilled if you concluded that I'm always so observant and generous. But allow me to assure you that I'm not! I quite often miss the life happening right before my eyes. But during luminous moments, when I'm attuned to myself and my surroundings, wonderful things can open up. A few days later, I saw the gentleman again at this restaurant and we had a lovely conversation.

Relearning Interdependence

Just as the incendiary word "craving" might lead us to condemn our human longings, so can the term "narcissism" become a denunciation of our humanity. We are born into the world with unavoidable needs. We want to feel safe and live free of threats. We need to earn a living to sustain ourselves and our family. We want to love and be loved and live a meaningful life. Pursuing such needs is not unseemly selfishness but part of a biological imperative to survive and thrive.

The natural growth process of any living being might be viewed as a movement toward a more expansive joy, which is different from craving and narcissism. We don't judge nature for seeking to enhance itself. Can we similarly honor the natural propensity of our organism to seek growth in ways that connect us with life?

Growth is often in the direction of "more." An oak tree, for instance, seeks more and more space to leaf upward and outward. Its roots stretch out deeper and wider to support this growth. This is its nature. Similarly, it is in our nature to want safety, love, and intimacy so that we may stretch out into a wider sense of aliveness and openness. When we don't find a skillful way to accommodate this longing, we suffer.

Trees have learned how to live in balance with nature; they have learned to be interdependent. By growing into itself, an oak tree takes its place in the world. It takes care of itself, but by doing so, it also serves others. In one way, oaks are "in it" for themselves. But perhaps less visibly, there is a way in which being for themselves supports the rest of nature. They provide oxygen for other living beings, acorns for squirrels, and a nesting place for birds. As the oak takes its place in nature, the world is nourished. This kind of growth is in stark contrast to the growth of a cancer, which is highly "narcissistic."

Cancer is out-of-control growth. Cancer cells are not team players; they have forgotten how to be interdependent. They have overlooked how to have a life-enhancing function within the larger scheme of things. They have no interest in the give-and-take of being part of a larger organism. They are opportunistic and oblivious to the havoc they wreak. Similarly, if we remain disinterested in how our own longing for expansive growth and connection affect our world—our partner, our friends, the natural environment—we are contributing to a global cancer that may one day destroy us.

The Human Experiment

Unlike trees, which have thrived for hundreds of millions of years, the human experiment is rather recent, beginning around 250 thousand years ago. Unlike a tree, we posses willpower and reason, which despite their notable advantages, are prone to disconnect us from nature and our natural longings unless we tap into an emotional, interpersonal, and ecological intelligence that reintegrates us with the natural world.

If we want our species to survive for as long as trees, we need to be more conscious about how we affect the life around us rather than thicken the walls of our isolationist bubble. We refine our sensitivity to ourselves and others by bringing mindfulness to our feelings and longings, noticing which ones to act upon and which ones to simply notice and allow to pass.

Just as our body has natural checks to inhibit the growth of cancer cells, so do we have the capacity to gently embrace our desires with quiet attention, which is a natural check for the cravings that isolate us. Using mindfulness to tame cravings that generate suffering, we come into ourselves in a way that connects us with people and life. We become more attuned to what serves us and the greater good. We move toward the same ordered kind of growth that exists in nature, one in which a friendly interdependence replaces the unyielding independence of narcissism.

Yearning for Others' Well-Being

Spiritual growth means feeling our connection with life so deeply that our longing for happiness includes the longing for others to be happy. Our heart opens wide enough to taste the suffering of others and yearns for their well-being; our happiness becomes inextricably linked with theirs. We exude a kindness and compassion that flow more naturally as we recognize that one of our vital needs is for others to be happy.

By not living with an awareness of our interdependence, we put our very survival at risk. Many years from now, it will become apparent whether or not we made it. If not, nobody will be around to write our tragic epithet: "Their highly specialized intelligence doomed them. Their lives became increasingly isolated from themselves and each other, until they ultimately severed themselves from the fabric of life. Becoming a cancer on the earth, they became another failed experiment of nature."

I'd prefer this option for the history books: "Our hard-won, integrated intelligence, balanced between intellect and feeling our own needs and the needs of others, our rights and our responsibilities to others and the planet, allowed us to take a dignified yet humble place within the larger fabric of life."

Whatever opens us to become more human is flesh of the God we can know.

—Peter Campbell and Edwin McMahon

Don't hope to be without problems—that's just laziness: accept life's difficulties. Don't expect your path to be free from obstacles—without them, the fire of your enlightenment will go out: find liberation within the disturbances themselves.

—Kyong Ho

The Romance of Enlightenment

W hen I was twenty, the term "cosmic consciousness" was sweep-ing my college campus, at least among a small subculture interested in such weighty matters. Wow, cosmic consciousness! That sounded better than drugs! Basking 24-7 in perpetual bliss, freedom, and peace. I could hardly wait for my enlightenment!

The notion that spiritual practice leads to our ultimate enlightenment or transcendence is, well, perhaps the Eastern equivalent of our Western notion of romantic love. The prospect of everlasting love or liberation renders everything else trivial.

Every religion has its own version of paradise. We want our pain to stop, our worries to end. The resplendent prospect of eternal bliss is quite compelling, especially if our childhood was scarred by trauma. We may cling to the hope of achieving the cosmic jackpot: total and complete liberation. Is this goal realistic or is it a grand distraction from a more humble spiritual path that opens our heart, deepens our compassion, and enhances our wisdom?

What Is Enlightenment?

The meaning of enlightenment or liberation has been long debated and generates as much confusion as clarity. People casually toss this word around without knowing what it means or whether it is even attainable.

Buddhist scholar D. T. Suzuki defines enlightenment quite dramatically as "the lightning-and-thunder discovery that the universe and oneself are not remote and apart, but an intimate, palpitating Whole."[1] I prefer the more sober description by scientist and spiritual teacher John Wren-Lewis, who portrays awakening as something quite ordinary. After a near-death experience, he wrote:

> The experience was . . . more like having a cataract taken off my brain, letting me experience the world and myself properly for the first time. . . . Perhaps the most extraordinary feature of eternity consciousness is that it doesn't feel extraordinary at all. It feels quintessentially natural.[2]

Many of us have been inspired by a taste of liberation. Perhaps while viewing a dazzling sunset or swimming in our lover's eyes, or during a meditation retreat, our usual self-consciousness shifted and a glittering intimacy with ourselves and life unfolded. Words fail us during such rapturous moments, but terms like awakening, God-consciousness, oneness, love, peace, radiant presence, or non-dual awareness point toward this liberating experience.

The Zen term *kensho*, which denotes an awakening experience, is described by Zen master Robert Aitken as "seeing into the true nature of things, where inner and outer are not different."[3] But lest we succumb to ego inflation, he soberly points out, "Kensho gives us a genuine glimpse of true nature but just a glimpse, requiring expansion and clarification . . . which is a lifetime process."[4]

A Path of Integration

Just as we are prone to become grandiose when falling in love, convinced that we're at the threshold of eternal bliss, we might conclude that we have attained some ultimate realization after having a "high" experience on our meditation chair, or during a sacred ritual, or even while doing the laundry. It takes humility and wisdom to recognize that this taste of liberation doesn't mean we have arrived. In fact, our work has just begun!

Perhaps we can declare that something happened right then, a moment of crystallization that is well worth marking. While it is happening, it may seem like an end point. But later, when we return to earth again, we realize it was a shining moment in a larger process. As the early Christian monks were fond of saying, "When you see a monk going up to heaven, pull him down by his legs!"[5]

An embodied spiritual life integrates the transcendent with the personal and interpersonal. Our spiritual being is intimately hitched to our life of emotions and everyday events. As Taoist and Confucian philosophers emphasize, our heavenly nature cannot be separated from our human nature.

Spiritual growth is a spiral staircase, not a straight line to liberation. We enjoy moments of awakening but then lose it when our Netflix movie is late or when our partner leaves crumbs on the counter—a sure sign that other parts of us need to awaken and be integrated.

The movement toward liberation is not linear. It takes much backing and filling as moments of awakening are assimilated into our bodily lived existence. As sorrows, fears, and frustrations are met with a wakeful and vibrant awareness, our spirituality becomes embodied in our daily life and interactions.

A Tricky Term

Early Buddhist texts often reinforce the alluring charm of enlightenment by showcasing nirvana as the ultimate fruit of practice. As the flame of desire is extinguished forever, we are no longer encumbered by the cravings that have kept us stuck on the wheel of death and rebirth.

Drawing upon original Pali texts, Buddhist scholar Walpola Rahula describes enlightenment in glowing terms:

> He who has realized the Truth, Nirvana, is the happiest being in the world. He is free from all "complexes" and obsessions, the worries and troubles that torment others. His mental health is perfect. He does not repent the past, nor does he brood over the future. He lives fully in the present. . . . He is joyful, exultant, enjoying the pure life, his faculties pleased, free from anxiety, serene and peaceful.[6]

Is it possible to attain such a rarefied state? Or are the eye-popping accounts of enlightenment a glamorized description of *something*? Do enlightened moments come and go or, as Rahula suggests, is it literally true that all "defilements," including desire, anxiety, and anger, are forever transcended?

I don't personally expect to get beyond such feelings. Nor can I say that I've met anyone who has. I believe that a more realistic aspiration is this: our relationship with our feelings transforms. Painful emotions and experiences still visit us, but they're not a big deal; we realize that pleasant and unpleasant feelings come and go. We engage with them compassionately, which allows them to shift more readily and opens us to whatever wisdom they may hold for us. Rather than view emotions as defilements, we simply see them as part of the human condition. Embracing feelings deepens our compassion for other's feelings, and sharing them allows us to feel closer to people.

Descriptions of enlightenment and the path toward awakening were developed thousands of years ago in a culture far different from our own. This was before Carl Jung did his pioneering work on the human shadow, illuminating how unconscious parts of ourselves sabotage us. It was before Bowlby's research that led to attachment theory and what children need to be psychologically healthy. And it was before the research of John Gottman, Susan Johnson, and others on what factors foster fulfilling, intimate relationships. As these modern streams of insight meet ancient wisdom, we can evolve in ways that give more grounding to our spirituality while helping us enjoy more interpersonal fulfillment.

The Humility of the Dalai Lama

I've felt most drawn to spiritual teachers who readily reveal their humanity and limitations. Notable among them is the Dalai Lama, who has never claimed to be enlightened. For example, he once revealed, "I can be kind to [children] for short periods only."[7] When asked about his weaknesses and faults, he responded: "Laziness . . . Other weaknesses are, I think, anger and attachments. I'm attached to my watch and prayer beads. Then, of course, sometimes to beautiful women."[8] When he dreams of alluring women, he reminds himself that he is a monk.

What we might consider to be weaknesses are simply aspects of being human. If we hold in our mind some picture of perfection and strive to be *that*, then we set ourselves up for being ashamed of our human side. Trying to fight feelings or eliminate traits that we find undesirable only ensures their continuation, often in unconscious ways that injure ourselves and others.

Lusting After Enlightenment

Without an attraction to spiritual awakening, our lives may be reduced to the pursuit of material allurements, transient pleasures, or self-aggrandizement. But a different danger lurks for the spiritually inclined in the Western world— and is increasing among Eastern nations that are burgeoning economically.

Our academic and social systems reward achievement and "excellence." Many of us grow up being shamed for not getting good grades, excelling at sports, or being socially popular. Spiritual teachings remind us that such external pursuits don't bring real happiness, thus prompting us to pursue spiritual development. We might enthusiastically jump on this train of a different color, not realizing that it may be powered by a more subtle kind of ambition—the desire to be special, different, or better than others.

The word "enlightenment" has become a hot potato. If we avidly pursue it, we may become too desirous, too attached to an outcome. Yet if we dismiss this sublime possibility, we may squeeze ourselves into a pair of tight shoes that restrict our movement toward something more expansive. Jack Kornfield wisely points out pitfalls in the language of enlightenment: "It is easy to get caught in the notion that there is a goal, a state, a special place to reach in spiritual life. Accounts of extraordinary experiences can create ideas about how our own lives should be, and lead us to compare ourselves to others."[9] A sober alternative to lusting after enlightenment is to live with simplicity and openness and remain open to a sacred sense of possibility.

Spiritual Materialism

We may pursue so purposefully some special experience that this search becomes a particular kind of materialism, what Tibetan teacher Chogyam Trungpa Rinpoche has aptly termed "spiritual materialism." As our ambition dons clothing of a different color, we miss the point of what spirituality is all about. As Trungpa explains, "The problem is that ego can convert anything to its own use."[10]

Soto Zen teachers have been especially wary, downplaying enlightenment in favor of simple attention to what is happening right now. We have enough on our plate to attend to our experience in the moment. The future takes care of itself as we greet whatever arises with a peaceful heart.

Stephen Batchelor offers a refreshing assessment of spiritual development that includes welcoming the full spectrum of feelings: "A compassionate heart still feels anger, greed, jealousy, and other such emotions. But it accepts them for what they are with equanimity."[11]

Spiritual practice is about shining a strong, steady light of awareness on our experience, which connects us to ourselves in a way that reduces suffering. It is about accommodating feelings, not transcending them. Being with our unfolding experience from moment to moment *is* the path. As Batchelor explains, "Awakening is no longer seen as something to attain in the distant future, for it is not a thing but a process—and this process is the path itself."[12]

It Takes as Long as It Takes

Clients who enter my psychotherapy office often want relief from their pain. Whenever I hear the question, "How long will it take?" I take a deep breath to compose myself before responding, cognizant that I may be treading on someone's hope for a quick fix.

Brief therapy can certainly be helpful, but it is difficult to place a timetable on matters of the soul. I usually explain that the process takes as long as it takes and depends upon their goals. By doing one's best and being gentle with oneself, the process moves as quickly as possible. This news is sometimes hard to swallow, but I'm delighted when clients knowingly nod their heads, now freed to simply do the work without a nagging preoccupation with rapid results.

Being overly ambitious in psychotherapy, intimate relationships, or spiritual life is counterproductive, like opening the oven every few minutes to see how well our cake is baking. Christianity offers a similar call for patience. We cannot control the workings of grace, which comes in its own time and way. However, we can put ourselves in a place where grace is more likely to alight. As Richard Baker Rōshi has commented, "Enlightenment is an accident. Meditation makes you accident prone."[13]

Holding Our Purpose Lightly

The pursuit of liberation doesn't mean being driven or preoccupied. We develop practices, attitudes, and relationships that support our movement in this direction. We live intentionally, with purpose and commitment, but it's not a big deal. We are attentive but not obsessive. We live ethically but without an obnoxious self-importance. We are mindful, but we don't "wear our mindfulness on our sleeve," exuding what the Zen folks call the "stink of enlightenment."

We never quite arrive. Just as our body is constantly changing, what we call "I" is always in process. There is no ultimate truth to "get," no identity to grasp, no final resting place. There may be times of stabilization, but we're always moving forward—whatever "forward" may look like—by continually uncovering blind spots and integrating our humanity into our spirituality and our spirituality into our humanity.

The goal of reaching some sublime state may motivate us initially, but then we settle into a rhythm of living day-to-day, doing what needs to be done. Any goal we may carry is held lightly. We may occasionally peek at the mountaintop, but we keep our focus on the step before us lest we stumble over the obstacles that present themselves. Gradually, we mosey our way toward greater openness, peace, and connection. But most of our attention is on the scenery that presents itself, which for most of us encompasses the frustrations and delights that revolve around our longing to love and be loved and its surrounding emotional life.

Relaxing into the moment allows us to reside in our unfolding experience. As Tibetan Buddhist teacher Ngakpa Chögyam puts it, "There is no need to look for enlightenment in any other place than where we are. It is there, unrecognized, in every moment."[14]

Rather than pursue an agenda that we consider spiritual, can we simply be fully present as the imperfect and precious beings that we are? An embodied spirituality is not so self-conscious; it's just the pursuit of ordinary life and a dance with the ebb and flow of happiness and sorrow, intimacy and aloneness, desire and satiation that are inherent in being alive.

Inhabiting the Moment

The seductive illusion of basking in a light that casts no shadow misses the simple truth that liberation flows from being awake to the joys and sorrows of this lived moment. Clinging to some goal of enlightenment, we are yanked out of the very moment that needs inhabiting if we're to move toward liberation. As Tibetan teacher Milarepa put it, "Do not entertain hopes for realization, but practice all your life."

Robert Aitken Rōshi recounts a Zen *koan* about a hundred-foot pole. Koans are questions or stories that cannot be solved or grasped by rational thought. He explains that on top of the pole is the person who is stuck on enlightenment. The koan asks, "How do you step from the top of a hundred-foot pole?"[15] An embodied spiritual life means stepping down from that pole and awakening in the world rather than breathing rarified air that is removed from intimacy with life.

Questionable Views of Liberation

What does it look like to be moving forward on a spiritual path? What is possible and not possible to attain through spiritual practice? Can we point to any experiential markers that assure us that we are on a path that actually leads somewhere?

Over the twenty-five hundred-year history of Buddhism, there has been a proliferation of many different ideas about liberation. These views often point toward a kind of perfection that rarely, if ever, exists. Here are some views about liberation that are as common as they are questionable:

- We transcend desire and longing, which no longer arise in our consciousness.
- Fear disappears, including survival fear and the fear of death.
- Nothing bothers us; we live uninterruptedly in serene non-attachment and equanimity.
- We do not need anything or anyone; we are totally self-sufficient.
- Emotions, such as sadness, hurt, loss, and shame, no longer visit us.
- Enlightenment is the final state of realization, the ultimate state of peace and equanimity.
- Upon experiencing a powerful opening or transcendent state, we are fully liberated.

A Process View of Spiritual Progress

Contrast this transcendent view of enlightenment with a more embodied process view of spiritual progress. The word "progress" is hazardous because such evaluations can lead to self-critical comparisons or suggest a linear path that just doesn't exist. Yet perhaps the lack of distinct markers presents an even greater hazard: clinging to distorted views of liberation. Please hold these lightly:

- The spiritual path is one of reducing suffering, not eliminating desire. Being spiritual doesn't mean exorcising our amygdala. Being in an animal body, we will always have inner promptings to lurch toward some things and avoid other things. Desires will continue to arise regardless of how "advanced" we are. However, when we have more spaciousness around our longings and emotions, we are less prone to slide into clinging and craving. We aren't as triggered when our longings are unmet. We are less driven or consumed by desire. We get a clearer sense about which longings to act upon (the ones that truly nourish us) and which ones to notice and relinquish (those that lead to suffering for ourselves or others). Such discernment enables us to make better choices and be more peaceful.

- Fear and anxiety continue to appear, but we are less overwhelmed by them. We hold them gently and seek support from friends when necessary. We recognize that fear is part of the human condition. Courage doesn't mean being fear-free; it means acting even though something in us feels afraid.

- We are affected when we're mistreated, abused, or traumatized and when we observe abuse and injustice around us. We may be disappointed when things don't go our way or if we fail to succeed at some venture, but such feelings pass quickly, and we don't cling to the belief that we're a failure or succumb to a crippling shame. We may be upset to witness sorrowful events around us as we become more sensitively attuned to life. Our heart quivers in sorrow as we see people suffer or the environment being damaged. If we feel moved to help, we do so as a wounded healer rather than a person who is above it all and has all the answers.

- We need people in order to live a fulfilling and meaningful life. We are interdependent beings, not independent ones. We interact with the community for emotional support and to earn a living. Life is enhanced through loving connections, but we also have the capacity to embrace solitude.

- We continue to experience emotions like hurt, sorrow, grief, fear, and embarrassment, but we learn to hold these feelings gently and gracefully; we are not so tormented by them. Rather than think something is wrong with us, we meet our feelings without shame. We experience them more poignantly because we're less defended, but we have less emotional reactivity as we develop inner resources to face them.

We are more likely to respond rather than react. We also have more awareness of our limits so that we don't overextend ourselves. Even so, there are times when equanimity deserts us and we may experience stress or loneliness, and we're okay with this. Or we're okay about *not* being okay with it.

- There is no end point to spiritual growth, no final destination. We are an evolving process, an ongoingness. Spiritual practice will not transform us into a person at perfect peace. Instead, our reptilian brain remains alive and well. We cannot flip a switch and turn off the "old brain," nor would we want to, because we need it sometimes to survive! However, spiritual practice can soften our instinctual reactions by cultivating greater spaciousness around our experience.

- Although we may have had profound spiritual experiences, we see ourselves as an awakening being, not an awakened one. There is always something beyond whatever we think we have attained—more integration of body, mind, and spirit, an ever-deepening sense of love, compassion, and wisdom. We humbly recognize that there are parts of ourselves that have yet to be embraced and integrated. As Buckminster Fuller was fond of saying, "I seem to be a verb."[16] We live interactively with our environment. We are happening.

Just as we will never find an unflawed, perfect partner, the goal of achieving some ultimate state of being will keep us leaning into a future that never arrives. Avidly pursuing such desires is like chasing a mirage; just as we think we have grasped the trophy, it slips away.

Spiritual practice means facing life on life's terms, not ours. This includes finding the quiet strength to embrace vulnerability, powerlessness, and not-knowing—not some spiritual athletics that we believe will lead us to become a superhuman, perfected being. Opening to how life is touching us from moment to moment is the essence of spiritual practice.

Meditation discipline is vital to dharma practice precisely because it leads us beyond the realm of ideas to that of felt experience. Understanding the philosophy of emptiness is not enough. The ideas need to be translated through meditation into the wordless language of feeling in order to loosen those emotional knots that keep us locked in a spasm of self-preoccupation.

—Stephen Batchelor

We cannot have an unobstructed connection with another person through a complex defense system that was designed to avoid direct experience.

—Jett Psaris and Marlena S. Lyons

Chapter Seventeen

Embracing Feelings— Embracing Life

❧

H earing the word "emotions" or "feelings," we may think of intense peaks and valleys of rage, fear, grief, or joy. But feelings are usually more subtle; they are the wordless ways we are touched by life. Opening to life means opening to the feelings that life brings. Where there is life there is feeling.

The word "feelings" is a shorthand term for something enormously complex—a blend of emotions, sensations, and meanings that arise as a result of being alive. Feelings are colored by our traumas, disappointments, triumphs, fears, and longings. They are the nuanced flavors of shifting situations and conditions that we encounter in life. They include a spectrum of mild to extreme emotions like apprehension/terror, annoyance/rage, embarrassment/shame, sadness/grief, and joy/ecstasy. Feelings also include bodily felt sensations, such as a heaviness in the chest, tightness in the throat, or jumpiness in the abdomen.

Feelings Embody Meaning

Feelings carry meaningful messages for our lives. They orient us in ways that allow us to move forward. Anger may signal that we are being violated and need to set a boundary. As we notice a tight band around our chest when our partner is critical, our frozen silence may yield to empowering words: "I feel angry when you talk to me that way!" Beneath that may lie the hurt of rejection and an underlying need for safety. "It really hurts when you raise your voice and tell me I'm selfish. I need gentleness from you." Queasiness in our stomach when our date orders his second martini may be screaming the message, "Stay away from him!"

Encoded within our body is a capacity to actualize our deepest longing for connection, love, and freedom. Dodging feelings rather than attending to them is a lost opportunity to learn something about ourselves and to connect more with each other and with life.

Emotions are often blurry at first—and slippery. Oftentimes, we can't quite put our finger on what's bugging us and what our feelings may be signaling about our lives. It is not always easy to find words that capture their complexity and delicacy.

Effects of Process-Skipping

Life happens. Feelings happen. A mindfulness practice that connects us with our feelings is an antidote to controlling other people or ourselves. Rather than telling others what to do or how to be, we can tell them how they affect us. Instead of being critical and blaming, we expose the tender feelings that have been poked.

Viewing feelings as an affront to our ego or threat to our well-being, we may rely upon alcohol, drugs, or other addictions to replace uncomfortable feelings with more pleasant ones. We may turn to positive affirmations or a spiritual practice as a one-dimensional strategy to transform unpleasant feelings into agreeable ones. We might judge feelings as positive or negative, which can lead us to avoid fear, sadness, and grief. What we call "negative feelings" are simply uncomfortable feelings.

Royal subjects in Europe during the Middle Ages who valued the notion of keeping their head firmly attached to their neck would never deliver bad news to the king! But if our ego, our inner king, intimidates and silences our authentic feelings, we will never receive the vital messages that serve our lives. Feelings are an ongoing feed of life's text-messaging, reminding us that a larger intelligence is operating, beckoning our lives toward ever-greater freedom and happiness.

Opening to Life; Opening to Feelings

Emotions teach us that life can't be avoided; they keep beseeching us until we turn toward them—hopefully, before we hit a crisis. They are life's way of trying to get our attention. As incarnate beings, we have a body that carries important information about how to move toward the love and connectedness that our soul yearns for. Refusing this invitation, we diminish our aliveness, remain distant from people, and might even invite illness.

Spiritual teachers who recognize the ill effects of pushing feelings away encourage us to *notice* emotions rather than *evade* them. This can be helpful, but merely noticing what we are experiencing might keep us removed from feelings that need exploration. By cultivating a broader mindfulness, we shine a light on elusive feelings that lie just beneath our awareness.

Equanimity: A Foundation for Being with Our Experience

Releasing or transforming difficult emotions begins by acknowledging them and being gentle with them. We spend so much energy dodging unpleasant feelings and scrambling to secure pleasant ones. It is natural to prefer pleasure over pain and to make efforts to create a life that's more likely to bring happiness. But wanting things to be different than they are distances us from what is occurring in the moment.

Living with greater equanimity and freedom means tapping inner resources to ride the waves of life's emotional tides. As the saying goes, "We can't control the waves, but we can learn how to surf." Growing more comfortable with our feelings, we are not thrown off center so easily; we regain our bearings more quickly.

The habit of avoiding feelings cuts us off from people in ways we barely detect. For example, if a person we're dating voices a desire to spend more time together, we might sense a squirmy feeling inside. We might notice a fear that we will be smothered, just as we were by our mother. Consequently, we might subtly recoil from this bid for more contact.

By pausing and bringing a tender curiosity to the fear of suffocation that was just activated, we might respond differently. If we meet this fear with mindfulness, it can soften, freeing us to see things more clearly. Perhaps we will recognize it as an old fear and realize that this person is not our mother. A helpful thought might also occur: we have the power to regulate how much contact we want, which wasn't much of an option with our controlling mother.

The key to a more stable joy and equanimity is bringing a compassionate attention to the full range of feelings stirring within us. As we acknowledge them, let them be, work with them, and share them with people we trust, our feelings settle. We can't meditate, pray, or wish feelings away; when we hold them gently, they are less likely to implode on us or explode on others.

Welcoming Felt Experience: A Door to Intimacy

A mindfulness practice that cultivates intimacy with ourselves supports a foundation for being intimate with others. Rich relationships unfold as we develop a taste for noticing, embracing, and expressing the various textures of feelings resulting from being alive and being together. A beautiful dance of intimacy can unfold between two people porous enough to reveal what they are experiencing inside and who receive each other with tender openness.

Our capacity for self-presence and self-intimacy is self-communicating. People notice when we are present and available. A gentle look, smiling eyes, and a warm heart emanating from our quiet depths invite people to savor a precious moment of uplifting contact. One of the joys of spiritual life is luminous engagement. We reside in the aliveness of what is and maintain an openness and curiosity about where that takes us.

Love invites us to trust another person with our heart. And our capacity to deepen love and sustain intimacy grows as we learn to trust ourselves, finding more ease in embracing whatever arises within us as a result of opening ourselves to another. Through a kind of mindfulness practice that tracks our felt experience, there can be a simultaneous awakening to inner experiencing and nourishing connections with others and with life itself.

The essence of working with another person is to be present as a living being. . . . I am just here, with my eyes, and there is this other being. If they happen to look into my eyes, they will see that I am just a shaky being. I have to tolerate that. They may not look. But if they do, they will see that. They will see the slightly shy, slightly withdrawing, insecure existence that I am.

—Eugene Gendlin

Without awareness of our sensations, we are not fully alive. Life is unsatisfactory for most people because they are absent from their experience much of the time.

—Charlotte Joko Beck

Chapter Eighteen

Focusing: Loving-Kindness toward Ourselves

As we have seen, the path toward liberation is not about avoiding longing; nor is it about trying to change our feelings or fix ourselves. We awaken to the beauty of who we really are as we welcome and embrace our ever-changing felt experience.

The path toward awakening invites us to bring a calm, loving awareness to the changing array of our pain and pleasure, hurts and joys, fears and triumphs, neither resisting them nor getting lost in them. We engage *with* our emotional process rather than try to extinguish it.

Expanding Our Awareness of Feelings

Bringing awareness to emotions is no stranger to Buddhist practice. Awareness of feelings is one of the Four Foundations of Mindfulness, along with mindfulness of the body, which is especially emphasized by the Buddhist teacher S. N. Goenke. Buddhist texts categorize five emotion-laden attributes as "mental factors," namely hatred, greed, envy, restlessness, and doubt. They are included in a long list of qualities that Buddhist texts identify as important subjects of mindfulness.

Some mindfulness approaches emphasize the careful "noting" of feelings, thoughts, and sensations, perhaps labeling them as desire, worry, sloth, anger, etc. When we feel desire, we know that there is desire in us; when we feel worried, we note that worry is present. We bring "bare attention" to the pleasant, unpleasant, or neutral quality of feelings.

As experiences come and go, we begin to understand the nature of *anicca*, the truth of impermanence. We learn not to identify with any inner or outer passing phenomena as we come to recognize that our experience is empty of anything permanent and solid. We simply notice how all experiences arise and pass away without claiming them as our own.

This process of objectification and neutralization has found broad appeal among those drawn to Buddhism. It gives ample permission to distance ourselves from painful and uncomfortable experiences. But the view that feelings and sensations are just impersonal phenomena and are not particularly meaningful may have unintended consequences. It is no wonder that many longtime meditators acknowledge that their practice has not improved their lives or relationships and may have harmed them by maintaining a split between their meditation practice and their daily emotional experience.

Here is how one friend described her experience on a meditation retreat:

It was on my fourth silent retreat when one of the last layers of defensive armor dissolved. The floodgates opened and the big, ancient feelings came roaring up—old pain and grief that I didn't know how to deal with. I went to the teacher and struggled to express how overwhelmed I felt, and all he could suggest was "let it go." Of course, I couldn't simply "let it go," so the ensuing shame was huge and lasted a very long time. I was too ashamed to talk about it anymore, since that would mean admitting that I'd failed to deal with it properly and was probably seriously disturbed, and a bad meditator to boot. It would have helped if someone suggested that I be loving toward myself and compassionate with my feelings, and told me how to gently be with them and explore them.

Through the dry practice of noting feelings and letting them go, we may consign them to the dark basement of our psyche, where they return to haunt us later. Viewing emotions like fear, sorrow, and anger as hindrances or defilements often leads to an aversion to them rather than welcoming them as part of one's practice and hearing whatever messages they may hold for our lives.

An additional pitfall to spiritual practice is that if we believe that our feelings are unimportant we won't hold others' feelings and needs with tender respect. We might see their emotions as something that calls for a tidy disposal. A natural extension of this attitude is to not take our agreements or commitments to others seriously. We might have agreed to something in the moment, but this is a new moment, and it is okay to casually change our mind or even forget what we agreed to. It is no big deal if they suffer over it; it is just unpleasant feelings that they can notice and relinquish rather than take personally. We might even consider it beneficial for their spiritual practice, a golden opportunity for them to release the attachments that we believe are creating their suffering.

This dismissive and disrespectful attitude reflects how we minimize our own feelings. There is a curious logic here that often becomes an accepted mindset in spiritual communities; personal feelings are viewed as the lowly workings of ego, a kind of dirty laundry that needs to be cleansed in the purifying waters of a more effective mindfulness practice. But there is no denying that this depersonalized view is destructive to intimacy, which requires a climate of trust nurtured by empathic responsiveness. Taking our experience seriously, though not somberly, with a welcoming attitude of wonder and curiosity, moves us toward inner freedom, wholeness, and loving connections with each other.

The Quandary of Letting Go

As we have seen, many spiritual paths instruct us to live in the present by letting go of our stories, feelings, and desires. But when attempts to achieve this feat fall short, as they often do, we are left with an aftertaste of shame and defeat.

I am not an avid fan of holding on to unhelpful things, but our limbic brain isn't wired to let go on demand. Our neocortex isn't very persuasive when it tries to instruct the limbic and reptilian brain to be quiet and behave itself. We need to get more creative in accessing and engaging mindfully with our intense emotions and desires.

The words "let go" can become a doctrinaire mantra that falls flat, especially when preached to people choking on human misery. These words don't convey compassion toward our ordinary struggles and discontent. Our well-meant admonition may fuel self-loathing and shame: "Why can't I let go? What's wrong with me?" A more helpful inquiry might be, "What is the art through which we might release what constricts us? How can we create an inner climate that fosters fluidity, freedom, and connection?"

Pursuing letting go as a goal may only amplify our clinging. Instead of allowing what is, we tightly hold a conviction that there is something we urgently need to do. A more useful approach is to bring a caring presence toward our felt experience and cultivate practices that help us open to our feelings and longings in a loving, non-shaming way.

We fumble our way toward inner freedom by welcoming our experience as it is. A common and painful obstacle to inner peace is judging ourselves for what we are experiencing, or believing that we're defective at our core. If there is *anything* wrong with us, it may be this: we believe that something is wrong with us.[1]

Much suffering is generated because we pathologize ourselves; we believe we are fundamentally flawed rather than hold all aspects of ourselves with loving-kindness and respect. As psychologist Carl Rogers knew, "The curious paradox is that when I can accept myself just as I am, then I can change."[2]

There is more entailed in loving ourselves than the common self-improvement clichés would let on. Loving and accepting ourselves doesn't mean remaining blind to our unconscious and unskillful habits, but rather making a mindful effort to be present, to discover and then compassionately accept whatever we are experiencing inside in the moment. The present moment is the only moment in which our experience can be encountered and transformed, and it is transformed only through its acceptance.

A Path of Embracing Feelings

Walking a path that welcomes our emotional process requires experimentation. An approach I have found especially helpful during the past thirty years is Focusing, which has notable parallels with meditation and spiritual practice. Focusing can be learned from a teacher or training group, and some therapists integrate it into their psychotherapy sessions.

In 1981, I completed my doctoral dissertation on the complementary effects of Focusing and meditation. I found that, when practiced together, they weave a well-integrated tapestry. Robert Aitken Rōshi, the dean of American Zen masters, echoes its usefulness for meditators in a communication to Eugene Gendlin: "I'm glad that you find many Buddhists interested in Focusing. I continue to recommend the practice from time to time in personal interviews, and students report worthwhile results."[3] Jack Kornfield has also recognized its value as a complement to meditation: "Focusing is a beautiful and meditative approach to psychotherapy and personal growth. It offers a deep parallel to the practice of mindfulness in a carefully developed and sensitive way."[4]

Focusing is a path of self-inquiry that welcomes nuanced experiences that we often overlook. We gently bring awareness into our bodies, which is where feelings and sensations reside. We allow and befriend whatever we are experiencing in a way that permits the stuck places to loosen up, moving us toward greater peace, freedom, and wisdom.

Origins of Focusing

Focusing is one of the most thoroughly researched approaches to personal growth. Eugene Gendlin, a philosopher, psychologist, and researcher at the University of Chicago, asked a simple question: "What are the key factors that make psychotherapy effective?" He never imagined that his findings would be of interest not only to psychotherapists, but to the spiritual community as well.

Gendlin and his research team could accurately predict after one or two sessions whether people would make progress in psychotherapy despite the orientation of the therapist. They discovered that those who were self-reflective in a specific kind of way benefited the most. Rather than scrambling to figure things out in their heads, these naturally gifted clients slowed down their speech, sensed inwardly with curiosity, and waited for words, images, insights, or meanings to arise that resonated with their most deeply felt experience. Uncovering what was freshly alive within themselves, they felt more connected, whole, and peaceful. Their lives moved forward not by analyzing themselves or their problems, but by being with an experience as it unfolds from within.

Uncovering Deeper Feelings

Sue, a middle-aged woman struggling after a relationship breakup, reported the following during a Focusing session. (My comments, meant to clarify how Focusing works, are in brackets):

Sue: I feel angry that he didn't give our relationship a chance. What a jerk he is!

Me: You're feeling really angry that he didn't give the relationship a chance. Would it be okay to sense how that anger feels inside you right now? Take your time and notice if anything more wants to come. [I invite her to sense the anger inside her. Perhaps something more will unfold as she stays with what she's noticing.]

Sue: Well, yes, I'm angry, but there's more there. [She begins to sense more vulnerable feelings beneath her initial rage and blame.] It's like a heaviness in my gut. Kinda like a knot there . . . a tight knot. [As I invite her to stay with the anger, the feeling, at first fuzzy, comes into focus.]

Me: There's a heaviness there . . . feels kinda like a tight knot. [Reflecting back what people say enables them to hear themselves in a new way, which may allow more to unfold.]

Sue: Yeah, it's a painful place. There's something in me that feels really hurt by that—like I don't matter to him. It makes me feel that I don't have any value as a person. That feels really sad. [She's getting in touch with a deeper feeling beneath her anger, and a sense of what this feeling is about arises. It's affecting her self-worth. The painful feeling begins to shift as she recognizes this.]

Me: It hurts to feel that you don't matter to him. And it makes you feel that you have no value.

Sue: Yeah . . . It reminds me of all the times I've felt ignored in my life . . . and not good enough . . . Hmmm, that's interesting . . . there's something familiar there . . . I let my worth and value be defined by how others see me. That's sad . . . Somehow I feel lighter to see that. My stomach feels less knotted now. [A memory comes, along with a curiosity about how she continues giving others the power to judge and define her. Recognizing this leads to sadness and then a feeling of lightness—a burden she'd been carrying begins to lift.]

If Sue had dealt with her feelings by strictly using the more narrow mindfulness method of "noting" her initial anger, it might have passed, but it probably would have cycled back again and again. Thorny emotions and issues are less likely to recur with the same ferocity or duration as we uncover the deeper feelings and the meanings they hold for us.

As we attend to what underlies our fixed perceptions and cognitions, we enter the life stream of our ever-changing experience. By attending to this flowing current of life in a gentle, loving way, we may notice a release or opening, which in Focusing language is called a "felt shift." Perhaps a tight place loosens or a heavy burden lightens. We feel freer, more alive, and more connected to our own being and with what's around us.

By attending to our ever-changing felt experience, we tap into a core creative process. Stuck places begin to untangle not through willpower, mental effort, or trying to let them go, but by granting them space to be and breathe. Our inner landscape shifts naturally as we permit our experience to be and to unfold. We may then appreciate in a more bodily felt way the Buddhist teaching about impermanence. We realize that everything changes, although this doesn't mean that what is here now isn't consequential or important.

CHAPTER EIGHTEEN

Connecting with What Is Real Feels Good

As we connect with what we are experiencing, we enter a natural pathway toward healing and well-being. Painful or difficult feelings shift as we accept them as they are rather than cling to opinions about what they mean, such as that we are flawed or a spiritual failure or need to work hard to fix ourselves.

A young woman was using Focusing to stay connected to what she was experiencing during childbirth. At one point that was keenly agonizing, she exclaimed, "I'm feeling afraid!" Trying to calm her, the midwife reassured her that she didn't need to be afraid. Not feeling heard, Sara bristled and shouted angrily, "But I *am* afraid!" Fortunately, her husband knew how to soothe her by calmly hearing her feelings and mirroring them back: "Yes, Sara, I can really hear that you're feeling afraid."

Just as suddenly as her fear arose, it began to subside. She simply needed to voice her authentic feelings and have them reflected back to her. Expressing what was alive for her freed her to take her next step in life. In fact, it enabled two lives to move forward. She gave birth to a beautiful baby girl.

Rather than fighting our feelings, fleeing from them, or being paralyzed by them, we can learn to accommodate them with equanimity. Being present with our experience as it unfolds is the "middle way" that moves us beyond the attachments and aversions that generate suffering. We even make room for our attachments and aversions; it is all part of the wondrous dance of life. No longer fighting ourselves, we find greater freedom to be ourselves, embrace our common humanity, and relish the mystery of being alive.

Attending to Our Felt Sense

Gendlin emphasizes that he didn't *invent* Focusing. He merely *observed* it in people who had successful outcomes in psychotherapy. Distilling the core elements that led to positive change, he crafted teachable steps so that others can tap into this natural process.

The core of Focusing is attending to our bodily felt sense, that vague, murky something that we can sense in our body yet can't quite articulate. For example, you may feel uncomfortable meeting a man at a party. You stay with your vague discomfort without trying to figure it out and without running from him or your feelings about him. Simply being mindful of your discomfort allows it to ease. You accept his offer to exchange business cards but aren't sure if you want to meet if he calls.

Later, you may sense that there is something about this man's friendliness that you don't trust. As you sense into this, you may be reminded of a former partner who seemed so kind at first but then became frequently critical and angry. You notice that you often shut down now to protect your heart when you meet a potentially kind man. You don't give him a chance or give yourself a chance to see whether this is a person you can trust. This meditative-like inquiry frees up some inner space so that you can check people out without immediately clinging to them or pushing them away.

Parallel Approaches to the Human Condition

Both Buddhism and Focusing are existential in nature. We are encouraged to attend directly to what stirs within, though in somewhat different ways. No longer fighting the feelings and sensations that course through us, we're less oppressed by them. There is an easing of the anguish and anxiety that arises from defending against what is happening inside us.

Focusing and mindfulness practice overlap in the following ways:

- Allowing our experience to be exactly as it is
- Being non-judgmental and accepting of whatever arises inside us
- Adopting an attitude of gentleness toward our experience
- Being compassionate with ourselves

However, there are some differences between the two in terms of how we relate to our feelings and unfolding experience.

Let It Go, Let It Be, Let it Unfold

In Buddhist retreats I attended long ago, the instructions for dealing with feelings went something like this: "Just let them go" or "Just notice them and let them pass." Through cool, detached observation, we realize that the nature of all mental and emotional phenomena is to arise and pass away. We learn not to get attached to any aspect of our experience.

Years later, it became apparent that these instructions had an unintended effect: many students were dissociating from their feelings and bodies. A split was being reinforced between body, mind, and emotions. And so the instructions were adjusted to obviate this danger: "If feelings or emotions arise, don't push them away—just let them be." This refinement fostered a gentler acceptance rather than a pushing away of unpleasant experiences.

A further evolution of these instructions may now be helpful in engaging with feelings and concerns that arise again and again in our minds and bodies. Like a hurting child, some feelings clamor for attention until we listen with loving-kindness. As much as we may try to attend to our breath, our mind may relentlessly move toward unresolved concerns: a gnawing conflict with our partner, a health quandary, or money anxiety may all compete for attention. Rather than see these feelings and issues as distractions, can we include them as part of our practice?

If our intention is to let feelings go, we may avoid important emotions or concerns that need attention. If we let them *be*, we bring mindfulness to the dimension of our life in the world as experienced from the inside. Going further, by *allowing feelings to unfold*, some new grace or insight may enter so that troubling issues resolve or are held less oppressively.

Allowing space in our meditation practice for how life affects us supports an integration of mindfulness with our life in the world. We then embody the teaching of ninth-century Chinese Zen master Huang Po: "On no account make a distinction between the absolute and the sentient world."[5]

A Way to Attend to Feelings

Here is a manner of attending to feelings that allows them to unfold without inflating or deflating our sense of self:

> If feelings arise just let them be; perhaps notice how they feel in your body right now. If anything more arises—perhaps other emotions, thoughts, images, memories, sensations, or a sense of what these feelings are about—just meet it in a caring, gentle way.

This compassionate attitude allows spaciousness around our experience. We dance with it in such a way that we can notice when we are merging with our feelings or are too removed from them. As Focusing teacher Ann Weiser Cornell explains, "Focusing is not about feeling as intensely as possible. Focusing is about keeping your feelings company."[6] Sometimes we may want to get very close to our feelings, such as when we allow ourselves to grieve. At other times, such as when feelings are traumatic or overwhelming, we may need a little distance from them.

Master couples therapist Dan Wile's work appears to help couples develop a certain kind of mindfulness that also resembles Focusing. He helps couples find what he calls a platform, a "nonaccusing and nonanxious vantage point,"[7] so they can observe what is happening inside them. This enables them to monitor their "ever changing internal landscape rather than to be swallowed up in it."[8] By bringing a gentle awareness to what we are experiencing rather than being debilitated by it, our feelings and wants can be shared with less emotional charge; we're then more likely to be heard.

A Complement to Meditation or a Way of Meditation?

Focusing invites us to greet all of our experience as welcomed guests, as expressed in Rumi's poem "The Guest House":

> This being human is a guest house
> Every morning a new arrival.
> A joy, a depression, a meanness,
> some momentary awareness comes
> as an unexpected visitor.
>
> Welcome and entertain them all!
> Even if they're a crowd of sorrows,
> who violently sweep your house
> empty of its furniture,
> still treat each guest honorably.
> He may be clearing you out
> for some new delight.
>
> The dark thought, the shame, the malice.
> Meet them at the door laughing,
> and invite them in.
>
> Be grateful for whoever comes,
> because each has been sent
> as a guide from beyond.[9]

Similar to meditation, Focusing is a way of being present that is non-striving and non-evaluative. We welcome experiences that arise as a result of being alive.

Focusing differs from methods of meditation designed to cultivate one-pointed concentration. We attend to a level of experience that lies somewhere between our usual distracted state and deeper levels of absorption. Those whose practice is directed toward concentration might complement their practice by allowing the gentle spirit of Focusing to enter their meditation or, perhaps, at times apart from meditation.

Focusing may be seamlessly integrated with vipassana or mindfulness methods of meditation, which broaden awareness to include experience as it unfolds. We allow edgy feelings, important decisions, or creative challenges to rest in the forefront of awareness. Similar to meditation, we maintain an attitude of openness to whatever is arising now.

Buddhist teacher Thich Nhat Hanh suggests bringing mindfulness to our feelings in a way that reflects the gentle spirit of Focusing:

> It is best not to say, "Go away, Fear. I don't like you. You are not me." It is much more effective to say, "Hello, Fear. How are you today?" Then you can invite the two aspects of yourself, mindfulness and fear, to shake hands as friends and become one.[10]

Rather than push away fear or other unpleasant feelings, we cultivate an attitude of gentleness and friendliness toward our experience. Thich Nhat Hanh offers the following suggestion, which clearly resonates with the Focusing attitude: "Do not fight against pain; do not fight against jealousy. Embrace them with great tenderness, as though you were embracing a little baby. . . . The same thing goes for all your emotions."[11]

Welcoming Feelings

While having close parallels to the practice of meditation, Focusing is more geared toward allowing life issues to arise. We sense their texture and allow space for a further unfolding of meanings or directions for our lives. Perhaps a niggling fear has a message for us—maybe to steer clear of a tricky situation or to notice how it is holding us back from voicing our feelings or desires in a relationship.

Focusing appears to weave seamlessly with the meditation instructions offered by meditation teacher Jason Siff. In his helpful book *Unlearning Meditation*, he encourages an "open, flexible, minimally structured approach to meditation,"[12] allowing thoughts, feelings, longings, or any other phenomena to arise as they will and consciously choosing to explore them if that seems useful. As Siff puts it:

> I see clinging to experiences and elaborating on them, or thinking about them, as being quite natural and nothing to be alarmed about. . . . I have heard many reports of meditation sittings where someone has written an article, composed a piece of music, planned an art project, or redecorated her house, and it was actually very productive and efficient to be doing this in meditation.[13]

Siff explains how in his own meditation, he allows feelings such as anger, fear, hurt, and longing to arise: "Sitting still with those feelings, I learned how to tolerate them and, eventually, how to quietly and gently explore them."[14] Extending the parameters of meditation to include an exploration of feelings and thoughts would seem to embrace Focusing as a form of meditative inquiry.

A pitfall of many traditional meditation practices is that if we are intent on returning awareness to our breath every time our mind moves in another direction, we're not available for other aspects of our experience. Rigidly adhering to standard meditation instructions, we may strain to do the meditation "correctly," which creates a tension that ultimately undermines our practice.

A pitfall of Focusing is that we may keep spinning our wheels in the quicksand of content. If our attention remains murky or scattered, we might skate on the surface of personal concerns without uncovering what lies beneath. Stampeded with a relentless parade of issues, we may not get much traction on any of them. Developing some initial concentration by meditating on the breath or the sensations of our hands touching each other might steady our attention. We might then focus more productively on feelings or issues seeking attention.

Focusing is akin to mindfulness practice, though in a more specific, bodily felt way. Many forms of meditation connect us to our body, but the Focusing variation puts attention mostly on bodily felt experiences that are linked with meaningful life issues. Connecting with our bodily felt experience of a particular life concern, we might create space for more clarity and resolution to emerge. At some point, these two practices may interweave in a way in which it is difficult to differentiate them. Whether we label what we do as Focusing or meditation is not as important as the quality of our presence to unfolding experience.

Weaving Focusing with Meditation

The path toward awakening opens up not when we try to fix or even improve ourselves, but as we create a holding environment for our experience as it is. By allowing our inner process to arise, incubate, unfold, and shift as it might, a new understanding or forward movement may emerge.

Through experimentation, we may learn to weave Focusing seamlessly into our meditation. While sitting, Bill noticed that thoughts about his new relationship wouldn't quit. Rather than pushing them aside or noting that he was thinking, he attended to the feelings connected with them. He soon became aware of a constricted place in his chest. Staying with this tight sensation in a tender way, he noticed memories of soured love and the specter of another heartbreaking rejection. He recognized a familiar fear that was preventing him from opening his heart.

Gently attending to this fear, he found some compassion toward himself, which allowed the fear to ease. It occurred to him that if he got hurt in this new relationship, he could hold this place in a caring way just as he had gently held the tight place in his chest. He realized that such pain would pass, as it had before. And he could feel empowered for having risked loving again rather than sitting on the sidelines, playing it safe but not really living.

Recognizing the wisdom of risking rather than being controlled by fear, he felt a new boldness to love and then see what would happen. Noticing his breathing ease, he became aware of the rhythmic sensations of his abdomen rising and falling. A delightful calm descended over him. He allowed himself to experience that until it shifted into something else.

Focusing offers a way to attend to nuances of experience that traditional meditation often overlooks. We notice whatever images, memories, meanings, words, or feelings arise. Inner knots disentangle themselves and tensions ease as we bring a steadied attention to concerns that arise on or off the meditation cushion.

Bringing a warm, loving awareness to what's alive inside us prepares the ground for a shift in how we experience stuck feelings or recurring issues. This opening may flow from simply embracing feelings that we normally resist. Or a shift might accompany newly felt insights.

For example, during meditation we might recall how our partner's words triggered a spasm of angry frustration but not understand what was activated within us. The stillness fostered by meditation might help us look more clearly at our vulnerable underbelly. It might occur to us that our sarcastic jabs defended us from an unpleasant hurt, which we are ashamed to acknowledge because we deem it to be a weakness. Staying with this awareness for a time, we might notice self-compassion welling up as we recognize how hard we're being on ourselves for having normal emotions. It occurs to us that expressing our hurt would be an important step forward.

Being gently mindful of our authentic feelings, we not only feel freer, we are also better positioned to relate to our partner from a more self-aware place, which invites the connection we want. In this way, weaving Focusing into meditation alleviates some personal suffering while easing our way toward more loving relationships.

Cultivating the Habit of Felt-Sensing

Focusing is often seen as an approach to problem solving, which might cast it as a solution-based approach. But this view would limit its potential scope. Beyond tidying up loose ends that dangle uncomfortably at the edge of our awareness, we can embody the Focusing attitude in our everyday lives. We can attend to anything that wants attention or clarification, such as where to go on a weekend or what color to paint our room. I'm using Focusing right now as I write, getting a "feel" for what I want to say and how to say it.

My own Focusing teachers, Ed McMahon and Peter Campbell, emphasize that Focusing can help us develop "the habit of bringing the gift of a listening, loving presence"[15] to all of our feelings. This includes being present for positive feelings as well as difficult ones.[16] This orientation takes us beyond problem solving into a realm of being present to life as it presents itself from moment to moment.

Being mindful of our ongoing felt-sensing, we might relish having our cat on our lap or savor a good meal—and know when we are full. When our partner returns from work, we might notice a warm feeling in our abdomen or a sparkling energy throughout our body, or an engaging smile that enlivens our face and invites contact. Being mindfully present with the fluidity of our felt experience, we're more available for the dance of living and loving.

Replenished by the Open Space

Focusing on a troubling concern may deliver us to a new shore. Then, rather than scan for the next issue to resolve, we can simply enjoy this new vista. Resting in this open space after something shifts offers a taste of liberation.

Refreshed by the waters of pure being, we may at times experience a moment of "Big Mind," a larger sense of presence and connection with life. As inner constraints melt, we may find ourselves dwelling in a tranquil aliveness. Tasting the presence of love and connection, we no longer long for it. We no longer seek it. We *are* it. A particularly sumptuous feast of connection arises during those moments when two people are resting in their own deeper being.

Rest assured that being human, our longings, thoughts, and concerns about our lives will reemerge. Spiritual teachings might have us believe that our ego has reasserted its ugly head and that we should get beyond it. But what is actually most egotistical is having an *attitude* toward our ego—a foul and critical one. We see it as something that interferes with our spiritual progress when, in fact, it is the vehicle through which we awaken.

Ego functions include thinking, planning, and orienting ourselves in ways that help us survive and thrive in the world. This part of us alerts us to present dangers and helps us anticipate and ward off future dangers. It allows us to gather, evaluate, and synthesize information so that we can gauge how best to proceed. Eliminating something that enables us to pay our bills, take care of us, and channel our creativity would sabotage our spiritual development, not support it.

As we embrace our unfolding experience without the contaminants of self-criticism or aversion, we can move fluidly between longing and satiation, desire and contentment, craving more and having enough, wanting to fix ourselves and being okay just as we are. By embracing these natural rhythms with poise and equanimity, we dance gracefully with what wants attention in the moment rather than push anything away.

Fresh Perspectives on Buddhist Teachings

Focusing can offer new perspectives on core Buddhist doctrines. As we stay with our felt sense of life concerns, we notice how feelings and sensations come and go of their own accord. We directly experience the Buddhist notion of impermanence. The fact that things are constantly changing becomes apparent with the direct experience of bodily felt shifts.

Focusing may also help us discover how our efforts are often misguided. The more we spin our wheels trying to figure things out in our minds, the more we stay stuck. As we experience how creative change happens through the skillful effort to see things as they are—and lovingly notice how that feels inside us—we are embodying the Buddhist notion of "Right Effort."

We might also realize how we stay stuck when we try to hold on to some idealized version of ourselves rather than allow our experience to be as it is. Thus we learn about *anatta*, the Buddhist notion that suffering is perpetuated by trying to hold on to a fixed sense of self. Recognizing how our experience is constantly shifting, we come to appreciate that no particular aspect of our psychophysical being can be declared to be our self. We realize that we are not a person who needs fixing, but a process that invites embracing. Both Focusing and mindfulness practice lead to the discovery aptly described by Zen teacher Charlotte Joko Beck: "Who I am is simply experiencing itself."[17]

The unique language taught by some Focusing teachers invites us to welcome our experience without aggrandizing or solidifying a rigid sense of self. Ann Weiser Cornell and Barbara McGavin emphasize phrases such as "part of me feels" or, even more helpful, "something in me feels" sad, afraid, constricted (or whatever) rather than saying, *I* feel sad, afraid, or constricted.[18] This language may feel strange at first, yet it conveys that there is more to us than our passing feelings and allows a spacious mindfulness around our experience, enabling it to move and shift more readily by not being consumed by whatever we're feeling inside. Expressing our feelings this way also allows them to be heard by others more easily—they are not so jabbing or final; they are always in process.

Focusing offers a way to bring compassion and loving-kindness to the clinging and craving that generate suffering. Rather than judge ourselves for clinging, we can notice what we're really feeling and wanting. For example, if we attend to our felt sense of attaching to someone who is harming us, we might notice a tight sensation in our abdomen or a jumpy feeling in our solar plexus. Staying with the felt sense of all this, we might recognize a fear of being alone and a longing to be understood. Bringing a gentle mindfulness toward our fear of loneliness and desire for a loving connection has a curious way of softening our clinging, allowing us to feel freer.

Too Attached or Not Attached Enough?

People who visit my therapy office express a peculiarly common viewpoint when the topic of Buddhism or meditation arises. As a student who attended one of my talks put it, "Buddhism is about being detached, right? You shouldn't be too happy, sad, or passionate about anything. You create a buffer so you're not too attached to anyone or anything." It's not easy to undo the unfortunate reputation Buddhism has gained as a path of chilly detachment.

A client, Stan, had an attraction to Buddhism that fit perfectly with his tendency to avoid intimacy. Stan's family moved frequently when he was young, uprooting one friendship after another. Unable to bear the pain of losing another friend, he vowed to not get too close to anyone. During college he found a refuge in Buddhism, which reinforced his belief that nothing lasts and that getting too attached creates suffering.

Stan came into my office complaining about a gnawing anxiety and low energy. Exploring this, he gradually realized that it was related to his distancing from people. His fear of getting too attached was keeping his emotions flatlined. "People find me boring. Whatever feelings I have, I keep to myself. I'm actually bored with myself! I get lonely. I think I'm being a good Buddhist by not getting attached, but I'm actually attached to being comfortable, I'm attached to my vow to stay detached. I have an aversion to pleasure and intimacy. I don't take risks that might lead to rejection. I've had a lot of loss in my life, and it was unbearable."

After working together for some time, Stan felt more alive and less anxious as he courageously opened himself to the joys and sorrows of interpersonal relating. Taking more risks to reach out, he felt less lonely and more connected. He also didn't bolt from therapy, as he had done with several therapists in the past. His fear of getting too dependent yielded to a willingness to share his feelings more honestly and allow someone (namely, me) to get closer to him. As he revealed his feelings and wants more openly, he created more healthy connections with important people in his life.

Embracing Experience Versus Bracing Against It

Focusing offers a way to embrace our experience rather than brace against it. We welcome our feelings rather than wallow in them or punt them away. We cultivate a warm and spacious presence toward whatever we're experiencing in the moment. Engaging intimately with what lives inside us connects us in a very immediate, authentic way with our partner, friends, and community.

It is beyond the scope of this book to describe the Focusing process in detail; I have done that in an earlier book, *Being Intimate*. Other helpful books are included in the bibliography. The Guide to Resources offers opportunities to learn Focusing.

Part Four

Intimacy with Community

The quest for truth cannot thrive outside the nourishment of mutual trust flowering into a commitment to friendship.

—Ivan Illich

We do not believe in ourselves until someone reveals that something deep inside us is valuable, worth listening to, worthy of our trust, sacred to our touch. Once we believe in ourselves we can risk curiosity, wonder, spontaneous delight, or any experience that reveals the human spirit.

—E. E. Cummings

Chapter Nineteen

Friendship: Awakening in Community

❧

A s I am writing, a friend who just returned from a trip overseas calls. Hearing his voice, something inside me smiles. My stomach relaxes and my chest lightens. I breathe a little easier. We exchange some stories and arrange to meet for lunch.

The joy and comfort of friendship has always been an important part of my life. Whatever I have learned from teachers becomes integrated through rich conversations and connections with friends.

Friendships and the Holy Life

There is a story that highlights the importance of friendship in the Buddhist tradition. Ananda was one of the Buddha's main students. One day, upon returning from a trip, Ananda made a poignant observation about the value of spiritual community: "Admirable friendship, admirable companionship, admirable camaraderie are half of the holy life."

Not missing a beat, the Buddha took this sentiment a step further. "Don't say that, Ananda. Don't say that. Admirable friendship, admirable companionship, admirable camaraderie are the whole of the holy life." In another discourse, the Buddha affirms that having such friends is "the first prerequisite for the development of the wings to self-awakening."

Buddhism and contemplative traditions direct us toward the inner life—the path of mindfulness and inquiry that leads to peace and freedom. Human relations aren't something we usually associate with Buddhism. But, clearly, the Buddha's rousing affirmation of friendship suggests that one of the great spiritual exemplars places preeminent value on human connections and, presumably, the intimacy and affection they afford. In short, we need each other. We awaken in relationship and in community.

Did the Buddha Value Friendship for Himself?

The Buddha's affirmation of friendship raises the question of whether he valued this not only for his students, but for himself as well. Since the Buddha is revered for being enlightened, some people assume that he no longer experienced human feelings like the rest of us, or anything that resembles the human need for companionship. He may appear as remote, even intimidating in his spiritual accomplishment. But given the Buddha's assertion that friendship is the *whole* of the holy life, it would seem that friendships were vital for him, too.

We can only wonder about the challenges faced by a very human Buddha. Did he and Ananda confide in each other about their hopes and concerns while sipping aromatic teas in the morning, or sharing freshly baked bread, or conversing late into the sultry nights in the Indian countryside? Of course, we can never know. But given the Buddha's validation of friendship, we may wonder why Buddhism is often viewed as the impersonal pursuit of an inward journey that brokers no room for the pleasures of human relating.

I can imagine how personal connections added meaning to the Buddha's life. We see over and over again in Buddhist texts that he was compassionate toward everyone he met. He appears to have affection for his students and exudes a kindness born of clear seeing into our sorrowful human condition. And during his final days at the age of eighty, he experienced excruciating pain, apparently as a result of food poisoning. Surrounded by his closest disciples, his dying process was a very human one, indeed.

Engaging Friendships

Some commentators believe that the Buddha's notion of friendship was limited to supporting each other's ethical values and path toward liberation rather than the intimacy and belonging that we seek in the West. Whatever the Buddha might have meant by friendship, the important questions for us are "What does it mean to be good friends in our time?" and "How can we support and encourage each other?"

A good friend is someone with whom we feel safe enough to open our heart and reveal our deepest feelings and concerns. We know we can call when we are hurting or just want some contact. Sharing thoughts, feelings, or laughing together, we feel renewed. Trusting that we won't be judged, we don't need to parse our words so carefully. We can be who we are.

Good for Our Health

Friendships not only help us awaken, they offer a sense of connectedness that is crucial for good health. Hundreds of studies have confirmed the health benefits of having a strong social network.

Most people are aware that smoking, obesity, and lack of exercise contribute to ill health. But who would have suspected that not having good friends may be as harmful as being obese or not exercising? A review of 148 studies that tracked the social interactions and health of over 308,000 people over an average of 7.5 years suggests something unexpected: being lonely is as bad for our health as smoking fifteen cigarettes a day or being an alcoholic.[1] Our modern-day trend toward isolation is fueled by factors like modern technology, more people living alone, and the stresses of work.

Researcher James Pennebaker suggests that social support helps keep us healthy. Talking about our feelings when experiencing loss and trauma increases immune functioning. "Social support only protects your health if you use it wisely; that is, if you have suffered a major upheaval in your life, talk to your friends about it. Merely having friends is not enough."[2]

Friendship and Feelings in Today's World

Some Buddhist communities promote the concept of spiritual friendship between teacher and student and among peers. But there has been little attention to the role of intimacy in those relationships and scant guidance about how to create a climate that fosters connections and resolves conflicts.

The meditation retreats I've attended rarely include time to relate to each other apart from preparing meals and washing dishes. I appreciate the value of retreating from our busy lives and minds, but retreating from meaningful, authentic relating is something that most people already do quite well.

Meditation retreats could be an ideal place to step back from life's busyness and practice speaking and listening to our spiritual friends from a calm, connected place within ourselves. Whether or not we are inclined toward retreats, we practice relational mindfulness by expressing our authentic feelings, thoughts, and longings in a clear and kind way and allowing ourselves to be moved by others' feelings and longings.

No One Is Exempt from the Human Condition

On the eve of the Buddha's awakening under the Bodhi tree, he struggled with a whirlwind of emotions. As the story goes, he was tempted by the armies of Mara, the god of illusion and evil, to abandon his foolish quest for awakening and return to the pleasures of normal life. He was presented with alluring visions of beautiful women, pleasure, power, and wealth—the hallmarks of his earlier life as a prince.

Gautama, before becoming the Buddha, sat steadfast throughout Mara's assault, neither grasping nor pushing away any pleasant or unpleasant experiences. As he greeted the arrows of greed and hostility with open-hearted serenity, they transformed into fragrant flower petals alighting around him.

Gautama emerged from this ordeal as the Buddha—literally an "awakened one." But a persistent Mara continued to stalk the Buddha. According to one version of the story, the Buddha warmly greets his old friend Mara, inquiring, "How have you been?" Mara grumbles about the difficulties of being an evil tempter. Listening sympathetically, the Buddha responds, "Do you think it is easy being a Buddha? Do you know what they do with my teachings, what they do in the name of the Buddha at some of my temples? There are difficulties being in either role, a Buddha or a Mara. No one is exempt."[3]

I wonder if the Buddha felt a sense of responsibility for the students who dropped everything to study with him. Did he have moments of irritation when students misused his teachings or when he observed the suffering caused by an oppressive caste system that he opposed? Did he experience sadness and grief when loved ones died or became ill? As the Buddha conveyed to Mara, no one is exempt from the human condition.

Repeated visits by Mara suggest that the Buddha was not immune from human emotions and temptations. Like all of us, he grappled with tricky emotions without drowning in them. A Christian parallel is the theological view that Jesus had the "Christ nature" while also being fully human. He felt agony when metal pierced his flesh on the cross. He had moments of doubt and perhaps fear, asking God, "Why have you forsaken me?" He appears to have had a close friendship with Mary Magdalene and enjoyed hanging out with prostitutes (presumably without the sex), perhaps because they were more down-to-earth and real than most other people of his time. Friendships were apparently important for him, too.

The ability to honor and engage wisely with our feelings makes the crucial difference between a disembodied kind of liberation where we remain distant from life (which is no liberation at all) and an awakening that becomes increasingly integrated into our bodies, lives, and relationships. Cultivating this integration enables us to accommodate unavoidably painful feelings while becoming increasingly free of unnecessary suffering.

Becoming amicably engaged with our feelings doesn't mean over-dramatizing our emotions, wearing our feelings, becoming our feelings (over-identifying with them), or probing for every little feeling to express. Nor does it mean attacking people with the sharp edges of our annoyances or desires. An emotionally engaged spirituality means being attuned to the subtle world of our felt sensing and choosing wisely when and how to share this. We remain awake to opportunities to connect authentically, understand each other, and enjoy a rich sense of community.

An Emotionally Engaged Spirituality

Some people may bristle at the prospect of an enlightened person continuing to have human feelings and longings like the rest of us mortals. But I do not believe that the Buddha wanted to be stripped of his humanity. To idealize him in that way would be to place him on a pedestal far beyond anything we can attain. The path toward liberation is not synonymous with erasing our humaneness. Allowing and sharing our feelings and longings with select people is an essential part of building relationships that form the basis of community life.

Since most of us don't live in spiritual communities, our path is to integrate spiritual practice with our lives in the world, developing what Joko Beck calls "ordinary mind" and "everyday Zen." Just as a socially engaged

Buddhism has developed to promote social justice and community well-being, there is a need today for an emotionally engaged spirituality. As we cultivate qualities of compassion, openness, and wisdom and apply them to our emotional and interpersonal lives, we become more whole and healed. A rich world of intimacy opens wide.

The most precious gift we can offer others is our presence.

—Thich Nhat Hanh

Let us be kinder to one another.

—Aldous Huxley's last words

Chapter Twenty

Finding Refuge in Community

﷼

I t was a cool autumn morning. I was looking forward to meeting a new spiritual community I'd heard about. I was just getting over a cold and wasn't at my best, but I didn't want to miss this opportunity. I figured I could drag myself there without too much struggle.

Arriving early with a friend, I met a vibrant woman who asked with a cheerful smile, "How are you this morning?" Reluctant to fake a social smile, I told her that I wasn't feeling great. Without pausing to wonder why, she responded, "What do you mean? It's such a beautiful day today!" My stomach immediately tightened and my chest constricted. I didn't feel welcomed as I was.

I am sure she was well-intentioned, but rather than being interested in my inner world, she wanted me to be somewhere else. She seemed to have some spiritual agenda about how people should feel and be. What I heard was, "Why aren't you happy? Aren't you a spiritual person?" I felt criticized and shamed in a subtle way. I listened to my body and trusted what it was telling me: just keep it light and move on.

Since there was no room for my authentic self, there was not much chance of connecting with her. Feeling rebuked, I reverted to superficial conversation. I soon discovered that this woman was one of the leaders of this spiritual gathering. I stayed for the meeting, but it became apparent that this was not the spiritual community I was seeking. It was not a safe place for me to be authentic.

CHAPTER TWENTY

Honoring Feelings in Community

Shortly after that, I attended the International Focusing Conference, where I had a very different experience. Nearly 200 people gathered from seventeen countries. Some of us had meditation practices, and we were also interested in honoring feelings. A small group of us gathered after the conference for a two-day meditation/Focusing retreat.

The retreat consisted of sitting meditation, walking meditation, and meeting once a day in Focusing partnerships. During this time, we paired up, taking twenty minutes each to attend to what we were experiencing in the moment. Our partner would simply listen in an open, empathic way, sometimes reflecting back our words or meanings without giving advice or opinions.

Whatever felt alive for us had a chance to get aired, heard, and released. As a result, these thoughts and feelings were less likely to clamor for airtime during meditation. By all accounts, the connection and openings that we experienced through Focusing were very helpful in furthering our meditation practice.

How rare and freeing it is to feel safe with another person, to know that our authentic feelings will be heard and accepted without being judged! Having had my spiritual and human side seen, accepted, and respected, I felt that these were people I wanted as part of my spiritual community. This was the piece I was missing years ago when I stole away from the retreat in New England to commune with my friend at the pizza parlor. I was missing an opportunity to process feelings and meanings that were arising for me during meditation, and needed the steadying effect of human connection.

The Power of Listening

The yeast that helps grow friendships and community is listening to each other's authentic feelings. The mirroring magic of feeling heard helps us awaken to parts of ourselves that often remain hidden. Our caring presence, kindness, compassion, and interest in another's world are priceless gifts.

Being human, we tend to carry insecurities about whether or not we are okay. We have wounds to our self-worth and doubts about our value. Perhaps we have been so judged and shamed for being authentic that our true feelings scurried down a rabbit hole, where they now become difficult to coax out—like my neighbor's cat hiding under the house.

We may have lived in darkness for so long that when the light of another's love or attention shines upon us, it blinds us. We may revert to our comfortable isolation. Opening our heart in a spirit of friendship, revealing the fears and hurts from which we've been running, can heal something deep within us.

Creating Refuge in the Sangha

The cornerstone of every Buddhist tradition involves the three refuge vows. We are invited to take refuge in the Buddha (our awakened being) and in the dharma (what is true and real). The third vow invites us to take refuge in the sangha, the community of practitioners. Unfortunately, this third vow often gets short shrift and is rarely elaborated. What might it mean to take refuge in the sangha in our culture?

The word "refuge" comes from a word meaning "to flee." Webster's defines it as "a place of safety; shelter; safe retreat." Taking refuge in the sangha means retreating from the distractions and difficulties of the world and finding safety in the community of people on the spiritual path.

Creating Emotional Safety in Spiritual Life

In addition to our basic needs for food, shelter, and safety, we also need *emotional* safety—the freedom to be ourselves without the threat of being criticized or shamed. We want to feel accepted for the full range of our feelings, thoughts, and wants. We want to relish the exhilarating freedom of being unguarded in revealing our humanity in our close relationships.

We may not realize that we also have the power to offer a generous serving of freedom to others by how we interact with them. The prevailing view in today's pop psychology culture is that no one has the power to constrain our freedom to be ourselves unless we grant him or her that power. This is true to a point; yet, without being warmly received and accepted, our freedom is limited.

We are free to be an isolated self, but such freedom confines us to a prison within our own skin. The freedom to love and be loved is meaningful to the extent that we receive each other openly and enter each other's world with curiosity and sensitivity. To find refuge in the sangha, including our partner and close friends, is to recognize that there is a way in which we need each other if we want a more deeply resonant kind of freedom, one that allows us to soar beyond the confines of our separate self.

Staying connected with ourselves in a way that allows a non-evaluative presence with others affords them the freedom to be authentic with us. Compassionate acceptance is a wonderful gift we can offer others, which then rewards us through the connection it fosters. Creating emotional safety supports a tender, open space with each other, leading to a precious intimacy that is one of the fruits of mindful living.

Sadly, many of us were raised in environments where we didn't feel welcomed as we are. Desperate for love and acceptance, we may have created a false self that we hoped would win approval and respect. I've often heard clients say, "I'm always trying to be somebody. It never occurred to me that I might be acceptable just as I am. I'm sad that I've lived most of my life trying to be someone I'm not."

This split between our authenticity and our fabricated self accounts for much of the anguish in our lives. We become divided, confused, and disconnected from our authentic heart. We may become anxious and depressed without realizing that this suffering stems from not allowing ourselves to be as we are. We may subtly hate ourselves because we're not being true to our authentic, luminous self.

Freud spoke of this dissociation when he commented that neurosis is measured by the difference between the idealized self and the actual self.

Healing this inner split requires the kind of mirroring that many of us did not receive in our families. Trusting that our authentic feelings will be heard and accepted in our close relationships frees us to reveal our tender heart.

Friendship Frees Us to Be Ourselves

Feeling safe to show ourselves has a way of amplifying what we are experiencing inside. Feeling heard and accepted as we are, we're suddenly freed to *be* who we really are. Aspects of ourselves that have restrained us become illuminated. A burden of shame and isolation lifts as we realize that we have sorrows and foibles just like everyone else in the human community.

The gift of the sangha then becomes not simply meditating together silently, but also availing ourselves of *interacting* deeply with each other—exposing our fears, hurts, and joys, revealing our longings, sharing our stories, and letting people into the sanctuary of our humanity. This tender sharing with trusted people brings our mindfulness practice soundly into our relationships.

Sharing the challenging aspects of our journey allows them to shift. Something in us relaxes as we give them space to breathe and be heard. Being less encumbered by whatever distracts, annoys, or frustrates us, we feel more freed up. We become more radiant and alive.

As a community of people on the spiritual path, the sangha can become a safe place to open our heart and support each other in our authenticity. Availing ourselves of this interpersonal refuge helps soothe the limbic brain, which is wired to seek secure connections. The calming effect of being heard frees us from the tug of a longing that is now being met, thereby easing our movement toward awakening.

There is enormous, untapped potential for integrating authentic sharing into our spiritual practice. Cultivating rich friendships can become an important part of our spiritual life. In fact, as the Buddha observed, it is the whole of the holy life.

Perfect enlightenment appears in many texts, but amid all the Western masters and teachers I know, such utter perfection is not apparent. Times of great wisdom, deep compassion, and a real knowing of freedom alternate with periods of fear, confusion, neurosis, and struggle. Most teachers will readily admit this truth.

—Jack Kornfield

Believe nothing; question everything.

—The Buddha

Chapter Twenty-One

Teachers and Spiritual Communities: Trust Your Guru or Yourself?

❦

Taking refuge in the sangha means finding friendship and solace in spiritual community. A spiritual teacher, who is typically steeped in a specific tradition, assumes the mantle of leadership in such communities, offering guidance and direction. But there has been a growing chorus of concerns about the danger of surrendering our power to a teacher.

Skepticism grows as we hear reports about reputedly enlightened masters displaying all-too-human foibles. Sex scandals, alcoholism, and chilling abuses of power have spread more heartache than healing in some communities. Questions abound about whether these teachers are truly enlightened if their behavior generates suffering among their followers.

Despite scandalous headlines, many students maintain a fierce loyalty to their beloved teacher. They excuse indiscretions with a common refrain: "You shouldn't judge an enlightened master. Our limited minds can't comprehend the conduct of a spiritual teacher." But might such comments be lamentable rationalizations that expose an unhealthy attachment to authority and a failure to trust one's own perceptions?

A non-judgmental attitude is an important part of any spiritual path, but there is a difference between being judgmental and being discerning. The former elevates us to a morally superior pedestal; the latter simply sees reality clearly. When we allow ourselves to recognize that the emperor has no clothes, we are faced with several choices. We may become suspicious of a teacher's spiritual attainment or motives, which may or may not be a fair assessment. Or we might inquire anew about the gifts and limitations of all teachers, appreciating their wisdom while recognizing that their humanity will forever interplay with—and sometimes color—their spiritual teachings.

Trusting Our Experience

Yearning to be a devoted student, we may feel compelled to comply with our teacher's perspective about what is best for us. The perennial danger of being part of any spiritual community is that we may minimize our own experience and not nurture the fragile seeds of our own insights. By trying too fervently to make our experience mesh with our teacher's views, we may not develop our own inner barometer of what is true and best for us. Meditation teacher Jason Siff expresses it clearly:

> We may be living with a rather simple narrative that we should believe everything about the teachings we are practicing and not question them, since they come from someone wiser and more spiritually developed than we are. But that view leads to dependence upon the teacher, or his or her tradition, and does not usually allow us to have critical thoughts about the practices we're doing and the teachings we're receiving.[1]

Surrendering our own discernment may lead to a cult-like situation in which we strive to be a clone of our teacher rather than notice what resonates for us and what doesn't fit.

Having a spiritual teacher who can offer wise guidance can be enormously valuable, especially if this spiritual parenting compensates for some developmental gaps in our childhood. But we betray ourselves when we don't develop our own innate sense of truth. In fact, the Buddha cautioned his students not to blindly follow his teachings, but to check it through their own experience. He invited us to investigate freshly what makes sense to us in the context of an ongoing dialogue with trusted teachers and peers.

A Personal Story

As a young writer many years ago, I interviewed a teacher widely revered as an enlightened master. I spent many hours preparing questions and then transcribing our long conversation. As a sign of respect, I sent him an advance copy to review before publication. After many months, I finally heard that he wanted to refine some of his responses.

Several more months passed, and I was prepared to give up the project, but I finally decided to write a letter to ask the teacher what was happening. His assistant contacted me and said that the teacher would like to meet me at the airport. I eagerly agreed. When the day arrived, I spotted his entourage. Sending his companions away, he sat down next to me and took my hand tenderly in both of his.

What happened next surprised and delighted me. He looked into my eyes and continued to hold my hand. I can't remember his exact words, but the following is close: "I'm sorry," he said. "It's my fault." "Did you like the interview?" I asked sheepishly. "Yes. It was a good interview. I just wanted to make some refinements and have been too busy to get to it. I want you to know that we will definitely complete it. I will contact you soon, and we will finish it."

I felt very touched that such an accomplished teacher would respond so kindly, humbly, and apologetically, taking time from his busy schedule to reassure me in such a personal way. My hurt was assuaged in that tender exchange. I looked forward to completing something that was meaningful to me.

Well . . . I'm sad to say than twenty-five years have passed, and I have yet to hear back from him! Although my disappointment might sound like sour grapes, I believe that this teacher has affected our world positively through his illuminating books and teachings. I'm sure that his intentions were good, and I can also imagine that life became very busy for him.

Yet still, "Right Speech," which is part of the Buddha's Eightfold Path, includes the guidance to refrain from agreements that we cannot keep and to keep the ones we make. As a psychotherapist and in my personal life, I've observed how broken agreements rupture trust and connection. Of course, things can change and agreements can be modified. Showing respect and sensitivity toward another's feelings by communicating these changes can go a long way toward preserving trust.

Embracing the Shadow in Spiritual Practice

My intention is not to trash gurus but rather to point out their humanity. All of us fall short; we sometimes disappoint and injure people. We all hold images of ourselves that are not always congruent with who we really are. A well-integrated spirituality means expanding our mindfulness practice to include our interpersonal world, bringing the dharma (the path of truth) to our relationships. Our spiritual path is then informed by the realization that we have the power to hurt others; our words and actions affect tender hearts.

Each bright thing carries its own darkness with it. When the light of mindfulness shines brightly, it produces a shadow as it strikes parts of our personality that are dense, solid, and impermeable. If we are to integrate our spiritual experiences with our emotional lives and relationships, then these dark sides of ourselves must be honestly faced and addressed.

I have no doubt that many spiritual teachers have experienced something so profound that it deserves a non-ordinary name. We might even call it an enlightenment experience—or, perhaps more humbly, an enlightening experience. But this doesn't mean they now can be absolutely trusted as perfected beings who will always offer flawless guidance.

Stories abound that are far more gruesome than my own modest tale: teachers who preach celibacy and then have sex with their students, chilling threats and manipulation of practitioners who chose to leave ("You'll writhe in the hell realms for many lifetimes!"), and other abuses of power and trust. So the question arises: How can a person be so accomplished in some ways, yet when it comes to interpersonal relationships or assuming a leadership role that requires sound judgment, be so undeveloped or perhaps even narcissistic? Can one be spiritually liberated while also being oblivious to the psychological suffering generated by insensitivity and boundary violations?

I had assumed for many years that accomplished teachers are also psychologically mature; I projected an image of flawlessness onto them. After hearing many disillusioning stories, I realized that many people we consider "enlightened" have yet to mature emotionally. The refined awareness gained on the mountaintop doesn't necessarily translate into healthy human relations down in the village.

Waking Down teacher Saniel Bonder, who lived in a spiritual community for many years, describes his changing views of teachers:

> When I was younger, I used to believe that some people were totally free of attachments and aversion. But after many years of studying great realizers of absolute consciousness, often through prolonged direct contact, I now find this notion silly—and scary. Those emperors have no clothes. And to the degree that they can get their students to believe their dogma, those students end up carrying a lot of the emperors' baggage—including the considerable psychic shadows and mind/body/spirit splits.[2]

Idealization eventually gives way to the discovery that our esteemed teacher has human blemishes—a disillusionment that often mimics what happens in our romantic relationships. Our degree of shock and consternation is proportional to our unrealistic expectations. The sobering conclusion: spiritual teachers are not exempt from the human condition.

Trusting Our Own Experience

Perhaps we need to find a middle way of being a little suspicious, but in a way that doesn't poison the well. Can we respect the wisdom of teachers while also acknowledging that they are human and flawed like everyone else? No longer looking for perfection in a teacher, we can learn and grow through our contact with them.

If we remain at the mercy of external guidance, we may surrender our power to someone who does not have a nuanced understanding of what we need for our emotional healing and spiritual growth. We might get attached to a teacher for whom our loyalty is more important than our need to awaken to our own innate wisdom, goodness, and beauty.

A large measure of cult immunity is provided by cultivating a sense of discernment about whether a teacher's views and suggestions resonate with us. By mindfully refining and trusting our own felt sense of things, we can sort out what we can accept, where we disagree, and what we want to ponder further. The wisest teachers invite us to listen closely to our own experience rather than blindly follow what they say, which often includes our flawed interpretations of what they mean. Bouncing up against their perceptions can help us clarify our own.

Awakening: The Beginning of a Journey

Perhaps a handful of fully enlightened beings walk amongst us, but I can't say that I've met any. Meditation teacher Jack Kornfield offers this illuminating view:

> For almost everyone who practices, cycles of awakening and openness are followed by periods of fear and contraction. Times of profound peace and newfound love are often overtaken by periods of loss . . . or the discovery of betrayal, only to be followed again by equanimity and joy. In mysterious ways, the heart reveals itself to be like a flower that opens and closes. This is our nature.[3]

We are only recently seeing the fruits of crossing Eastern traditions with spiritually friendly forms of psychotherapy. This skillful blending of spirituality and psychology offers a fresh possibility of creating an embodied path that connects us with our true nature, each other, and our community. We are all in this together. You are more developed in certain aspects of the journey and others are more skillful in other ways. With humility and grace, we can help each other awaken to ourselves, each other, and life itself.

Conclusion

With each passing year, I notice a more tender appreciation for the precious gift of being alive. I sense a growing longing to live and love more fully and leave this earth awash in rich relationship and with minimal regrets. I recognize that embracing the nuanced feelings and longings that arise from being alive is an essential part of any spiritual path.

Diverse religions have the common aim of opening our hearts to love. But in practice, religious life has often been lived "above the neck." However compelling our beliefs about love, God, or truth might be, they are limited to lofty ideas in our mind if we don't take the elevator down to the ground floor of our body and hear what it knows and needs in order to live an emotionally healthy spiritual life.

A vibrant spirituality invites us to embrace all parts of our being. Wars and conflict throughout the world are external reflections of our internal emotional war. Creating a world where peace and justice prevail requires building a critical mass of people who are cultivating equanimity within themselves and developing loving-kindness toward their own vulnerabilities. This gentle attentiveness to our inner life creates the foundation for being responsive to the needs and sensitivities of our partner, friends, and community—and beyond that—our world.

A Key to Happiness

This book is an invitation to explore the individual and interpersonal aspects of awakening. Soothing and inspiring us, close relationships are a vehicle for self-discovery and true happiness. And our relational life grows more fulfilling as we develop a calm and welcoming mindfulness toward the full range of our experience.

Being human means that heartbreaking losses and betrayals will inevitably visit us. But we are less likely to lose ourselves as we cultivate a reliable inner refuge. Developing a growing trust that we can embrace whatever feelings arise within us as a result of loving and being loved is tremendously empowering. There is a silent sanctuary awaiting us when life becomes challenging.

Our journey toward personal growth and spiritual development eases as we deal gracefully with our soulful longings and the jagged emotions that orbit around them. As we live more comfortably in our bodies, we can notice and express feelings with greater equanimity rather than exude blame and ooze irritability. Lowering our shields and extending a warm transparency, we invite people toward us. Staying present to our feelings and longings and engaging with them wisely allows a deepening connection with ourselves, others, and life itself.

Creating harmonious relationships and a secure world rests upon our capacity to meet a variety of human yearnings. We can meet some portion of our longing for connection and inner freedom by cultivating intimacy with ourselves. Through practices such as quiet sitting, Focusing, and bringing mindfulness into daily life, we can stay close to ourselves.

But in addition to inward practices, we need to cooperate with how we are biologically wired to need support from outside of ourselves: nourishing food, safe shelter, and gainful employment. We're also hardwired to need fulfilling, trusting relations with our fellow humans. Something withers within us without empathic connections that allow us to feel heard, accepted, and understood. The salve of such intimacy eases our existential angst of isolation while enhancing our happiness.

The path of connecting with ourselves nurtures a warm intimacy with our own being. By allowing ourselves to be just as we are, which really means allowing our experience to be just as it is, we become simultaneously present to ourselves and deliciously available to meet others' hearts. We welcome our sacred longings and all the passionate energies they evoke. We celebrate the juiciness of connecting deeply and we gently embrace the agony and ecstasy of being alive. Moving gracefully with what life brings us, we offer a reverential bow to the promise and challenges of dancing with fire.

Self-Inquiry or Discussion Questions

I suggest that before asking yourself these questions, you allow a few slow, deep breaths and take some time to attend gently to your body. As your attention rests inside your belly or chest, you may make the following inquiries.

Some of you might consider contemplating these questions with a partner, friend, or group of friends with whom you feel safe and comfortable. If so, practice listening with an open heart. In a group discussion, refrain from offering advice (this is not group therapy), but instead notice what touches you from listening and what themes are emerging that may be important for your group to pursue. Above all, be gentle and kind with yourself and others. Feel free to "pass" or skip to another question, and take responsibility to explore and share only what feels comfortable for you. If difficult feelings come up around these questions, you may want to consult a qualified psychotherapist, especially a spiritually-oriented one.

- Do you consider your feelings and desires to be a part of your spiritual practice? If so, in what ways do you include them? If not, how do you typically deal with feelings and desires in your daily life or when they come up during your spiritual practice? Does the way you engage or don't engage your feeling life work well for you?
- If you have a meditation practice and feelings or longings arise, do you include them as part of your practice or perhaps deal with them later?

- What is your relationship in general with your feelings and longings? How do they fit into your life? Do you allow them space or do you tend to dismiss, minimize, or bypass them? Is your attitude toward your feelings usually warm and welcoming? Or is it judgmental or something else?
- Have you had experiences of deep intimacy with and acceptance from another as described in the book? What were those experiences? How did you feel? How do you feel inside when you feel deeply heard by another person?
- How do you usually respond when someone shows kindness and caring toward you? Are you able to "let it in" when someone shows kindness and caring toward you? Do you notice any beliefs or feelings that get in the way of receiving love and welcoming intimacy?
- What are your associations with the word "intimacy" as described in the book? What are your associations with the word *love*?
- Does the expression "intimacy with yourself" have any appeal to you? How would it feel to direct some of the love, kindness, and caring that you might feel toward a partner, friend, or pet toward yourself? How difficult is this to do? (It is difficult for most of us!)
- What is it about relationships that you find soothing? What are some ways you soothe yourself apart from relationships?
- Do you think that you are skilled at soothing yourself in healthy ways? What are some of the ways you soothe yourself apart from relationships?
- Do you think you make it safe for people to approach you, feel safe with you, and trust you?
- Are there some ways you might make it safer for people to come toward you?
- Do you notice what you say to yourself (perhaps critically) when you're experiencing feelings such as shame, fear, hurt, or sadness?
- Are there times when you feel deeply peaceful with yourself? If so, what are some of the experiences you remember, whether in the recent or distant past?

- Have you noticed any relationship between those times when you feel at peace with yourself and your ability to feel connected with others?
- What practices or activities help you feel inner peace?
- What have spiritual teachers or leaders communicated to you about desire and the need for human connection? Have you experienced any subtle sense of shame around any needs or feelings because they seemed spiritually incorrect? Or do you feel that feelings are welcomed as a part of the practice?
- What has your experience been with spiritual communities? Did you feel free to be yourself or did you sense some kind of subtle pressure to go along with others' viewpoints?
- Are there ways in which your spiritual practice may have contributed to your feeling badly about yourself? How about your desires?
- Were there sections of the book that were especially meaningful, evocative, or important for you? If so, how were you affected by them?

Notes

Introduction

Epigraph. Pierre Teilhard de Chardin, *Toward the Future* (New York: Mariner Books, 2002), 86–7.

1. This story is my adaptation from the story in Paul Reps, *Zen Flesh, Zen Bones* (Garden City, NY: Doubleday, 1961), 10.

2. Gregory Kramer, *Meditating Together, Speaking from Silence* (Seattle, WA: Metta Foundation, 2002), 15.

3. Dalai Lama, *Worlds in Harmony: Dialogues on Compassionate Action* (Berkeley, CA: Parallax, 1992), 91.

Chapter One

Epigraph. Viktor Frankl, *Man's Search for Meaning* (New York: Pocket Books, 1971).

Epigraph. Charlotte Joko Beck, *Everyday Zen: Love and Work* (San Francisco: HarperOne, 2007), 77.

1. Dalai Lama, *In My Own Words: An Introduction to My Teachings and Philosophy*, ed. Rajiv Mehrotra (Carlsbad, CA: Hay House, 2008), 1, 3.

2. Mother Teresa, *The Greatest Love* (Novato, CA: New World Library, 2002), 94.

3. Deborah van Deusen Hunsinger. *Pray without Ceasing: Revitalizing Pastoral Care* (Grand Rapids, MI: Eerdmans, 2006), 53.

4. Harvey Cox, *The Future of Faith* (New York: HarperCollins, 2009), 2.

5. Jack Kornfield, *A Path with Heart: A Guide through the Perils and Promises of Spiritual Life* (New York: Bantam, 1993), 6–7.

6. Tara Brach, *Radical Acceptance: Embracing Your Life with the Heart of a Buddha* (New York: Bantam, 2003), 8.

7. Jack Kornfield, quoted in Tony Schwartz, *What Really Matters: Searching for Wisdom in America* (New York: Bantam, 1995), 332.

8. Dean Ornish, *Love and Survival: The Scientific Basis for the Healing Power of Intimacy* (New York: HarperCollins, 1998), 13, 42.

Chapter Two

Epigraph. Brach, *Radical Acceptance,* 156 (see chap. 1, n. 6).

Epigraph. John Tarrant, "Let Me Count the Ways," *Shambhala Sun,* September 2011, 30–31.

1. See Allan Schore, *Affect Regulation and the Repair of the Self* (New York: W. W. Norton, 2003).

2. See John De Graaf, David Wann, and Thomas H. Naylor, *Affluenza: The All-Consuming Epidemic* (San Francisco: Berett-Koehler, 2005).

3. See Edwin McMahon and Peter Campbell, *Rediscovering the Lost Body-Connection within Christian Spirituality* (Minneapolis: Tasora, 2010), 181–198.

4. See John Welwood, *Toward a Psychology of Awakening: Buddhism, Psychotherapy, and the Path of Personal and Spiritual Transformation* (Boston: Shambhala, 2000).

Chapter Three

Epigraph. Robert Aitken and David Steindl-Rast, *The Ground We Share: Everyday Practice, Buddhist and Christian* (Boston: Shambhala, 1996), 5.

Epigraph. Martin Buber, *I and Thou* (New York: Charles Scribner's Sons, 1958), 11.

1. Kathleen Doheny, "10 Surprising Health Benefits of Sex," *Web MD,* http://www.webmd.com/sex-relationships/ guide/10-surprising-health-benefits-of-sex.

Chapter Four

Epigraph. From Paul Hawken's commencement address at the University of Portland, May 3, 2009.

Epigraph. Friedrich Nietzsche, *Human, All Too Human: A Book of Free Spirits,* 1878.

1. Rick Hanson and Richard Mencius, *The Buddha's Brain: The Practical Neuroscience of Happiness, Love, and Wisdom* (Oakland, CA: New Harbinger, 2009), 96.

2. Quoted in Sidney D. Piburn, *The Dalai Lama: A Policy of Kindness* (New Delhi: Motilal Banarsidass, 2002), 101.

3. David Bulwa and Steve Rubenstein, "Mad Scramble for Bonds Home-Run Ball," *San Francisco Chronicle,* August 8, 2007, 17.

Chapter Five

Epigraph. John Gross, *Oxford Book of Aphorisms* (Oxford: Oxford University Press, 2003), 256.

Epigraph. Nathaniel Hawthorne; see http://www.worldofquotes.com/author/ nathaniel+hawthorne/1/index.html.

1. Attributed to Adolph Hitler.

2. Jim Dreaver, *End Your Story, Begin Your Life: Wake Up, Let Go, Live Free* (Charlottesville, VA: Hampton Roads, 2011), 21.

3. See John Gottman, *Seven Principles for Making Marriage Work: A Practical Guide from the Country's Foremost Relationship Expert* (New York: Crown, 1999).

4. John J. Prendergast and G. Kenneth Bradford, eds., *Listening from the Heart of Silence: Nondual Wisdom and Psychotherapy,* vol 2 (St. Paul: MN: Paragon, 2007), 13.

5. David Brazier, *The Feeling Buddha: A Buddhist Psychology of Character, Adversity, and Passion* (New York: Palgrave, 2002), 54.

Chapter Six

Epigraph. John Tarrant, *Bring Me the Rhinoceros and Other Zen Koans that Will Save Your Life* (New York: Harmony, 2004), 116–7.

Epigraph. Anton Chekhov; see http://batr.org/quotes.html.

1. *Hsin Hsin Ming: Verses on the Faith-Mind* by Seng-Ts'an, trans. Richard B. Clark (Toronto: Coach House, 1973).

2. David Chadwick, *Shine One Corner of the World: Moments with Shunryu Suzuki* (New York: Random House, 2001), 117.

3. Thich Nhat Hanh, quoted in Stephen Batchelor, *The Awakening of the West: The Encounter of Buddhism and Western Culture* (Berkeley: Parallax, 1994), 274.

4. *Dōgen's Extensive Record: A Translation of the Eihei Kōroku,* trans. Taigen Dan Leighton and Eihei Koroku (Boston: Wisdom, 2004), 257–8.

5. Susan Johnson refers to the anger in such instances as an "attachment protest."

Chapter Seven

Epigraph. Susan M. Johnson, *The Practice of Emotionally Focused Marital Therapy: Creating Connection* (Florence, KY: Brunner/Mazel, 1996), 18.

Epigraph. Amir Levine and Rachel S. F. Heller, *Attached: The New Science of Adult Attachment and How It Can Help You Find and Keep Love* (New York: Penguin Group, 2010), 21.

1. Thomas Lewis, Fari Amini, and Richard Lannon, *A General Theory of Love* (New York: Random House, 2000), 86.

2. Ibid., 71.

3. Johnson. *The Practice*, 19.

4. Ibid., 169.

5. Henry David Thoreau, *WaldenPond* (Los Angeles: Empire, 2012), 66.

Chapter Eight

Epigraph. Cornelia Funkhe, *Inkheart* (Somerset, UK: Chicken House / Scholastic, 2003).

Epigraph. Mark Epstein, *Open to Desire: Embracing a Lust for Life* (New York: Penguin Group, 2005), 132.

1. Alfred Kazin, ed., *The Portable Blake* (New York: Viking, 1968), 252.

2. John Welwood, *Perfect Love, Imperfect Relationships: Healing the Wound of the Heart* (Boston: Trumpeter, 2006), 121.

3. Stephen Batchelor, *Verses from the Center* (New York: Penguin, 2000), 33.

4. Kazin, *The Portable Blake*, 134.

5. Pema Chödrön, *When Things Fall Apart: Heart Advice for Difficult Times* (Boston: Shambhala, 1997), 51.

6. Shunryu Suzuki, *Zen Mind, Beginner's Mind: Informal Talks on Zen Meditation and Practice* (New York: Weatherhill, 1972), 32.

7. Eugene Gendlin, quoted in Ann Weiser Cornell, *The Power of Focusing: A Practical Guide to Emotional Self-Healing* (Oakland: New Harbinger, 1996), 17.

8. Gershen Kaufman, *Shame: The Power of Caring* (Rochester, VT: Schenkman, 1985), ix.

9. Stephen Batchelor, *Buddhism without Beliefs: A Contemporary Guide to Awakening* (New York: Riverhead, 1997), 8.

Chapter Nine

Epigraph. Lewis, Amini, and Lannon, *A General Theory*, 37 (see chap. 7, n. 1).

Epigraph. Joseph Campbell and the Power of Myth with Bill Moyers, PBS television series, Mystic Fire Video (2001), episode 2, chapter 4.

1. Chödrön, *When Things Fall Apart*, 51 (see chap. 8, n. 5).
2. Johann Wolfgang von Goethe and Otto von Wenckstern, *Goethe's Opinions on the World, Mankind, Literature, Science and Art* (Charleston, SC: Bibliobazaar, 2008), 3.
3. Buber, *I and Thou*, 11 (see chap. 3, second epigraph).
4. Nyoshul Khenpo and Lama Surya Das, *Natural Great Perfection: Dzogchen Teachings and Vajra Songs* (Boston: Snow Lion, 2009), 11.
5. Dalai Lama, *The Art of Happiness, Tenth Anniversary Edition: A Handbook for Living*, (New York: Riverhead, 2009), 161.

Chapter Ten

Epigraph. W. B. Yeats, "A Prayer for Old Age," in Richard J. Finneran, ed., *The Collected Poems of W.B. Yeats* (New York: Scribner, 1996), 282.
Epigraph. Jill Bolte Taylor, *My Stroke of Insight: A Brain Scientist's Personal Journey* (New York: Plume, 2009), 75.
1. P. Lal, trans. *The Dhammapada* (New York: Farrar, Straus & Giroux, 1970) 39.
2. Rick Hanson, "What Puts People at Ease," *Just One Thing Online Newsletter*, August 18, 2010, no. 37, http://www.rickhanson.net/writings/just-one-thing.
3. Dalai Lama, *The Art of Happiness,* 161 (see chap. 9, n. 5).
4. Harvey Aronson, *Buddhist Practice on Western Ground: Reconciling Eastern Ideals and Western Psychology* (Boston: Shambhala, 2004), 134.

Chapter Eleven

Epigraph. Chödrön, *When Things Fall Apart*, 10 (see chap. 8, n. 5).
Epigraph. Unpublished poem by Rob Foxcroft, used with permission.
1. For additional helpful phrases, see Sharon Salzberg, *Lovingkindness: The Revolutionary Art of Happiness* (Boston: Shambhala, 1995), 30–31.
2. Quoted in Joe Hyams, *Zen and the Martial Arts* (New York: Bantam, 1982), 134.
3. Jack Kornfield, *Path with Heart*, 107 (see chap. 1, n. 5).

4. For some people, the opposite may be true. They may cry easily but resist expressing anger and outrage. The point is to identify what's most authentic for us in any given moment.
5. Chödrön, *When Things Fall Apart*, 122 (see chap. 8, n. 5).
6. Quoted in Frederic Brussat, Mary Ann Brussat, and Thomas Moore, *Spiritual Literacy: Reading the Sacred in Everyday Life* (New York: Scribner, 1998), 283.
7. Quoted in John Woolman and Amelia M. Gummere, *The Journal and Essays of John Woolman* (Charleston, SC: Nabu Press, 2010), 166.

Chapter Twelve

Epigraph. Kornfield. *Path with Heart*, 107 (see chap. 1, n. 5).
Epigraph. Quoted in Martin Buber, *Tales of the Hasidim: Book One: The Early Masters and Book Two: the Later Masters* (New York: Schocken, 1991), 252.
1. George Lyman Kittredge, *The Complete Works of William Shakespeare* (New York: Grolier, 1958), 1233.

Chapter Thirteen

Epigraph. Søren Kierkegaard, *Works of Love* (Port Washington, NY: Kennikat, 1972), 19.
Epigraph. Sobonfu Somé, *The Spirit of Intimacy: Ancient Teachings in the Ways of Relationships* (Harper Collins, 2002), 12.
1. Quoted in Kornfield, *Path with Heart*, 332 (see chap. 1, n. 5).
2. For more about the difference between romantic love and mature love, see my book *The Authentic Heart* (Hoboken, NJ: John Wiley & Sons, 2001).

Chapter Fourteen

Epigraph. Jon Kabat-Zinn, *Coming to Our Senses: Healing Ourselves and the World through Mindfulness* (New York: Hyperion, 2005), 26.

Epigraph. Jason Siff, *Unlearning Meditation* (Boston: Shambhala, 2010), 32.

1. Batchelor, *The Awakening of the West*, 120 (see chap. 6, n. 3).
2. Brach, *Radical Acceptance*, 25 (see chap. 1, n. 6).
3. Wikipedia, "Research on Meditation," http://en.wikipedia.org/wiki/Research_on_meditation.
4. Ibid.
5. Jon Kabat-Zinn, *Wherever You Go There You Are* (New York: Hyperion, 1994), 4.
6. Tarrant, "Let Me Count the Ways," 33 (see chap. 2, second epigraph).
7. Mark Williams et. al., *The Mindful Way through Depression: Freeing Yourself from Chronic Unhappiness* (New York: Guilford, 2007).
8. See Steven Hayes, *Get Out of Your Mind and Into Your Life: The New Acceptance and Commitment Therapy* (Oakland: New Harbinger, 2005).
9. For more information, see chapter 14, "Spirituality and Emotionally Focused Couple Therapy: Exploring Common Ground," in James L. Furrow, Susan M. Johnson, and Bren Bradley, eds., *The Emotionally Focused Casebook* (New York: Routledge, 2011).

Chapter Fifteen

Epigraph. Albert Einstein, *The World As I See It* (New York: Open Road/Philosophical Library, 2011), 11.
Epigraph. Anaïs Nin; see http://en.wikiquote.org/wiki/Ana%C3%AFs_Nin.

1. Aitken and Steindl-Rast, *The Ground We Share*, 22 (see chap. 3, first epigraph).

Chapter Sixteen

Epigraph. Edwin McMahon and Peter Campbell, *Please Touch* (Landham, MD: Sheed & Ward, 1969), 15.

Epigraph. Quoted in Brazier, *The Feeling Buddha*, 58–9 (see chap. 5, n. 5).

1. Quoted in Jim Dreaver, *The Ultimate Cure* (Woodbury, MN: Llewellyn, 1996), xiv.

2. John Wren-Lewis, "The Dazzling Dark: A Near-Death Experience Opens the Door to a Permanent Transformation," http://www.nonduality.com/dazdark.htm, 2.

3. Aitken and Steindl-Rast, *The Ground We Share*, 9 (see chap. 3, first epigraph).

4. Ibid., 9.

5. Aitken & Steindl-Rast, *The Ground We Share*, 11.

6. Walpola Rahula, *What the Buddha Taught* (New York: Grove, 1959), 43.

7. Don Lattin, "Dalai Lama Begins Bay Area Visit with Praise for Humanitarians," *San Francisco Chronicle*, May 17, 2001, A6.

8. Claudia Dreifus, "The Dalai Lama Comes Down to Earth," This World, *San Francisco Chronicle*, December 5, 1993, 13.

9. Jack Kornfield, *After the Ecstasy, the Laundry: How the Heart Grows Wise on the Spiritual Path* (New York: Bantam, 2000), 101.

10. Quoted in Brach, *Radical Acceptance*, 10 (see chap. 1, n. 6).

11. Batchelor, *Buddhism without Beliefs*, 89 (see chap. 8, n. 9).

12. Ibid., 10.

13. From Goodreads, http://www.goodreads.com/quotes/150731-enlightenment-is-an-accident-meditation-makes-you-accident-prone.

14. Ngakpa Chögyam with Khandro Dechen, *Spectrum of Ecstasy* (New York: Aro, 1997), 27.

15. Aitken and Steindl-Rast, *The Ground We Share*, 10.

16. Buckminster Fuller, *I Seem to Be a Verb* (New York: Bantam, 1970).

Chapter Seventeen

Epigraph. Batchelor, *Buddhism without Beliefs*, 88–89 (see chap. 8, n. 9).

Epigraph. Jett Psaris and Marlena S. Lyons, *Undefended Love* (Oakland, CA: New Harbinger, 2000), 75.

Chapter Eighteen

Epigraph. Eugene T. Gendlin, "The Small Steps of the Therapy Process: How They Come and How to Help Them Come," G. Lietaer, J. Rombauts, and R. Van Balen (eds.), *Client-Centered and Experiential Psychotherapy in the Nineties* (Leuven: Leuven University Press, 1990), 205.

Epigraph. Charlotte Joko Beck, *Nothing Special: Living Zen* (San Francisco: Harper, 1993), 159.

1. Not all shame is bad. We sometimes need a small dose of shame to recognize when we've hurt someone or violated our values. Psychopaths are so egotistical that they have no shame.

2. Carl Rogers, *On Becoming a Person* (New York: Mariner, 1995), 17.

3. David Rome, "Searching for the Truth That Is Far Below the Search," *Shambhala Sun*, September 2004.

4. Personal communication.

5. Beck, *Everyday Zen*, 33 (see chap. 1, second epigraph).

6. Cornell, *The Power of Focusing*, 36 (see chap. 8, n. 7).

7. Daniel B. Wile, *After the Fight: A Night in the Life of a Couple* (New York: Guilford, 1993), 33.

8. Ibid.

9. Coleman Barks, trans., *The Essential Rumi, New Expanded Edition* (San Francisco: HarperOne, 2004), 109.

10. Thich Nhat Hanh, *Peace Is Every Step* (New York: Bantam, 1991), 53–54.

11. Thich Nhat Hanh and Melvin McLeod, *Your True Home* (Boston: Shambhala, 2011), 16.

12. Siff, *Unlearning Meditation*, 90 (see chap. 14, second epigraph).

13. Ibid., 159–160.

14. Ibid., 32.

15. McMahon and Campbell, *Rediscovering*, 93 (see chap. 2, n. 3).

16. Peter Campbell and Edwin McMahon, *Bio-Spirituality: Focusing as a Way to Grow* (Chicago: Loyola, 1997), 152.

17. Beck, *Everyday Zen*, 91 (see chap. 1, second epigraph).
18. See Ann Weiser Cornell and Barbara McGavin, *The Focusing Student's and Companion's Manual* (Berkeley, CA: Calluna, 2002), 4.

Chapter Nineteen

Epigraph. Lee Hoinacki and Carl Mitcham, eds., *The Challenges of Ivan Illich* (Albany, NY: State University of New York Press, 2001), 235.

Epigraph. E. E. Cummings; see http://en.wikiquote.org/wiki/E._E._Cummings.

1. Sample, Ian, "With a little help from your friends you can live longer." Guradian.co.uk, July 27, 2010, http://www.guardian.co.uk/lifeandstyle/2010/jul/27/friendship-relationships-good-health-study.
2. James Pennebaker, *Opening Up: The Healing Power of Expressing Emotions*, (New York, Guilford, 1997), 110.
3. Kornfield, *After the Ecstasy*, 24 (see chap. 16, n. 9).

Chapter Twenty

Epigraph. Thich Nhat Hanh, *Living Buddha, Living Christ* (New York: G. P. Putnam's Sons, 1995), 20.

Epigraph. Aldous Huxley; see http://www.betterworld.net/heroes/pages-h/huxley-quotes.htm.

Chapter Twenty-One

Epigraph. Kornfield, *After the Ecstasy*, 124–5 (see chap. 16, n. 9).

Epigraph. The Buddha; see http://www.sonoma.edu/users/d/daniels/buddhapage.html.

1. Siff, *Unlearning Meditation,* 100 (see chap. 14, second epigraph).
2. Saniel Bonder with Laura Airica, *Healing the Spirit/Matter Split: An Invitation to Wake Down in Mutuality and Fulfill Your Divinely Human Destiny* (Petaluma, CA: Mt. Tam Empowerments, 2005), 63.
3. Kornfield, *After the Ecstasy,* 124–5.

Bibliography

Aitken, Robert, and David Steindl-Rast. *The Ground We Share: Everyday Practice, Buddhist and Christian*. Boston: Shambhala, 1996.

Amodeo, John. *The Authentic Heart: An Eightfold Path to Midlife Love*. Hoboken, New Jersey: John Wiley & Sons, 2001.

_____. *Love & Betrayal: Broken Trust in Intimate Relationships*. New York: Ballantine, 1994.

Amodeo, John, and Kris Wentworth. *Being Intimate: A Guide to Successful Relationships*. New York: Penguin, 1986.

Aronson, Harvey. *Buddhist Practice on Western Ground: Reconciling Eastern Ideals and Western Psychology*. Boston: Shambhala, 2004.

Batchelor, Stephen. *Verses from the Center*. New York: Penguin, 2000.

_____. *Buddhism Without Beliefs: A Contemporary Guide to Awakening*. New York: Riverhead Books, 1997.

_____. *The Awakening of the West: The Encounter of Buddhism and Western Culture*. Berkeley: Parallax Press, 1994.

Beck, Charlotte Joko. *Everyday Zen: Love & Work*. San Francisco: HarperOne, 2007.

Beck, Charlotte Joko. *Nothing Special: Living Zen*. San Francisco: Harper, 1993.

Bolte Taylor, Jill. *My Stroke of Insight: A Brain Scientist's Personal Journey*. New York: Plume, 2009.

Bonder, Saniel with Laura Airica. *Healing the Spirit/Matter Split: An Invitation to Wake Down in Mutuality and Fulfill Your Divinely Human Destiny*. Petaluma, CA: Mt. Tam Empowerments, 2004.

Brach, Tara. *Radical Acceptance: Embracing Your Life with the Heart of a Buddha*. New York: Bantam Books, 2003.

Brazier, David. *The Feeling Buddha: A Buddhist Psychology of Character, Adversity, and Passion*. New York: Palgrave, 2002.

Brussat, Frederic, Mary Ann Brussat, and Thomas Moore. *Spiritual Literacy: Reading the Sacred in Everyday Life*. New York: Scribner, 1998.

Buber, Martin. *Tales of the Hasidim: Book One: The Early Masters and Book Two: The Later Masters*. New York: Schocken Books, 1991.

Buber, Martin. *I and Thou*. New York: Charles Scribner's Sons, 1958.

Buddhaghosa, Bhadantacariya. *The Path of Purification*. Translated by Bhikku Nyanamoli. Colombo, Ceylon: A. Semage, 1964.

Campbell, Peter, and Edwin McMahon. *Bio-Spirituality: Focusing as a Way to Grow*. Chicago: Loyola Press, 1985.

Campbell, Joseph. *Joseph Campbell and The Power of Myth with Bill Moyers*. 1988. Montauk, NY: Mystic Fire Video, 2002. DVD.

Chödrön, Pema. *When Things Fall Apart: Heart Advice for Difficult Times*. Boston: Shambhala, 1997.

Chögyam, Ngakpa with Khandro Dechen. *Spectrum of Ecstasy*. New York: Aro Books, 1997.

Cornell, Ann Weiser. *The Power of Focusing: A Practical Guide to Emotional Self-Healing*. Oakland, CA: New Harbinger, 1996.

Cornell, Ann Weiser, and Barbara McGavin. *The Focusing Student's and Companion's Manual*. Berkeley, CA: Calluna Press, 2002.

Cox, Harvey. *The Future of Faith*. New York: HarperCollins, 2009.

Dalai Lama. *The Art of Happiness, 10th Anniversary Edition: A Handbook for Living*. New York: Riverhead Books, 2009.

_____. *In My Own Words: An Introduction to My Teachings and Philosophy*. Edited by Rajiv Mehrotra. Carlsbad, CA: Hay House, 2008.

_____. *Worlds in Harmony: Dialogues on Compassionate Action*. Berkeley: Parallax Press, 1992.

De Graaf, John, David Wann, and Thomas H. Naylor. *Affluenza: The All-Consuming Epidemic*. San Francisco: Berett-Koehler Publishers, 2005.

Doheny, Kathleen. "10 Surprising Health Benefits of Sex." *Web MD*. http://www.webmd.com/sex-relationships/guide/10-surprising-health-benefits-of-sex.

Dreaver, Jim. *End Your Story, Begin Your Life: Wake Up, Let Go, Live Free.* Charlottesville, VA: Hampton Roads, 2011.

Einstein, Albert. *The World as I See It.* New York: Open Road/Philosophical Library, 2011.

Epstein, Mark. *Open to Desire: Embracing a Lust for Life.* New York: Penguin Group, 2005.

Finneran, Richard J. *The Collected Poems of W. B. Yeats.* New York: Scribner, 1996.

Frankl, Viktor. *Man's Search for Meaning.* New York: Pocket Books, 1971.

Fuller, Buckminster. *I Seem to Be a Verb.* New York: Bantam Books, 1970.

Funkhe, Cornelia. *Inkheart.* Somerset, UK: Chicken House/Scholastic, 2003.

Furrow, James Love, Susan M. Johnson, Brent Bradley, and John Amodeo. "Spirituality and Emotionally Focused Couple Therapy: Exploring Common Ground." In *The Emotionally Focused Casebook: New Dimensions in Treating Couples,* edited by James L. Furrow, Susan M. Johnson, and Bren Bradley, 343–372. New York: Routledge, 2011.

Gendlin, Eugene. *Focusing.* New York: Bantam, 1982.

Gendlin, Eugene T. "The Small Steps of the Therapy Process: How They Come and How to Help Them Come." In *Client-Centered and Experiential Psychotherapy in the Nineties,* edited by G. Lietaer, J. Rombauts, and R. Van Balen. Leuven: Leuven University Press, 1990.

Goethe, Johann Wolfgang von, and Otto von Wenckster. *Goethe's Opinions on the World, Mankind, Literature, Science, and Art.* Charleston, SC: Bibliobazaa, 2008.

Gottman, John. *Seven Principles for Making Marriage Work: A Practical Guide from the Country's Foremost Relationship Expert.* New York: Crown Publishers, 1999.

Gross, John. *Oxford Book of Aphorisms.* Oxford: Oxford University Press, 2003.

Hanson, Rick. "What Puts People at Ease" *Just One Thing Online Newsletter,* August 18, 2010, no. 37. http://www.rickhanson.net/writings/just-one-thing.

Hanson, Rick, and Richard Mendius. *The Buddha's Brain: The Practical Neuroscience of Happiness, Love, and Wisdom.* Oakland, CA: New Harbinger Publications, 2009.

Hayes, Steven. *Get Out of Your Mind and Into Your Life: The New Acceptance and Commitment Therapy.* Oakland, CA: New Harbinger, 2005.

Hoinacki, Lee, and Carl Mitcham, eds. *The Challenges of Ivan Illich*. Albany, New York: State University of New York Press, 2001.

Hopkins, Andrea. *The Book of Courtly Love: The Passionate Code of the Troubadours*. San Francisco: HarperCollins, 1994.

Hunsinger, Deborah van Deusen. *Pray Without Ceasing: Revitalizing Pastoral Care*. Grand Rapids, MI: Wm. B. Eerdmans Publishing Co, 2006.

Johnson, Susan M. *Hold Me Tight: Seven Conversations for a Lifetime of Love*. New York: Little, Brown and Company, 2008.

_____. *The Practice of Emotionally Focused Marital Therapy: Creating Connection*. Florence, KY: Brunner/Mazel, 1996.

Kabat-Zinn, Jon. *Coming to Our Senses: Healing Ourselves and the World Through Mindfulness*. New York: Hyperion Books, 2005.

Kaufman, Gershen. *Shame: The Power of Caring*. Rochester, VT: Schenkman Books, 1985.

Kazin, Alfred, ed. *The Portable Blake*. New York: Viking Press, 1968.

Khenpo, Nyoshul, and Lama Surya Das. *Natural Great Perfection: Dzogchen Teachings and Vajra Songs*. Boston: Snow Lion Publications, 2009.

Kierkegaard, Søren. *Works of Love*. Port Washington, NY: Kennikat Press, 1972.

Kittredge, George Lyman. *The Complete Works of William Shakespeare*. New York: Grolier, 1958.

Kornfield, Jack. *After the Ecstasy, the Laundry: How the Heart Grows Wise on the Spiritual Path*. New York: Bantam Books, 2000.

_____. *A Path with Heart: A Guide Through the Perils and Promises of Spiritual Life*. New York: Bantam Books, 1993.

Kramer, Gregory. *Meditating Together, Speaking from Silence*. Seattle, WA: Metta Foundation, 2002.

Lattin, Don. "Dalai Lama Begins Bay Area Visit with Praise for Humanitarians." *San Francisco Chronicle*, May 17, 2001.

Leighton, Taigen Dan, trans. *Dōgen's Extensive Record: A Translation of the Eihei Kōroku*. Boston: Wisdom Publications, 2004.

Levine, Amir, and Rachel S. F. Heller. *Attached: The New Science of Adult Attachment and How It Can Help You Find and Keep Love*. New York: Penguin Group, 2010.

Lewis, Thomas, Fari Amini, and Richard Lannon. *A General Theory of Love.* NewYork: Random House, 2000.

McMahon, Edwin, and Peter Campbell. *Rediscovering the Lost Body-Connection Within Christian Spirituality.* Minneapolis, MN: Tasora Books, 2010.

———. *Please Touch.* Landham, MD: Sheed & Ward, 1969.

Mother Teresa. *The Greatest Love.* Novato: New World Library, 2002.

Ornish, Dean. *Love & Survival: The Scientific Basis for the Healing Power of Intimacy.* New York: HarperCollins, 1998.

Pennebaker, James. *Opening Up: The Healing Power of Expressing Emotions.* New York, Guilford Press, 1997.

Piburn, Sidney D. *The Dalai Lama: A Policy of Kindness.* New Delhi: Motilal Banarsidass, 2002.

Prendergast, John J., and Bradford G. Kenneth, eds. *Listening from the Heart of Silence: Nondual Wisdom and Psychotherapy,* Volume 2. St. Paul, MN: Paragon House, 2007.

Psaris, Jett, and Marlena S. Lyons. *Undefended Love.* Oakland: New Harbinger, 2000.

Rogers, Carl. *On Becoming a Person.* New York: Mariner Books, 1995.

Rome, David. "Searching for the Truth That Is Far Below the Search." *Shambhala Sun,* September 2004.

Salzberg, Sharon. *Lovingkindness: The Revolutionary Art of Happiness.* Boston: Shambhala, 1995.

Sample, Ian. "With a Little Help from Your Friends You Can Live Longer." *The Guardian,* July 27, 2010. http://www.guardian.co.uk/lifeandstyle/2010/jul/27/friendship-relationships-good-health-study.

Schwartz, Tony. *What Really Matters: Searching for Wisdom in America.* New York: Bantam Books, 1995.

Seng-Ts'an. *Hsin Hsin Ming: Verses on the Faith-Mind.* Translated by Richard B. Clark. Toronto: The Coach House Press, 1973.

Siff, Jason. *Unlearning Meditation.* Boston: Shambhala, 2010.

Some, Sobonfu. *The Spirit of Intimacy: Ancient Teachings in the Ways of Relationships.* New York: Harper Collins, 2002.

Suzuki, Shunryu. *Zen Mind, Beginner's Mind: Informal Talks on Zen Meditation and Practice.* New York: Weatherhill, 1972.

Tarrant, John. *Bring Me the Rhinoceros and Other Zen Koans That Will Save Your Life*. New York: Harmony Books, 2004.

_____. "Let Me Count the Ways." *Shambhala Sun*, September, 2011.

Teilhard de Chardin, Pierre. *Toward the Future*. New York: Mariner Books, 2002.

Thich Nhat Hanh and Melvin McLeod. *Your True Home*. Boston: Shambhala, 2011.

Thoreau, Henry David. *Walden*. Los Angeles: Empire Books, 2012.

Watts, Fraser, and Kevin Dutton. *Why the Science and Religion Dialogue Matters*. West Conshohocken, PA: Templeton Press, 2006.

Welwood, John. *Perfect Love, Imperfect Relationships: Healing the Wound of the Heart*. Boston: Trumpeter Books, 2006.

_____. *Toward a Psychology of Awakening: Buddhism, Psychotherapy, and the Path of Personal and Spiritual Transformation*. Boston: Shambhala, 2000.

Wile, Daniel B. *After The Fight: A Night in the Life of a Couple*. New York: Guilford Press, 1993.

Williams, Mark, John Teasdale, Zindel Segal, and Jon Kabat-Zinn. *The Mindful Way through Depression: Freeing Yourself from Chronic Unhappiness*. New York: Guilford Press, 2007.

Woolman, John, and Amelia M. Gummere. *The Journal and Essays of John Woolman*. Charleston, SC: Nabu Press, 2010.

Wren-Lewis, John. "The Dazzling Dark: A Near-Death Experience Opens the Door to a Permanent Transformation." *Nonduality.com*. http://www.nonduality.com/dazdark.htm.

A Guide to Resources

For information about my psychotherapy practice, my other books, as well as articles and video/audio links: www.johnamodeo.com

For resources to learn more about Focusing, including workshops in your area, or referrals to Focusing-oriented therapists:
The Focusing Institute: www.focusing.org

For articles, information, and links related to Focusing Oriented Therapy:
International Association for Focusing Oriented Therapists (IAFOT): www.focusingtherapy.org

For an educational website about Focusing, especially its connection to spirituality and working with children using Focusing:
The Institute for Bio-Spiritual Research: www.biospiritual.org

Couples Therapy

For referrals for couples therapists who use Emotionally Focused Therapy:
International Centre for Excellence in Emotionally Focused Therapy (ICEEFT): www.iceeft.com

For programs and retreats related to the practice of mindful awareness, called vipassana (insight) meditation:
Spirit Rock Meditation Center: www.spiritrock.com

For programs, classes, and retreats related to vipassana (insight) meditation (founded by Tara Brach):
Insight Meditation Community of Washington (IMCW): www.imcw.org

Index

Related Quest Titles

Everyday Dharma, by Lama Willa Miller

The Meditative Path, by John Cianciosi

The Opening of the Wisdom Eye,
by the Fourteenth Dalai Lama

The Zen of Listening, by Rebecca Z. Shafir

To order books or a complete Quest catalog,
call 800-669-9425 or (outside the U.S.) 630-665-0130.

More Praise for John Amodeo's *Dancing with Fire*

"With masterful, lucid simplicity, *Dancing with Fire* gives us a vision of how to make a fervent quest for spiritual freedom dovetail with an equally ardent search for love and intimate connection. John Amodeo has created a founding treatise for the new, embodied wholeness so many of us yearn to find. Yet reading it doesn't feel like listening to a sage give a lecture; it feels like having a conversation with a trusted friend. If you want to 'curl up by the fire' with a book full of authentic Buddhist wisdom, this may be just the book you need."

—**Saniel Bonder,** founder of Waking Down in Mutuality;
author of *Healing the Spirit/Matter Split*

"Spiritual awakening, personal growth, fullness of relating, learning to be a more healing presence for others, fulfillment through intimacy: these are all just different names for the same thing. The fact that a split has developed—many splits, in fact—among therapy, spirituality, and personal growth is a sign that something has gone wrong. There has to be a reintegration. This book is an important landmark on the path to such wholeness."

—**David Brazier,** psychotherapist, leader of the Amida Order, and
author of *The Feeling Buddha*

"We owe John Amodeo a debt of gratitude for providing all of us with valuable insights on the connection between mindfulness and deepening intimacy in relationships. Whether you see yourself as nurtured by spiritual practice or psychological growth, read on and your heart will be touched, your mind opened. I highly recommend this fine book as an important guide for all those who seek genuine happiness and greater awareness."

—**Charles Garfield,** PhD, clinical professor of psychology at the University of California San Francisco School of Medicine, founder of the Shanti Project, and author of *Sometimes My Heart Goes Numb*

"This book is a masterful, sensitive, and heartfelt reflection on the valuable contributions available in the teachings on mindfulness in the Buddhist tradition, placed into rich and dynamic dialogue with the equally significant insights coming forth from the field of attachment theory and Sue Johnson's practical work on repairing and enhancing intimacy and connection in human relationships."

—**Harvey B. Aronson,** PhD (Buddhist Studies), LCSW, LMFT, LCDC; founding codirector of Dawn Mountain Tibetan Buddhist Temple, Houston, Texas; author of *Buddhist Practice on Western Ground*

"Blending mindfulness with contemporary psychology, Amodeo brings what often remains lofty conversation into our kitchens and bedrooms. He shows how meditative awareness can help us develop more vital relationships while helping us embody spiritual realization more fully in everyday life. The writing style is warm and inviting, like having a conversation with a wise and gentle friend. This book is a wonderful contribution to the emerging relationship yoga of the West."

—**Jett Psaris,** PhD, coauthor of *Undefended Love*

"If there was ever a book to guide us in the pursuit of 'daily life as spiritual practice,' this is it. In his clear, heartfelt, and entertaining style, John Amodeo shows us how to bring mindful, loving attention to all aspects of our personal and interpersonal life—especially the painful or difficult aspects. He shows how the practice of seeing, feeling, and embracing the suppressed or wounded parts of ourselves creates a sense of empathy and unity with other humans and with all of Life."

—**Susan Campbell,** PhD, author of *Getting Real* and *The Couple's Journey*

"A bold adaptation of Eastern spirituality to bring about loving, intimate connections."

—**Dan Wile,** psychologist and author of *After the Fight* and
After the Honeymoon

"This compelling and fascinating book has been long overdue. All too many people on a so-called 'spiritual path' are actually looking for more subtle and effective ways of short-circuiting the inherent pain in life. John Amodeo clearly illuminates the lack of any contradiction between practicing mindful living and creating intimacy in one's relationships. His distinction between extinguishing desires and attachments and working skillfully with them offers a clear path toward living with engagement and open-heartedness."

—**Charlie Bloom,** coauthor of *101 Things I Wish I Knew
When I Got Married* and *Secrets of Great Marriages*

"John Amodeo's brilliantly written, incisive, and heart-centered book provides a multilayered, in-depth journey demonstrating why we need both the spiritual teachings on mindfulness along with Western approaches, like Focusing and Emotionally Focused Therapy, to live a truly awakened, embodied life of sacred intimacy with oneself, one's relationships, and life itself!"

—**Laury Rappaport,** PhD, professor and director of Mind-Body Dept., Five Branches University;
author of *Focusing-Oriented Art Therapy*

"*Dancing with Fire* is a beautifully written, lucid, and honest account of how to merge a feeling-based intimacy with authentic spirituality. I've been a reader of John Amodeo's work for a long time, and he is simply one of the best at what he does: blending Buddhism and psychotherapy with wisdom gleaned from thirty years of clinical practice and life experience, all mixed in with a healthy dose of levity."

—**Jim Dreaver,** author of *The Way of Harmony* and
End Your Story, Begin Your Life

"Brilliant, liberating, clarifying wisdom for meditators of every persuasion! One of the most helpful books ever written on spiritual practice."
—**Deborah Boyar,** PhD, senior teacher, Waking Down in Mutuality; Somatic Experiencing practitioner

"A coherent, intelligent, loving book that weaves Eastern spirituality with our need for deep, loving personal relationships—showing how a spiritual path toward awakening and the path toward fulfilling intimate connections can nourish and support each other."
—**Bret Lyon,** PhD, co-creator of Healing Shame workshops, focusing trainer, and Somatic Experiencing practitioner

"Writing with a tender heart and deep wisdom, John Amodeo reveals the missing link between spirituality and relationships. This powerful book illuminates how to embrace the longing at the core of the human condition. It explores how to live with passionate emotions in a way that furthers connection with self and others by moving from a state of shame to learning to dance in the fire of authentic desires. A great book for therapists, meditators and anyone who wants a better life and better relationships."
—**Sheila Rubin,** LMFT, RDT/BCT; co-creator of Healing Shame workshops and Life-Stories workshops; adjunct faculty of JFK University and the California Institute of Integral Studies

"Profoundly wise and beautifully written, this book is for anyone who ever wondered how to reconcile the spiritual journey with the paths of self-healing and intimacy with others. John Amodeo is a gifted writer at the top of his form. His book is not just about authenticity and connection; it actually offers those experiences as one reads. A life-changing book."
—**Ann Weiser Cornell,** PhD, author of *The Power of Focusing* and *The Radical Acceptance of Everything*

About the Author

John Amodeo, PhD, a licensed marriage and family therapist for over thirty years, has been engaged in Buddhism and spiritual practice for forty years. He is the author of *The Authentic Heart* and *Love and Betrayal* and has been a writer and contributing editor for *Yoga Journal*. He is a Focusing Trainer and has trained in Somatic Experiencing for trauma. He lectures internationally on love and relationships and has led workshops at centers such as Esalen Institute, the Omega Institute, and the New York Open Center. He has been a featured guest on CNN, CNBC, Donahue, and New Dimensions Radio and has been interviewed or written articles for publications that include *The Chicago Tribune, The Dallas Morning News, The San Jose Mercury News,* and *Cosmopolitan*. With Susan Johnson he coauthored a chapter on EFT and Buddhism in *The Emotionally Focused Casebook*. An adjunct faculty member of Meridian University, he lives in the San Francisco Bay Area. Visit www.johnamodeo.com for additional information.

Photograph by Laury Rappaport